THE SHIP THAT WOULDN'T DIE

THE SHIP THAT
WOULDN'T DIE

THE SAGA OF THE USS *NEOSHO*
A WORLD WAR II STORY OF
COURAGE AND SURVIVAL AT SEA

DON KEITH

NAL
CALIBER

NAL Caliber
Published by the Penguin Group
Penguin Group (USA) LLC, 375 Hudson Street,
New York, New York 10014

USA / Canada / UK / Ireland / Australia / New Zealand / India / South Africa / China
penguin.com
A Penguin Random House Company

First published by NAL Caliber, an imprint of New American Library,
a division of Penguin Group (USA) LLC

First Printing, April 2015

LIBRARY OF CONGRESS CATALOGING-IN-PUBLICATION DATA:

Keith, Don, 1947–
The ship that wouldn't die: the saga of the USS Neosho—
a World War II story of courage and survival at sea/Don Keith.
p.   cm.
Includes index.
ISBN 978-0-451-47000-3
1. Neosho (AO-23: Fleet oiler)   2. Coral Sea, Battle of the, 1942.
3. Survival at sea—Coral Sea.   4. World War, 1939–1945—Naval operations, American.
I. Title. II. Title: Saga of the USS Neosho—a World War II story of courage and survival at sea.
D774.C63K45   2015
940.54'2659—dc23   2014038731

Printed in the United States of America
10   9   8   7   6   5   4   3   2   1

Set in Sabon
Designed by Spring Hoteling

This book is dedicated to the yeomen, stewards, machinists, cooks, watertenders, radiomen, pharmacist's mates, storekeepers, firemen, engine men, shipfitters, seamen, electrician's mates, and all the other sailors who helped turn the tide of the sea war in World War II by performing bravely and well their crucial but unspectacular jobs, and doing so with little notice and no glory whatsoever.

And thus they'll fight for ages on 'til warships sail no more,
Amid the boiler's mighty heat and the turbine's hellish roar.
So when you see a ship pull out to meet a war-like foe,
Remember faintly if you can, the men who sail below.

—From "The Snipe's Lament," author unknown

CONTENTS

CONTENTS

CONTENTS

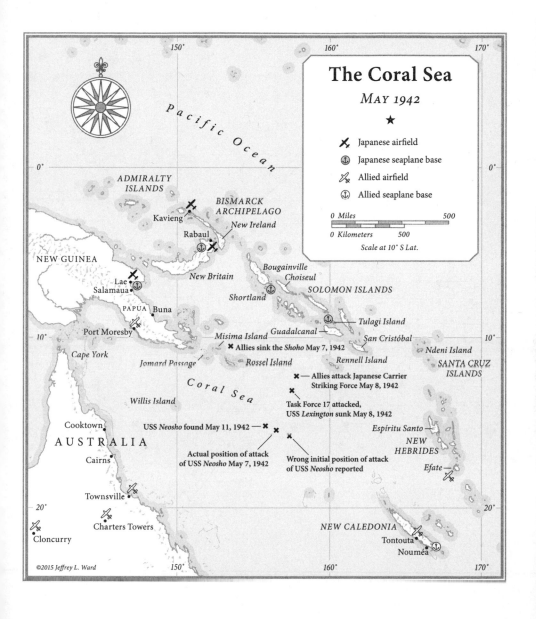

The Coral Sea

MAY 1942

★

✘ Japanese airfield

⚓ Japanese seaplane base

✘ Allied airfield

⚓ Allied seaplane base

0 Miles   500

0 Kilometers   500

Scale at 10° S Lat.

Pacific Ocean

ADMIRALTY ISLANDS

BISMARCK ARCHIPELAGO

Kavieng

New Ireland

Rabaul

NEW GUINEA

New Britain

Bougainville

Choiseul

Lae

Salamaua

SOLOMON ISLANDS

Shortland

PAPUA

Buna

Tulagi Island

Port Moresby

Misima Island

Guadalcanal

San Cristóbal

Cape York

Ndeni Island

Allies sink the *Shoho* May 7, 1942

Jomard Passage

Rossel Island

Rennell Island

SANTA CRUZ ISLANDS

Coral Sea

Allies attack Japanese Carrier Striking Force May 8, 1942

Willis Island

Task Force 17 attacked, USS *Lexington* sunk May 8, 1942

USS *Neosho* found May 11, 1942

Espíritu Santo

Cooktown

AUSTRALIA

NEW HEBRIDES

Actual position of attack of USS *Neosho* May 7, 1942

Wrong initial position of attack of USS *Neosho* reported

Cairns

Efate

Townsville

Charters Towers

NEW CALEDONIA

Cloncurry

Tontouta

Nouméa

©2015 Jeffrey L. Ward

THE SHIP THAT WOULDN'T DIE

PROLOGUE

May 6, 1942, in the Coral Sea,
between the Solomon Islands and Australia

"Abandon ship! Everybody, get off the ship!" the wild-eyed, red-faced sailor yelled as he ran through the vessel's forward compartments. "She's goin' down, boys, if she don't blow up first!"

Another sailor, busy passing up ammunition to the gun crew above, had no reason to doubt the truth in what his shipmate was screaming. From his station in the number one magazine—where shells were stored to feed the forward-deck gun—the barely twenty-year-old sailor could see nothing that was going on outside the hull, but could certainly feel the thuds and tremors, and heard the thunder as his big ship took vicious hits at the bow and amidships.

After a morning of cruel teasing, the vessel was now catching full-bore hell from a sizable and determined swarm of Japanese dive-bombers. Though the guns on his ship were firing back, it was clear—even down here in the dark, smoke-filled magazine—that the enemy planes were homing in, inflicting what could be mortal damage.

One near hit exploded in the water just on the other side of the ship's starboard hull from where the sailor worked. The resulting shock wave almost knocked him and his buddies to the deck. The men regained their balance, and eventually their hearing, as they kept hoisting shells up to those who were manning the bow gun, doing their best to fend off their attackers.

Each man working in the magazine fully expected a bomb to crash through the deck above him at any second and light off the explosive ordnance stacked all around. They also knew the likelihood of some stray spark touching off the fumes from the cargo of fuel oil they carried in the big tanks directly below their feet.

The high-pitched chatter on the ship's communications system confirmed that their vessel was taking one hell of a drubbing. Shipmates were dying.

"Let's get the hell out of here!" the man next to the sailor yelled. "If all that fuel below . . ." But the man turned and disappeared before he finished stating the obvious, his words overcome by the roar of explosions and the rattle of the ship's antiaircraft guns.

The young sailor paused, looked around, and ran after his buddy. He took a detour to grab his life vest, which he kept stowed beneath his bunk.

It was not there. Some son of a bitch had apparently decided he needed it worse than his shipmate did. The sailor knew he would have to go into the sea without it.

Once topside, what he saw almost stopped his bounding heart. An enemy plane, its flaming wreckage still discernible as an Imperial Japanese Navy dive-bomber, had crashed into the stack deck, aft of the bridge. Bombs had found the fire room and engine room, letting loose superheated steam and setting fire to leaking oil. Gray-black smoke clouded the sky as it climbed toward the midday sun. Flames swirled upward from back there. There was chaos on the deck. Even as some men fought the fires and tended to the injured, others were running or jumping overboard, some bleeding, some badly burned.

For the moment, no more enemy planes could be seen, no bombs falling, no machine guns strafing the deck. As he considered the near-fifty-foot jump into the water without a life vest, the sailor wondered if it might be the better option to wait right where he was, to see if the attack was over, if the ship might stay afloat for a while. He might be able to help fight the fires and care for the injured, too.

But something else felt out of kilter. The deck. Beneath his feet, the deck—normally solid and dependable except in the heaviest seas—was tilted just enough for him to notice. Somebody nearby dropped a wrench, and the sailor watched as it slowly slid away along the deck plates toward the far side of the massive vessel.

They were listing already, taking on water.

The ship was actually going to sink beneath them, go down suddenly, just as their escort destroyer, the USS *Sims*, already had. Some of the men stationed topside had witnessed that ship's quick death as it happened. The sailor had heard them talking about it over the communication system.

He hesitated no longer and ran to the starboard rail. Where were the lifeboats? Off to his right, one whaleboat hung at a skewed angle, dangling alongside the ship's hull, halfway down to the water. Only one man was aboard the boat. It looked like the gunnery officer, the sailor's direct boss whenever they were at battle stations. He was clearly having trouble launching the craft by himself.

But why was he trying it alone? That was not the way the drills went. If they were abandoning the ship, that whaleboat should have carried an assigned crew of men who were familiar with how to get the vessel launched quickly but safely and then knew what to do with the craft once they were in the water.

There were no life rafts anywhere in sight on deck, either. The sailor could see empty rafts—at least a half dozen—riding along the wave tops several hundred yards out from the ship, just beyond where burning oil covered the sea's surface. He could see no other lifeboats out there yet.

On each side of him, men ran over and leaped into the sea without hesitation. A couple of them, he noticed, were officers.

If the officers were getting off the USS *Neosho* as quickly and by any means they could, then its sinking was certainly imminent. His best chance to survive was to get into the water as well. Then, assuming he lived through the impact with the surface after jumping that far, and that a shark did not find and swallow him, he would try to swim away from the doomed ship. Swim far enough away so that the big oiler would not suck him all the way to the bottom with her when she plunged downward.

The sailor took one more look down and swallowed hard.

It was a hell of a long way. The waves were murky, blanketed with thick oil. Back toward the stern, the slick burned brightly, an arc of smoky fire stretching from beneath the ship out to a hundred yards or so. The nearest life raft was a daunting swim away, partly through oil, then over rolling, white-capped waves. The thing seemed to be getting smaller, drifting farther out all the time.

One of his buddies stood next to him then, taking in the same panorama of smoke, fire, mayhem, and panicked and wounded sailors. The man took a deep breath, held his nose, and leaped feetfirst.

The sailor climbed the rail, looked down once more, then up at a serene, cloudy sky from which so much deathly hail had just rained down on them.

He crossed his arms over his heart, closed his eyes tight, held his breath, and stepped off his listing ship into the Coral Sea.

PART ONE
PEARL HARBOR

We have witnessed this morning the attack of
Pearl Harbor and a severe bombing of Pearl
Harbor by army planes, undoubtedly Japanese.
It's no joke. It's a real war.

> —From first-known broadcast radio news report
> from Hawaii, December 7, 1941

CHAPTER ONE
Meatballs for Breakfast

December 7, 1941,
Pearl Harbor, Oahu, Hawaii

Surely the most powerful instinct hardwired into man is survival. It often manifests itself as a fight or flight for self-preservation when faced with a deadly threat. When we encounter a mortal menace, the hypothalamus in our brain immediately kicks into gear and issues a series of commands. Nerve cells amp up to force heightened awareness. Adrenaline surges into our bloodstream. Our heart rate zooms, pumping more blood than normal to organs and muscles, especially to extremities to fuel a fight or a quick getaway.

This mechanism explains how people can survive an ordeal that should kill them. It may also be the reason that they sometimes panic and do exactly the wrong thing.

At a berth at Ford Island in Pearl Harbor, a young sailor named Bill Leu was passing a typical early morning with his shipmates in the engine room of a U.S. Navy ship when suddenly someone came running through, yelling something improbable, impossible.

They were under attack.

Leu had just come off duty after a long night in the ship's engine room. A member of the "black gang," the "snipes"—or, as Leu termed it, the "lowest of the low" when it came to duty aboard a naval vessel—he was officially a fireman third class. Yet he and his fellow firemen were typically described by using a term—the black gang—left over from a time when ships ran on steam power produced by burning coal.

Leu had been in a black mood that morning, for sure. Saturday night in Pearl Harbor, near Honolulu in beautiful Hawaii, and he had spent it down in the bowels of the USS *Neosho* (AO-23), the huge tanker ship on which he served. Spent it staring at the oil-streaked mugs of the other sailors who drew the short straw instead of getting leave, drinking and dancing with some of the friendly hula girls at one of the clubs near Waikiki.

Now, once they finished pumping the last of the fuel oil out of her seemingly bottomless tanks, an empty *Neosho* would head out to the northeast and away from the pleasures of Hawaii. She would ride high on the water, rolling and swaying all the way back to the fuel depots at San Pedro, in Los Angeles. There they would fill her up once more and do the same thing all over again, making yet another quick turnaround for the "milk run" back to Hawaii. About the only thing they could look forward to was trying to time the circuit to put them back in Honolulu for weekend liberty, and then maybe home for Christmas.

A native of Skykomish, Washington, Leu had chosen the Navy of his own free will. He could not complain much about life aboard the tanker ship. For the most part, it was all right, even if it was hot and greasy and dirty and loud. He liked his shipmates, and there was usually a day or two of shore leave at one or the other end of the circuit, even if the Navy did keep them awfully busy lately.

Once he was out of high school, Leu's mother told him he could live at home rent-free for one year while he worked and saved money for college. He labored hard on a railroad section gang for a bit, then worked part-time in a mill while helping his father in his struggling grocery store in Skykomish, a tiny logging town in the mountains east of Seattle.

Soon Leu decided he was hardly college material, but he certainly had no interest in returning to the section gang or the mill. The Navy began to look more and more inviting. Posters in the recruiting office featured artists' renderings of beaches, exotic ports, smiling men in their dress whites, and long-haired girls waiting to welcome sea-weary sailors. As it turned out, Leu would not have much of an ocean view where he worked and bunked on the ship.

He was assigned duty on the brand-new "fleet replenishment" vessel, a *Cimarron*-class "tanker" or "fleet oiler," the largest and fastest of its type built to that point. The ship had been dubbed the *Neosho*, named, as all oilers were, for a river. The Neosho River is a tributary of the Arkansas and winds almost 500 miles through Kansas and Oklahoma. The vessel's size was imposing, even to a teenager who had seen plenty of ships operating in the waterways around Seattle.

A colossal craft designed to carry a cargo of almost 150,000 barrels of oil, the *Neosho* was 553 feet long and 75 feet wide, yet capable of reaching a speed of 18 knots. First launched in 1939, the tanker soon underwent more work to prepare her for a specialized job, refueling ships in a fleet while at sea. The ship was at nearby Bremerton shipyards when Bill Leu reported aboard for duty in May 1941, just two months before her final conversion to fleet tanker was to be completed. Then, in July, she and her crew went to work, transporting fuel from various ports on the West Coast to the storage tanks at military facilities in Pearl Harbor. It was interesting enough duty. Leu learned a lot about Navy life, and it was certainly more fun than his previous jobs. Besides, there was no war going on—at least not one involving the United States—so as long as they followed all the precautionary rules for handling the fuel they carried and everyone did his job correctly, it was as safe as riding a cruise ship.

"The Japs are bombing us! The damned Japs are bombing us!"

After coming off duty, Leu and his buddies had been below in the engine room when the peaceful morning exploded. Guys just back from downtown were bragging about their adventurous night on liberty, while the ones who had stayed aboard groused about an evening stuck in purgatory. Above the din of their complaints came what sounded like thumps, along with the roar and whine of aircraft engines.

They thought little of it. Somebody speculated that the noise was likely the damn Army flyboys deliberately torturing the sailors at Pearl Harbor with a blaring early-morning drill. The pilots would know that many of the swabbies were hungover and hurting so early on a Sunday.

That was when the red-faced sailor came running from compartment to compartment, proclaiming that they were under attack.

Leu felt the first surge of adrenaline and rapid heartbeat as he dashed to the ladder that led to the upper deck of his ship. He knew precisely what to do even before the klaxon sounded to tell them. He and his shipmates had been subjected to seemingly endless drills in preparation for moments such as this. As he raced toward his duty station, the grating, distinctive General Quarters alarm began sounding throughout the ship, sparking in him a new burst of energy.

He had a long way to go, all the way from the engine room aft to the ship's five-inch gun at the bow. Once topside, he was galloping full speed along a catwalk. Smoke was everywhere. The overwhelming clamor of airplane engines, antiaircraft guns, and explosions was excruciating.

Then he glanced over and saw something that would stick in his mind for the rest of his life. He stopped in his tracks and stared, wide-eyed.

A lightning-quick airplane buzzed so close, he thought its single propeller might clip the top of one of *Neosho*'s masts. It was a Japanese B5N "Kate" bomber, zooming so low and so near to Leu's ship that the young sailor could clearly see the pilot's face. The flier had his canopy open and was laughing as he pulled up and away, toward the few puffy clouds overhead. The plane had just dropped a deadly load, aimed at one of the seven U.S. battleships moored two abreast, all very near where Leu's ship was tied up.

The torpedo ran true and struck home. The impact of the blast pressed against his face and chest, nearly sucking all the air from his lungs, and flinging him to the deck. The explosion temporarily deafened him.

Heart pounding, Leu almost fell down, but he caught the handrail for balance and watched the plane for a few seconds as it roared away. The bold, red, rising-sun symbols were clearly visible on the aircraft's fuselage and on the underside of its wings.

"Meatballs." That was what some called the Japanese rising-sun emblem.

Leu could scarcely believe what he was seeing and hearing, what he was feeling. Across the water, the big warship USS *Oklahoma* had already been listing crazily, even before the laughing pilot's bomb struck home. Now, not even a football-field length off the stern of the *Neosho*, the *Oklahoma* was clearly capsizing as frantic sailors fled her decks, diving into a big, blazing pool of black, oil-covered water.

Men were dying by the hundreds. Leu watched from where he stood, mouth open in disbelief, observing the surreal scene.

But his instincts and adrenaline had already kicked in. All he could think of now was getting to his station as he was trained to do. And then doing whatever he could to try to erase the grins off the faces of those damned Japanese pilots.

Seaman Harry P. Ogg had drawn somewhat better duty aboard the *Neosho* than did Bill Leu. Like his shipmate, Ogg had experienced a tough upbringing during the Great Depression, working the fields of south Texas around Harlingen for pennies a day and then helping out in the little grocery store run by the grandmother who raised him. Later, the family moved up to Corpus Christi, and that was where Ogg went to high school.

He was a senior, struggling with math, when a good friend suggested that he quit school and that the two of them join the Navy together. Ogg had often listened to the audacious stories conjured up by the merchant seafarers around Corpus Christi. It sounded like an adventurous life, visiting exotic ports of call far from the choking dust, chattering cicadas, and backbreaking labor he had experienced most of his young life. Besides, as a seaman first class, he would be paid a whopping twenty-one dollars a month—much more than he made in the sun-baked fields—plus three square meals a day.

Ogg's job aboard the *Neosho* was to shadow the officer of the day and relay messages between him and the captain. On the morning of December 7, he had drawn early duty, which meant an early breakfast, served before 0600. Always an early riser from his days in the fields, first dibs on breakfast was something Ogg considered a nice benefit of his job on the tanker. The food was pretty good, and getting to it early meant it was plentiful, too.

After eating, he went as usual to assist the quartermaster in raising the ship's flag, her "colors." Since the ship was still hooked up and in the process of off-loading fuel to the storage tanks on Ford Island, the men were careful to keep the distinctive "Baker" flag hoisted. That was their way of making sure that anyone approaching their craft by air or water would be aware that the ship was discharging dangerous cargo. In this case, it was high-octane aircraft fuel that was being pumped from one of the ship's compartments into storage tanks ashore.

Just as they finished raising the flag and were climbing a ladder to the catwalk, Ogg first heard and then saw something odd. Five or six airplanes were approaching from the north over Ford Island at high speed, clearly diving, racing directly toward *Neosho*. They were "flat-hatting," a term Ogg had heard the Army pilots use for flying way too low to be safe.

"Jesus!" the quartermaster exclaimed. "Don't they see we're flying 'Baker'? They're not supposed to be coming anywhere close to us."

An officer approaching from the other direction stopped

to look, eyes wide. His jaw fell open in horror. No one bothered to salute him.

"Boys, look at that 'meatball' on their sides," the officer shouted. "That's Japanese. They're Japs!" Just then the phalanx of aircraft passed directly overhead, made a swooping turn, and zoomed back toward them, this time even more precariously low, seemingly a few dozen yards above the clear green water of the harbor. Ogg and the other two men on *Neosho* were standing on one of the highest parts of their ship. They felt the wind the planes had ginned up as they roared overhead, their screaming engines deafening.

Ogg and the others watched with shock as the pilots pointed their noses not toward the tanker but directly for the USS *Oklahoma*, the closest of the seven big battleships tied up in tandem nearby.

The officer had to yell to be heard over the ruckus of what was clearly an actual air assault, not an Army prank. His words made it somehow official: "Damn! We're in a war now!"

As the officer turned and dashed away toward the ship's bridge, Harry Ogg remained frozen in place, still disbelieving what he was witnessing. For some reason, he glanced at his wristwatch.

It was 7:55 a.m.

As the Kates and Aichi D3A "Val" airplanes bore down on the *Oklahoma*, Ogg was thinking that if only he had a rock, he could throw it and likely hit one of the bastards. They were close enough that he could see the face of the pilot of the nearest bomber. The airplane's canopy was open, and Ogg could easily make out his Asian features and the determined expression on the man's face. He wore some kind of unusual helmet, with a dashing little white tassel on top.

Something big and solid fell from beneath the Japanese aircraft and the pilot immediately pulled up and away toward the high morning sky, barely avoiding crashing into the battleship's rigging. The fallen object left a white trail through the green water as it ran just below the surface straight toward the warship. Ogg could see men standing on the deck of the *Oklahoma*, watching with as much curiosity and amazement as he and the quartermaster were.

Then, with an earsplitting boom, a flash of fire, and a miasma of smoke and debris, the torpedo hit home.

Someone running past told Ogg to go to his General Quarters station, but the alarm sounded simultaneously with the order and Ogg was on his way, anyway. His adrenaline had kicked in.

His assigned station was near a locker filled with rifles. A gunner's mate was supposed to be there with the key to the locker so that each man could be issued a rifle and ammunition, but he was nowhere to be seen.

Fat lot of good we can do with thirty-aught-six rifles against dive-bombers, Ogg thought. But at least they could do something besides watch and shake their fists while the airplanes pounded the regal vessels lined up helplessly unprotected along "Battleship Row."

Somebody, somewhere, with some rank, sent orders for them to grab fire axes and break into the lockers to get their weapons. Or maybe it was just one of the sailors standing there in the maddening confusion, frustrated, who issued his own command. At any rate, they did just that, and were soon shooting furiously at the meatballs on the planes' wings as they roared overhead before banking hard and unleashing more hellfire on the battlewagons.

Meanwhile, the bright, sunny morning had turned dark as

night. Impossibly thick, black smoke eclipsed the early tropical sun. Thunderous explosions and the raucous whine of the airplane engines and the continual clattering of the guns on the decks of the ships split the air until Ogg could hear hardly anything at all.

Still, he kept firing, kept trying to get lucky with a well-placed rifle bullet into an open cockpit. Like trying to pick off armadillos in the cotton fields back home with a .22 rifle from the bed of a bouncing truck.

Someone grabbed his shoulder, shouting something in his ear.

"What?" he screamed back. He tried to read his shipmate's lips.

"The captain says we got to make a run for it!"

"What?"

"We got to get under way, away from the mooring!" the man yelled.

Ogg shrugged his shoulders. So? The skipper had the wheel and the engine order telegraph on the bridge. He could steer them anywhere he wanted them to go.

"We're still tied up. Nobody's over there on the dock to untie our lines. Captain says we got to cut 'em loose ourselves!"

Then Ogg understood. Once untethered, they were going to steam right through an open stretch of water while under attack from scores of Japanese planes, with a series of massive tanks beneath their feet that still held thousands of gallons of some of the most flammable liquid on earth.

He dropped his impotent rifle, grabbed one of the axes they had used to break into the gun locker, and ran after the other man.

• • •

Captain John Spinning Phillips was proud of the big tanker he skippered, pleased with the vital service she performed to keep ships and airplanes ready for whatever might be coming their way in the next few troubled months and years.

If an army traveled on its stomach, a modern navy required fuel oil if it was to carry out its mission. Wind and coal no longer provided propulsion for most seagoing fighting vessels. And with aircraft carriers rising in importance, that meant aviation fuel had to be delivered for those airborne war machines, too. Whatever components made up a fleet, they all demanded fuel wherever they might be located—a fact that assured that there would be oilers in the mix, filled with the quencher for the incessant thirst of the warships and carrier-based aircraft.

The *Neosho* had been launched and commissioned directly into the Navy in 1939, unlike many of the similar models, then finally completed and placed into service in July 1941. The other tankers were originally turned over new to Standard Oil or the Keystone Tankship Corporation as merchant vessels to be used under contracts between the Navy and the shipping companies. Should war ever break out, the contracts stipulated that the ships could be taken back by the Navy. The *Neosho* had skipped the civilian service step.

With the ominous hubbub going on around the Pacific Rim and the saber rattling of the Japanese Empire, more than a few people had remarked to Phillips that the name *Neosho* sounded more like one of Emperor Hirohito's ships than an American vessel.

"No, it's about as American as it gets, a river in Kansas with an Indian name," had become his standard rejoinder. *Neosho* was an Osage word meaning "clear water."

Captain Phillips had finished his breakfast just before

eight o'clock. He was making his way to the bridge to oversee the off-loading of the last of their cargo of fuel and preparations to get under way back to California when the first Japanese aircraft roared directly over his ship. The captain was as stunned as Leu, Ogg and the rest of his crew.

Phillips began issuing orders. General quarters were to be sounded. The battery of three three-inch, twenty-three caliber antiaircraft guns and the single five-inch, fifty-one-caliber gun were to be manned immediately. He also instructed the gunnery crews to fire at will as enemy targets came into range.

As Phillips stood on the bridge of his ship, watching his men shoot in futility, he came to a frightening realization. He and the *Neosho* were sitting squarely in the midst of what were obviously the attackers' primary targets. Though he surely dreaded it, the captain understood exactly what had to be done.

So far, the planes were dropping bombs and torpedoes primarily aimed for the battleships, most of which were sitting in a line two abreast along the eastern shoreline of Ford Island. Each warship had her bow aimed directly at the *Neosho* except for the *California*, which lay to the tanker's southwest, a few hundred yards away. Those battleships were so close that, from where he stood, Phillips could feel the shudder of direct hits and the searing heat from out-of-control fires. He watched men jumping overboard, landing in oil-fed flames on the water's surface.

The assault on the battleships had been single-minded and relentless, but the *Neosho* was moored right there in the middle of them. Inevitably, the oil tanker would become a target, intentionally or not. With a direct hit, she would be nothing more than a massive incendiary bomb. Although they had off-loaded much of their fuel, there was more than enough high-octane gas still aboard Phillips's tanker to cause a monstrous blaze. The vapors left in the bunkers alone, even more volatile than the fuel, would be enough to ignite an enormous explosion.

They were still secured to the onshore storage tanks. If the ship exploded, those would certainly be destroyed as well. If a single bomb or torpedo found the *Neosho*, the resulting inferno would create even more of a disaster than the one that was already playing out all around them. The storage tanks would be vital to those warships—if any—that might survive this hellish attack.

Then, in an instant, that disaster grew worse. It would be more than enough to push Phillips to do what he knew he had to do.

Only a few minutes after sounding General Quarters, Phillips and all of his crew members who were topside felt, heard, and witnessed a cataclysmic explosion. They would later learn that a single bomb had found the exact path to the magazine on one of the battleships, the USS *Arizona*, berthed about eight hundred yards away. Debris from the detonation rained down on the *Neosho*.

Of all the deaths during the Pearl Harbor assault, half came at that instant as the result of that single blast.

Captain Phillips was now even more acutely aware of what might happen if his ship took a hit. His action report would show that he had another realization, even as he watched in horror all that was happening all around him.

His replenishment vessel was the only one of its type and size anywhere in that part of the world at the time. It would take days to get another one out to the middle of the Pacific. If the *Neosho* ended up on the sandy bottom of the harbor or blown apart, no serious response to this attack—and Phillips was savvy enough to already know there would be one—could be mounted until far too much precious time had been lost.

There was one other problem. The *Oklahoma* had capsized just a few hundred feet from the *Neosho*'s bow. USS *Maryland*, resting between the *Oklahoma* and the dock, starboard side toward the shore, was now not only fully exposed to the attackers but also effectively hemmed in by the *Neosho* and her sunken sister. The battleship could not move if her captain were to decide to try to make a run for the mouth of the harbor and the open sea.

Phillips took one glance across the smoke-shrouded harbor, at the swarm of attacking Japanese aircraft, at the blazing, smoking battlewagons, and came to a quick decision. There seemed to be a momentary lull in the assault's ferocity. He would try to take his ship away from the mooring, across the way to a safer location on the other side of the harbor, even if he could not see his destination at that moment. That would take them away from the battleships, away from the fuel storage tanks, and give the *Maryland* a way out of her corner. Though the tanker would be an easy target during the transit across the open harbor, the captain knew he had to do what it took to give them the best odds of saving the *Neosho* as well as the onshore storage tanks.

Phillips gave the order to make immediate preparations to get under way to Merry Point, Berth M-3, a distance of no more than a mile. Such a short trip was nothing on a normal day. On this particular bloody Sunday morning, that single mile across no-man's-land looked more like a hundred.

"Captain, there's nobody on the dock to cast off our lines from the bollards," someone reported. No wonder. Nobody would be waiting around over there, exposed to shrapnel and machine-gun fire, just in case the big tanker might decide to take a cruise.

"Get some men with axes and chop the lines!" Phillips ordered.

At 0842, they were loose and backing away from the dock with, at least for the moment, fewer Japanese buzzing around. Some planes still zoomed around overhead, viciously strafing with gunfire anything beneath them. The occasional bomb or torpedo still plummeted down, aimed for what remained of the nearby warships.

Maybe the attack was about over. Maybe these were stragglers, mopping up.

But from what Phillips was hearing on the radio, there would soon be a second wave coming in from the north. At least as many planes as in the first assault.

That confirmed his decision. The "fight" was not working out so well. It was time for "flight." The time to move was right damn now.

He had to get a virtually defenseless *Neosho* and her fume-filled fuel tanks away from the storage facility on Ford Island, away from the blazing battleships. Then, without help, he would have to maneuver dangerously close to the hulk of the capsized *Oklahoma*, steam across the harbor, and somehow make it to a marginally safer berth across the way.

And he had to get all this done in one hell of a big hurry.

CHAPTER TWO
Merry Point

Bill Leu was so busy at his battle station at the bow of the *Neosho*, where the number one gun was located, that it came as a shock to him and his shipmates when the ship abruptly began to move beneath them. After finally getting access to the magazine, the men had to use a rudimentary method of hauling shells up to the three-inch deck gun located just above them. They hooked boxes that held the shells to a block-and-tackle and lifted them topside, one container at a time. Each box held only three shells. Once topside, the shells were handed along from one man to another—Leu was one of those men—to the point where they could be loaded into the gun and fired. It seemed to be a lot of work for no results.

"We hit the sky every time," Leu later sardonically reported.

Aiming at and hitting the diving and zooming attack planes with the types of guns the *Neosho* carried was almost impossible. Leu wished for a machine gun, convinced that they had shown up for a gunfight with a knife.

Leu had already witnessed the awful explosion of the *Arizona*. As he worked, passing the shells, he also saw the *Nevada*, docked at the far end of Battleship Row from the *Neosho*, suddenly move away from her mooring. She appeared to be attempting to make a run for it, to get away from her sister ships, even though she was already listing noticeably from flooding through open wounds in her hull.

As she steamed into clear view in the harbor, Leu could see Japanese planes buzzing the fleeing battleship like bees around their hive, peppering the *Nevada* with bullets and bombs. As Leu would learn later, the ship's captain had, indeed, decided to pull away. With the harbor commander's permission—or urging—he wanted to try to get away from the far end of Ford Island to a position where his big vessel would not block the harbor's ship channel should she go down.

Leu, busy passing ammunition, was unable to watch her complete the valiant effort. The *Nevada* would soon deliberately run aground across the channel from Hospital Point. There, in the mud, dangerously exposed, she would continue to fight back, shooting down more of the attack planes. Her wreck would not block the harbor, either. Sixty of her crew members lost their lives. Two of her crew would receive the Medal of Honor for their actions that day, and their ship would live to fight once more, pulled from the mud, overhauled, and sent back into battle the following October.

Unbeknownst to the crew of the *Neosho*, they were about to try the same trick as the *Nevada*. Leu was surprised when he felt the ship moving, backing away from their berth. Though the attack had lessened a bit in the last few minutes, there were still planes in the sky, bullets raining down on the battleships, and bombs and torpedoes falling. The order came to keep firing at anything overhead, to step it up if at all possible if it appeared any of the aircraft were zeroing in on the oiler.

Bill Leu gasped. From his vantage point, he could clearly see that they were moving straight back, toward the upturned bottom of the *Oklahoma*. Having so far avoided getting blown out of the water by the Japs, they were now about to collide with a sunken one of their own, and as fast as they were reversing, it would be quite a jolt when they hit. He braced himself for impact.

But then, seemingly only yards from crashing into the doomed battleship, the *Neosho* swung around and pointed her bow toward the far side of the harbor. As they left behind the awful phalanx of listing and burning battleships, Leu could only shake his head in admiration as he heaved the next shell. The skipper and crew had done a fine job of getting under way from a mooring without the help of a tugboat.

As he glanced up, Leu could see off to their starboard the awnings that had been erected on the decks of *California* in preparation for church services later that morning. But no service would be conducted this day. Instead, prayers would be uttered in panic and amid chaos, spoken in hoarse whispers, not calmly in unison and in response to a chaplain.

Away from their berth and no longer covered by a black shroud of billowing smoke, the *Neosho* was dangerously exposed, alone in open water. At least she was far enough away from anything else that if she took a hit, the resulting blast would only claim the ship and her crew of nearly three hundred men. Inevitably their movement drew the attention of the attacking aircraft.

Bill Leu and his shipmates, bracing themselves against the

back-and-forth sway of the ship as she steamed a deliberately erratic course, stepped up the relay, passing shells even faster. The three-incher fired furiously into a sunny sky, even as the Japanese continued to launch their own brand of lightning bolts and thunder.

Harry Ogg had already deduced that the Japanese attackers were fixated on the battleships and destroyers. Still, he assumed they would start shooting at the big oiler and the onshore fuel storage tanks once the pilots were sure they had done in their primary objectives. Certainly when a fresh wave of planes thundered in from the north, anything not already ablaze would become targets.

Ogg continued to angrily fire his rifle at the buzzing fighters, as ordered, still hoping an accidental bullet might find a crucial engine component or strike one of the planes' three crew members. Someone had told him that Japanese aircraft ran with less armor in order to achieve more speed and maneuverability. Over and over, he had witnessed confirmation that the dive-bombers were both fast and maneuverable, but he saw no evidence that the rifle bullets were of any particular concern to the attackers.

After getting word to cut the lines to the bollards, Ogg understood that the skipper intended to make a dash across the harbor, over to where the tenders usually went. Tenders were small boats that carried the sailors from their duty ships to Merry Point Landing so that they could catch a ride into town for liberty. Someone said the captain might be planning to hide the ship behind one of the big warehouses over there, or they just needed to get as far away from the battleships as they could. But first they had to steam across the open harbor without getting themselves killed.

Sure enough, just as they cleared one of the done-for battleships and swung the bow toward Merry Point, Ogg spotted two Japanese planes that appeared to veer away from yet another run at Battleship Row and head in their direction.

It was immediately clear they were pointing toward the *Neosho*, not at one of the blazing, smoking battleships behind her.

Ogg aimed his rifle, fired, and prayed.

Captain Phillips watched through his binoculars as the stern of his big ship just avoided clipping what was left of the *Oklahoma*. Then, with enough clearance available so that they would not swing back into the overturned vessel, he ordered top-forward speed and aimed the bow of his oiler toward the other side of Pearl Harbor.

They would zigzag as much as they could without running aground, trying to give the Japanese as tough a target as possible. Meanwhile, his men would continue to punch the sky with what meager antiaircraft fire they could manage. Maybe one of the bastards would accidentally run into enough shrapnel to do some damage. Or maybe his guys would bother them enough that the planes could not get a good attack angle on the oiler.

Only minutes after leaving Ford Island behind, an approaching plane appeared to take a hit from his ship's bow gun. The aircraft began a decided sideslip at low altitude and disappeared from view into the clouds of smoke.

Just then, two other aircraft bore down on his vessel as she steamed across the harbor. The deck gunners had seen the planes, too, and directed as much fire their way as they could manage. Simultaneously, both aircraft turned sharply, showing the tanker their underbellies, and flew off to harass some-body else.

In just over half an hour after fleeing Battleship Row, the *Neosho* sidled up to a berth next to USS *Castor* (AKS-1), a supply vessel. Somehow, Phillips and his tanker had made it across the harbor with no damage, though two bombs had landed near enough to rattle not only the ship's infrastructure but the crew's nerves. Harry Ogg heard that one crew member had taken a bullet in the leg, but Captain Phillips's action report would not mention any casualties. That was despite the fact that, as Phillips noted in his report, the men at their gunnery stations on deck were in dangerously exposed positions.

Crew members on the *Castor* immediately began transferring ammunition across to the tanker, just in case the next wave had a different set of priority targets. As they worked, a lone Japanese plane approached from the north and strafed them, then roared off toward the Pacific. Amazingly, nobody was hit.

Soon after taking on the ammunition, crew members aboard the *Neosho* watched as a second wave of about 170 planes zoomed in from the north—the first had consisted of 181 aircraft—and resumed pounding the battleships, cruisers, destroyers, and other vessels. The attack was still concentrated on the very territory along Ford Island where the *Neosho* had so recently been moored.

From their new berth at Merry Point, the crew could now do little more than watch the assault and listen to the ominous thumping of exploding bombs and torpedoes. When attackers were slow to pull up from their bombing runs or strayed too near, *Neosho*'s guns targeted them as best they could. In reality, though, there was still little expectation of doing any real damage.

The Japanese would lose only twenty-nine airplanes that morning, less than 10 percent of their total attack force. The oiler's gun crews had gotten one of them.

Finally, at 1136, Captain Phillips allowed his men to relax. The second assault had been over for more than two hours and the anticipated third wave of attackers never showed up. He finally had the chance to draw a big breath and reflect on just how proud he was of the way his crew had responded to the events of this awful day.

"The gunnery discipline of the battery was excellent, as was the discipline of the ship control, repair parties, and engineering personnel," he later reported. His officers had performed well, too, including several naval reservists who had limited real-world experience. Of course, Phillips was one of only a few men on the ship who had actually served during wartime.

The *Neosho* was the only vessel moored along Battleship Row that morning that suffered no damage.

Phillips would soon receive high recognition for his own performance that day. His clearheaded thinking and quick action during those few hours at Pearl Harbor would earn him the Navy Cross, the second-highest honor for valor bestowed by the Navy. The citation read in part, "Commander Phillips realized the serious fire hazard of remaining alongside the dock as well as being in a position that prevented a battleship from getting under way, got under way immediately. Mooring lines were cut, and without the assistance of tugs, Commander Phillips accomplished the extremely difficult task of getting the ship under way from this particular berth in a most efficient manner, the difficulty being greatly increased by a battleship having capsized in the harbor. The conduct of Commander Phillips throughout this action reflects great credit upon himself, and was in keeping with the highest traditions of the United States Naval Service."

Phillips had made several correct assumptions that morning that led to his decision to cut his lines and risk racing across the harbor. One, not mentioned in his Navy Cross citation or in his own cryptic action report, was soon validated.

In President Roosevelt's speech the next day requesting a declaration of war from Congress, he urged American forces to "gain the inevitable triumph." That would have been almost impossible to fulfill if the *Neosho* had gone up in a fireball while sitting in Berth F-4 at Ford Island, or even if she had been damaged and made temporarily less than seaworthy. The skill, quick thinking, and daring of Phillips and his brave crew did more than simply avoid another catastrophic blast among all the others mushrooming around them that day. Their survival assured that a rapid American naval response to the Japanese attack would even be possible.

Allowing the *Neosho* to survive was only one of the mistakes the Japanese made that morning. Others included not waiting for the aircraft carriers to return from patrol, not being more aggressive in attacking fuel storage tanks and repair facilities, and not targeting submarines that were moored nearby.

The *Neosho* would be the only oiler available in the central Pacific for weeks. Fleets do not travel far without fuel. Carrier-based aircraft are useless without aviation gasoline.

With a war now to be waged, this particular vessel had become even more crucial to the U.S. Navy. Americans—furious, demanding revenge, and clamoring to go to war—were united in the cause. An immediate response was required to preserve morale and to assure the Japanese that their sneak attack had not, as intended, jammed the gears of the American war machine in the Pacific. Nor had it shocked the people of the United States into inaction.

The *Neosho* had an even more important job to perform. She would now be able to do it as no other ship and crew could. She would get to it, beginning the very next day.

CHAPTER THREE
Fat Girl

Battleships have long carried a great deal of panache among the world's navies, especially since the early 1900s. Once called "dreadnoughts" after the 1906 British Royal Navy vessel that bore that name, twentieth-century battleships were distinguished by their array of immense guns, their use of steam propulsion, and, to be sure, their size. They were well suited to do what warships are supposed to do: destroy and kill. As larger and more deadly ships were put into commission, naval tacticians naturally assumed that future sea battles would most often start between, and be dominated by, big battleships. Before the vessels could actually see each other, they would begin hurling huge shells from their large-caliber guns. Ultimately the clashes would end with surviving dreadnoughts firing point-blank at closer range until a ship surrendered, fled, or was sunk, much as had happened with sailing ships in another era.

The Japanese had been among the first to commit to building a larger fleet of the more sizable battleships, starting with *Satsuma*, which was laid down in 1904. The Russo-Japanese War of 1904 and 1905 confirmed for the Imperial Japanese Navy that sea battles would be fought at great distances, requiring deck guns capable of launching ordnance at enemy vessels and shore installations from well beyond the horizon. They were certainly aware of the fright value of a massive ship, guns booming, dropping shells out of the sky onto faraway targets. The IJN's continued infatuation with dreadnoughts carried over into the beginning of World War II. Japan built the two largest and most heavily armed battleships ever constructed, the first two of the proposed "three sisters." The *Yamato* and the *Musashi* were each more than 860 feet in length and displaced an amazing 72,000 tons. The *Yamato* was commissioned a week after the attack on Pearl Harbor. The *Musashi* followed soon after, in the summer of 1942.

The decision to concentrate the Pearl Harbor attack on warships moored along Battleship Row was driven by a prejudice that had been held by many in the Japanese navy for at least the previous half century. Yet for some officers, airpower had altered the balance at sea. Planes had successfully operated off ship decks since the Japanese first launched an air raid off a vessel in September 1914. Admiral Isoroku Yamamoto, commander in chief of the Combined Fleet, had been a strong proponent of carriers since before the war, even as his colleagues' commitment to the "three sisters" battleships persisted.

A new era of sea warfare required a different kind of capital ship. One reason for this was simply because of the vulnerability of the battleships, and especially to the specific ordnance that could be delivered by airplanes in wave after wave, overpowering the big ships' defenses.

Quick progress in aircraft technology between the wars assured that carriers would soon play a bigger role than battleships in modern combat. Airplanes could launch off aircraft carriers and then range out hundreds of miles from their mother ship to hunt and pounce on those extremely large and inviting targets. Then they could return to a continually moving base, refuel, and return to the skies from an entirely different point in the ocean.

It did not take the Japanese long to realize the changing nature of nautical warfare, and to come around to Admiral Yamamoto's way of thinking. The third of the "sisters," the *Shinano*, was already well under construction in the Yokosuka Naval Arsenal on Tokyo Bay when the decision was made to convert her to an aircraft carrier instead.

As the world's navies evolved to take advantage of emerging technology during World War I and after, the fuel used to propel many of their vessels changed, as well. Coal was no longer the primary fuel burned to make steam in ships' boilers to power their engines. Prior to World War I, warships had to make their way to coal stations at strategically located and friendly ports around the world (there was a massive one at Pearl Harbor), or rely on ships, called colliers, which came to them at sea. Colliers were typically lashed to warships long enough for a sufficient load of coal to be transferred over, much of the work being done by hand. With bigger battleships, this operation could take as long as twelve hours.

The rise of aircraft carriers brought a need for a different kind of replenishment ship. The flattops now required oil to make steam in their own huge boilers. The airplanes that flew off the carriers' decks had no need for coal, either. They thirsted for aviation fuel.

The tanker, or oiler, became a vital part of any country's navy, and a key member of a fleet or task force. With thousands of airplanes in the fleets of the world to keep filled up, the need was for bigger and bigger replenishment ships.

The U.S. Navy's first oiler, the *Arethusa* (which eventually carried the hull number AO-7), was built by the British. Acquired by the United States in 1893, she was at first used primarily to carry water. She began delivering oil to the Atlantic Fleet in 1910. Later classes of oilers were bigger but slower. Some tankers were actually purchased from commercial shipping companies as needed.

By the time the first three *Cimarron*-class tankers were launched in 1939, the ships had become huge, but were still able to steam remarkably fast for their bulk. Those first three were the *Cimarron* (AO-22), the *Neosho*, and the *Platte* (AO-24). Each was designated a "T3-S2"-type vessel. The T meant they were tankers. The 3 indicated that each ship had a length greater than five hundred feet. S2 was for the type of propulsion. S meant steam turbine and 2 indicated the ships were propelled by twin screws.

They were propelled rather quickly, too. Despite their size and weight when fully loaded, they could scurry along at 18 knots, about 21 miles per hour. Speed and range were important. They would be called upon to steam from distant locations, where the fleet might be operating, to depots where they could refill their storage tanks, and then hurry back loaded with oil and catch up with the fleet again. That was a tall order. Even the older carriers such as the *Lexington* were capable of better than 32 knots (37 miles per hour).

The *Neosho* was laid down at Federal Shipbuilding and Drydock Company in Kearny, New Jersey, along the Hackensack River, with an official start-of-construction date of June 22, 1938. She was commissioned more than fourteen months later on August 7, 1939, with Commander E. A. Mullan as her first skipper. His job was to take the big ship through her sea trials and, eventually, transit down the East Coast, through the Panama Canal, and on to the Puget Sound Naval Shipyard at Bremerton, Washington. There she underwent more conversion to meet the specific requirements of a fleet tanker, which were different from those of a ship bound for commercial tanker use. These included installing weapons, equipment for refueling ships while at sea, and even more fire-prevention gear and systems. There she also continued to assemble her crew of about three hundred men.

She was officially placed into service on July 7, 1941. The next month, in a change-of-command ceremony, the keys to the *Neosho* were passed from Commander Mullan to her new captain, an experienced forty-six-year-old named John Spinning Phillips.

Commander Phillips was born February 28, 1895, in Alexandria, Virginia, but grew up in Oradell, New Jersey, fewer than twenty miles up the Hackensack River from the shipyard in which the *Neosho* would be constructed more than forty years later. Appointed to the U.S. Naval Academy in Annapolis, Maryland, in 1914, Phillips was an active student, singing bass in both choir and glee club. He performed well academically, earning a 4.0 grade point average in languages. He made both the wrestling and tennis teams but was forced to give them up due to a bad knee. His true passions, though, were dancing, which appealed to the ladies, and golf, a game he picked up at the age of fifteen. He excelled at both.

Phillips graduated as part of the academy class of 1918, though he actually received his degree and commission in 1917. Right out of the academy, Phillips found himself in the midst of World War I. Because of the conflict raging across the globe, his class had been rushed to completion and assignment.

He served as an officer aboard USS *South Dakota* (ACR-9), an armored cruiser, escorting troopship convoys from the East Coast of the United States to the midpoint of the Atlantic Ocean. There British warships picked up the convoy for the remainder of the crossing while the cruiser would either meet an American-bound convoy or hustle back to the United States to do it all over again.

Phillips immediately experienced the tension and tactics of a shooting war. German U-boats were inflicting heavy losses on shipping, and the *South Dakota* and her crew were in constant danger. It was stressful duty. The young ensign learned a great deal about running a warship in enemy waters, as well as handling a crew that was continually under threat from a vicious and well-trained enemy.

In peacetime, with solid war experience on his résumé, Phillips continued his naval career, but swapped sea duty in enemy waters for more humdrum chores. He taught at the Naval Academy for two two-year tours and also served as professor of naval science and tactics at Northwestern University in Evanston, near Chicago, where he taught mostly naval reservists. That, too, was good experience. Once he assumed command of his own ship—and when he again found himself in the middle of a war—many of his officers would be reservists, hastily called up for active duty. He would understand well their value, as well as their limitations.

Phillips eventually worked at the Bureau of Naval Operations in Washington, DC, which afforded him plenty of time for golf. He felt he was well on track for possible flag command at some point in his career, but for that, he needed to actually captain a ship.

By 1938, rumblings of war led to a new assignment for Phillips that would plug that hole in his résumé. Ordered to return to sea duty, he was to become the skipper of a brand-new tanker just about to go into service out on the West Coast. Her first job would be to make runs from the mainland to Hawaii to deliver loads of fuel oil to various military storage facilities there. With Japan's bluster and aggressiveness, it was crucial to keep the tanks full at Pearl Harbor, at the air bases on Oahu, and at other locations around the Pacific Rim. Phillips's new command assignment and the launch of his ship came just in time for his crew to play a crucial role in that chore.

His first view of the *Neosho*, berthed in Bremerton, had to have impressed Phillips. Ever the golf enthusiast, Phillips thought a time or two about setting up a golf tee aft on his ship's poop deck, next to her single big smokestack. Then he would see how close he could come to driving a ball over the towering bridge amidships and try to reach the forecastle of his tanker. That would be some kind of drive, but the experiment would have to wait for another time and place.

At 553 feet long and 75 feet wide, she was only 50 feet shorter than the battleships and fully two-thirds the length of some of the aircraft carriers that she would soon be refueling at sea. No wonder the *Cimarron*-class tankers had earned the nickname "Fat Girls." She was certainly longer and wider than Phillips's previous ship, the cruiser *South Dakota*. The *Neosho* and her sisters were, at the time of their construction, the largest tankers in the world.

She was capable of carrying a stunning amount of volatile liquid cargo in her twenty-six tanks, each separated—and isolated for reasons of fire prevention—from the others by strong bulkheads. That also allowed her to carry different mixtures of petroleum, depending on the needs of the Navy.

The *Neosho* was of the "three-island" type of bulk oil carrier. She had a long, relatively flat deck with three raised sections: the poop, or "stack," deck at the rear of the ship with the distinctive single smokestack towering above it; the bridge, about two-thirds of the way from the stern; and the forecastle at the bow. She also displayed two towering steel masts rigged with powerful cargo-handling booms. In addition to fuel oil, the new, larger tankers were also called upon to carry freight—thus the booms—and even, at times, passengers.

Phillips had studied production documentation for the *Neosho* and knew already that because of his ship's primary cargo, she carried a sophisticated carbon dioxide system for extinguishing fires. Shipbuilders had to meet other fireproof construction requirements as well.

Steam, which propelled the big vessel, was supplied by four Babcock & Wilcox water tube boilers, designed to provide 450 pounds per square inch of pressure at 750 degrees Fahrenheit. This produced almost 7,000 horsepower via each of the twin steam turbines, which were capable of turning *Neosho*'s big screws at 96 rpm. Along with other equipment, the ship also had two General Electric 400-kilowatt generator sets that produced a 230-volt alternating current for the electrical needs of the ship.

Big pumps, located in pump rooms at the stern and amidships, were used to off-load fuel, either to ships at sea, often while they were moving—that was why she was called a "fleet tanker"—or into storage tanks at a depot when delivering to a port facility. A complicated maze of pipes, valves, and other plumbing handled all that fuel and made sure the right mixture got into the right tanks on the ship being refueled or into shore storage facilities.

Another set of pipes and fixtures carried the steam generated by *Neosho*'s boilers to the turbines. Safety mechanisms were built into this system, as well—the steam that drove the turbines could boil a man to death in seconds should there be a sudden rupture in a line.

Phillips was likely not surprised to learn that his ship carried limited defensive firepower. She projected nothing near the glamour of a battleship or carrier. The *Neosho* was a working ship, a blue-collar vessel, not a warship. Her job was to haul fuel oil, and that was primarily what she was designed to do.

Even so, different tankers in her class were equipped with slightly different weapons to provide at least marginal self-defense capability. At her commissioning, the *Neosho* had available four five-inch gun mounts, four twin forty-millimeter antiaircraft gun mounts, and four twin twenty-millimeter antiaircraft gun mounts. According to military records, though, shortly after the start of the war and throughout her short service, the tanker carried only one five-inch gun, three three-inch guns, and eight twenty-millimeter guns. As Commander Phillips noted in his action report, during the attack on Pearl Harbor his deck guns were good for little more than trying to harass and keep dive-bombers from getting too close to his ship and its volatile cargo.

In early 1940, the U.S. Navy had mostly completed the transfer of its Pacific Fleet Headquarters from San Diego, California, to Pearl Harbor. The reasoning was that if Japan did eventually drag the United States into the war, Hawaii would be a more strategic location from which to oversee defense of the West Coast of the mainland as well as other Navy outposts around the Pacific Rim, from the Philippines to the Aleutian Islands. Of course, there were no oil wells in Hawaii, so all fuel for ships and aircraft based there had to be imported. The Los Angeles area was the closest place to find it.

By the time the *Neosho* went into service, her sister ship, the *Cimarron*, had already been hustling, making regular runs from the big fuel depot at San Pedro, near Long Beach, across the Pacific and over to Pearl Harbor. Then the *Cimarron* was sent back to the East Coast when the *Neosho* was ready to take up her delivery route in the Pacific.

As soon as John Phillips was on her bridge, her crew assembled and trained, and final conversion work completed and tested in the summer of 1941, *Neosho* was hurried into service making the milk run out of San Pedro to Pearl, taking the place of her portly sister.

Bill Leu had come aboard in May. His assessment of his ship was simple: "She was a big ship. She was a good ship."

Harry Ogg, who had watched commercial oil tankers coming and going out of Corpus Christi, had never seen anything the size of his new ship. While still in Bremerton, Ogg's primary duty was one of the most common in any nation's navy: chipping off old paint and reapplying new in its place. Metal and wood had to be protected from salt air. He did not mind the job. The weather was cool and damp, not hot and dusty like back home, and he enjoyed the camaraderie with his shipmates.

It was not long before the *Neosho* headed down the coast to San Pedro to pump aboard her first load of high-octane fuel. Ogg still had to chip and paint while they were in port, but at sea he enjoyed easier duty as a gofer for the ship's officers.

Both Ogg and Leu noticed how the officers on the *Neosho* always seemed to be in a hurry, pushing the load-out in California as quickly as possible, steaming at near top speed across to Oahu, unloading at various depots around Pearl Harbor over the next two days, and then immediately pointing their big vessel back eastward. Word was their ship was the primary supplier of fuel to the growing base in Hawaii, and with all the tension between the United States and Japan, the Navy wanted to be sure tanks on the island were always topped off. The crew sometimes had overnight liberty, either in California or on Oahu. The time ashore was usually occupied by softball games with crew members from other ships or a run into town for the typical pursuits of sailors on shore leave.

Ogg found that he enjoyed life in the Navy. Washington, California, and Hawaii were impressive places for a guy from rural Texas whose previous longest trip away from home had been only to Louisiana. Traveling all the way to the Pacific Northwest and shipping out aboard his new home for the next year were truly amazing adventures for a kid off the farm.

Meanwhile, Ogg and Leu were trained diligently for their assigned duties, learning the procedures of General Quarters (sometimes referred to as "battle stations"). They were required to know what to do at their own particular duty stations if there was an accident or, if war did come, an enemy assault.

"I can remember training on the ship in case of an attack, where the ammunition was, where the rifle was, and all that," Ogg later recalled. He had no reason to expect his ship would ever come under enemy attack, yet they drilled anyway. It broke the monotony. "We were just supposed to follow instructions."

Commander Phillips would later cite all that training as one of the reasons they were able to ward off Japanese Kates and Vals as the *Neosho* maneuvered out of the berth at Ford Island and steamed across Pearl Harbor. Even with their limited firepower, Phillips was convinced that his gun crews had persuaded the attacking pilots to seek another target as the big ship zigzagged across to the relative safety of Merry Point.

His crew also trained on how to handle any damage to the equipment in their work areas if there should be an accident or if they came under attack. Damage control would be an important factor in whether or not they survived an accident or assault, the officers and chiefs assured them.

Bill Leu was certainly aware of the importance of keeping the boilers working, the turbines spinning, the two screws turning. Officers warned the crew that they might someday have to dodge a warship or maneuver the tanker to avoid an air assault.

In wartime, a ship that was dead in the water was simply dead. Yet before December 7, the young sailors had difficulty imagining ever getting pounced on by an enemy.

Both Ogg and Leu noticed that their ship seemed to be highly valued by the Navy. Even before surviving the attack at Pearl Harbor, when conducting exercises with other vessels, the tanker was treated as a prized asset, usually shielded by submarines, destroyers, and cruisers, just as the carriers were.

But now, with the nation at war, she was even more critical. The *Neosho* was the only tanker of her size and capabilities that America's Navy had in the Pacific when the war started, the only replenishment ship around to put to use as what was left of the fleet fanned out to seek some modicum of revenge against the Japanese.

With smoke still rising from the smoldering hulks along Battleship Row, with bodies still being fished from the harbor's placid waters, the *Neosho* was immediately ordered to follow and support the warships that were still available—primarily the destroyers and cruisers at first and soon the aircraft carriers—as they operated in the Pacific. Older, smaller tankers would continue the milk runs. Newer, bigger ones would be on the scene as soon as they could get there. The *Platte* was being refitted at San Diego when the war started, but got under way to Hawaii on December 17 to accompany and refuel the carrier task force that included USS *Enterprise* (CV-6). It would be April 1942 before *Cimarron* could be redeployed to the Pacific, to support the task force that was sending planes out to bomb Japan.

Bill Leu later remembered the days after the attack at Pearl, going out first with the "remnants of the fleet, just some cruisers and destroyers looking for the Japanese, but I don't think they looked very hard because we didn't have much left. We went out to fuel them, though. And then we . . . hurried back to the States and had eight twenty-millimeter machine guns put on her, tacked on our deck so we could better defend ourselves." Leu had finally gotten his wish for a weapon that might be more effective during an enemy dive-bomb attack.

Once they became part of Task Force 17—which eventually included the aircraft carriers *Lexington* (CV-2) and *Yorktown* (CV-5)—their duty became even more hectic and dangerous.

"About January . . . we started going out to the task force and we'd fuel them," Leu recalled. "And we fueled cruisers, destroyers, and . . . two aircraft carriers. And when we were out there fueling them, we were the most important ship in the task force. They'd all protect us, you know.

"One time, we got a torpedo across the bow and we were fueling the *Chicago* (CA-29), a heavy cruiser . . . and I'll never forget the way they cut their lines and took off [when they realized there was an enemy submarine nearby]. They wanted to get the hell out of there. They didn't want to be around a tanker."

Captain Phillips and his crew shadowed the carriers, fueling them as needed and pumping over aviation gas. When the oiler's cargo tanks approached empty, they ran back to Pearl to replenish them.

As in the First World War, John Phillips found himself on the bridge of a ship operating in hazardous enemy waters, scanning along with his lookouts for submarine periscopes. This time, though, unlike his stint on the *South Dakota* in the Atlantic, there was just as big a threat from above.

Phillips had already witnessed up close the damage carrier-based Japanese dive-bombers could do, and how difficult it was to avoid their bombs and torpedoes. He was usually protected by a destroyer escort when making the run back to Hawaii, and he knew those guys would do all they could to defend his big floating gas station. Still, any Japanese submarine or plane would likely appreciate the value of this particular plump target.

Soon there was proof of it. Word came that one of the older tankers, USS *Neches* (AO-5), had been sunk by a Japanese submarine on January 23, 1942. She had been 120 miles west of Pearl Harbor, taking fuel to the same ships that *Neosho* was replenishing. Fifty-seven sailors were lost.

On March 1 a sister to the *Neches*, the *Pecos* (AO-6), went down, sunk by dive-bombers. This was an even worse tragedy, as she carried over 300 passengers, survivors who had been rescued from another sunken Navy ship, in addition to *Pecos*'s crew of 317. Only 231 men were pulled from the water after *Pecos* slipped beneath the waves. Almost 400 were lost. Many of those who initially survived the sinking—in some cases sailors who had lived through both sinkings—were machine-gunned by Japanese aircraft while in the water, and killed.

Phillips knew that should he be caught in the open he would have to rely heavily on his escort destroyer to scare away any attackers, as well as on his brave crew to man what deck guns they had at their disposal. Meanwhile, it would be critical that others in the crew work unwaveringly to give them the steam power they needed to run fast and steer an erratic course, making their ship as hard to hit as possible. If they were close enough to their own fleet, warplanes off the carrier decks might be able to come to their aid, but that was unlikely on the runs from the South Pacific to Hawaii and back, as well as any other time they were away from the main force or if the fleet was tied up in battle.

In those situations, the *Neosho* and her escort would be on their own.

Everyone aboard the tanker was aware of the value of their contribution to the war effort, even if they would likely never show up in the newsreels or on the covers of magazines. Phillips had watched from the bridge as his brave men worked to pump fuel over to the aircraft carriers *Yorktown*, *Lexington*, and other ships. Often the seas were so rough that the men had to lash themselves to something solid to keep from getting washed over the side. So rough, it was a sickening tango to keep the *Neosho* close enough to the receiving vessel to stay attached while avoiding a collision.

Yet there was no choice. If a ship was low on fuel, regardless of treacherous weather or roiling seas, the sailors aboard the *Neosho* had to hook up and pump some over.

Nobody could be allowed to run dry.

Despite the anger, the clamor for payback, and the swelling patriotic ardor, it was quickly evident to many Americans that the push for a powerful answer to the December 7 attack was going to be more difficult than what most had expected. By May 1942, it was clear that the war was not going at all well for the Allies.

Nothing they had done so far had even slowed the Japanese in their continuing violent expansion. Despite the blunders made by the Imperial Japanese Navy in their attack on Pearl Harbor, the U.S. response had so far failed to slow the aggressive march down the spine of islands through the Pacific from the Home Islands to the Solomons and New Guinea.

Battles were being lost. Territory was falling to the enemy. There appeared to be nothing the Allies could do to stop the well-tuned war machine of the Japanese Empire.

If the Japanese continued to capture lands that gave them the slave labor and the crucial petroleum and other natural resources necessary to sustain the war effort, this particular fanatical enemy might well prove to be impossible to defeat. The rest of the world was beginning to believe, too, that the sneak attack on Pearl Harbor had been just as successful as the Japanese had claimed.

Then came word, thanks to superior American communications intelligence and the breaking of the Japanese naval code, that the enemy was next aggressively aiming a two-prong operation at the southern end of the Solomon Islands. Japan was quickly moving to establish bases close enough to

Australia to launch regular air attacks on that country's major cities and military facilities, while keeping a close eye on Allied comings and goings in the region.

Tulagi and Port Moresby were the locations to be captured and where Japanese bases were to be established. Both invasion forces would be supported by land-based planes from airfields farther north, as well as by two other battle groups. The main support force consisted of a small aircraft carrier—the *Shoho*—four heavy cruisers, and a destroyer. Farther away, over the horizon, additional cover was to be provided by aircraft off the decks of two bigger aircraft carriers, the *Shokaku* and the *Zuikaku*, as well as by cruisers and destroyers that made up that contingent, dubbed the "carrier striking force."

The Allies recognized this as a prime opportunity to attempt to blunt the point of the Japanese spear. If they could prevent Japan from establishing these strong strategic bases, they would, for the first time in the five-month-old war, finally have something positive to tout.

It would certainly not be easy. Japan's two big carriers had a fierce contingent of aircraft, and well-trained pilots to fly them. Both carriers had been a part of the fleet that launched the attack on December 7, and many of the planes and pilots were among those that devastated Pearl Harbor.

Weather was a concern as well. Storms were common in the area at that time of year. Not lost on the Allies was that this could well be a different kind of battle, one in which most of the actual fighting would be conducted by aircraft attacking each other's fleets. One in which neither side's warships might ever catch sight of the other's. In such a battle, weather would be a significant factor affecting aircraft and the carriers' ability to launch them. Cloud cover could even prevent each side from actually locating the other at sea.

At any rate, with the advance intelligence available to them and aided by the element of surprise, the Allies decided that this would be the best opportunity so far to attempt to stop the enemy. All available assets were put into place in an area southwest of the Solomon Islands, southeast of New Guinea, and northeast of the Australian coast.

The carrier *Yorktown* was there already. The *Lexington* had just undergone an overhaul in Hawaii and was speeding back to join the force. The *Neosho* and newly arrived sister tanker *Tippecanoe* (AO-21)—the last of the smaller *Patoka*-class oilers, a vessel that could carry only about half the fuel that the *Neosho* could—were the oilers in the task force. Designated as Task Group 17.6 (Fueling Group), the group under the command of Captain Phillips—the oilers and their escorts, the destroyers USS *Sims* (DD-409) and USS *Worden* (DD-352)—were kept busy refueling the thirsty carriers, destroyers, and cruisers as the fleet assembled and prepared for the inevitable battle. Meanwhile, more cruisers—more ships that would need fuel—were on the way from the Australian navy. Scout planes off the *Yorktown* were already busy, out looking for any signs of the enemy fleet in the steamy haze, thick fog, and muddling rain clouds.

May 1, 1942, found the Allied fleet as ready as they could be, waiting for the command to launch all aircraft and initiate the first devastating strike against the enemy. Strike, that is, when some pilot finally spotted the Japanese fleet or any elements of the attack force headed for Port Moresby.

They waited for the inevitable in the warm jade-green waters of the Coral Sea.

After serving aboard the *Neosho* for the rest of December and the first four months of 1942, shadowing various carrier task forces, Harry Ogg was abruptly transferred off the tanker when he and seven shipmates were designated for duty aboard new construction back in New Jersey.

Several weeks later, Ogg was aboard a train on his way across the country when he heard the news about the fate of his former ship.

All he could do was pray for his old shipmates.

PART TWO
THE CORAL SEA

With the losses we have sustained, it is necessary to revise completely our strategy of a Pacific War. . . . A very powerful striking force of carriers, cruisers, and destroyers survives. These forces must be operated boldly and vigorously on the tactical offensive in order to retrieve our initial disaster.

—Rear Admiral Chester W. Nimitz,
December 10, 1941

CHAPTER FOUR
Operation MO

If the war was going poorly for the Allies, then it was proceeding spectacularly well for the Japanese. Yet the stunning success of the Japanese following the attack on Pearl Harbor was actually causing distress in the higher reaches of the empire's military hierarchy. The longtime friction between the Army and Navy was openly sparking.

Though it had been less than half a year since Pearl Harbor and the U.S. entry into the war, the Japanese found themselves months ahead of even their most optimistic schedule. The Imperial General Headquarters argued vigorously among themselves about how aggressively they should continue to push to seize more territory to add to what the Japanese had cleverly named the "Greater East Asian Co-Prosperity Sphere." In mid-December, that "sphere" reached east to Wake Island, the Marshalls, and the Gilberts, south to the islands just north of Australia, and west into vast swaths of mainland China.

Some, primarily in the Japanese army, wanted to be a bit more conservative, to shore up what they held already, to build stronger defenses in case the Allies someday got their act together. On the other hand, the Navy advocated utilizing the momentum it had gained and grabbing all the strategically valuable territory it could as long as the opposition remained relatively ineffective.

Their argument became even more heated after U.S. bombers, modified for long-range, carrier-based raids, hit key targets on the main island of Honshu, including Tokyo, on April 18, 1942. Known as the Doolittle Raid, damage from the planes' bombs was minimal, yet the raid demonstrated to the world—including the shocked Japanese—that the Allies still possessed the capability of hitting the enemy where they lived, and even to possibly injure or kill their beloved emperor.

Despite their differences on strategy, after the shocking raid all elements of the Japanese military agreed on one point—another decisive victory was needed, and it might just as well have some tactical value.

Admiral Isoroku Yamamoto and the Imperial Japanese Navy wanted to take Australia. Such a bold invasion would send the obvious message that the empire had not finished expanding the "co-prosperity sphere," and that the Doolittle Raid had not quelled by one iota the enthusiasm for growing the empire. At the same time, it would also effectively allow Yamamoto to put a stop to what few attacks the struggling Allies were launching from Australia.

The Japanese army, already stretched thin by all the impressive advances—and the considerable casualties that came with them—championed a more cautionary plan. They advocated taking a couple of key tactical outposts first and then making a bolder move—if warranted—later in the year. The army prevailed for the time being.

Operation MO, as it was dubbed, was made a top priority, even though it was a compromise between the military leaders. It was the Japanese army's plan, but it had grudging appeal to the navy because it would still expand territory, if only minimally, and send the obvious signal to the Allies and the world—including the empire's Tripartite Pact partners in Nazi Germany and fascist Italy—that Japan was still aggressive. It would also confirm that the Allies in general and the United States in particular were powerless to prevent it.

Also, if successful—and it almost certainly would be, because the Allies were not only ill prepared to stop them but, as far as anyone knew, totally unaware of what was happening—the plan would give the Japanese effective control of the Coral Sea. That would put Australia to the southwest and the key shipping lanes to and from the island continent squarely in the gun sights and periscopes of their warships and submarines. It would also make the Allied bases in Australia an easily reachable distance for aircraft off Yamamoto's carrier decks, as well as the new land bases that would be established at the two captured outposts.

There was one other psychological plus: General Douglas MacArthur would soon move his headquarters from Melbourne on the southern coast of Australia to Brisbane, on the eastern coast. The Japanese knew that from their new outposts at Port Moresby and Tulagi Harbor, they could give the American general a daily dose of bombs to go with his breakfast. Of course, the invasion of Australia would be the logical next step, once the island continent was softened up more and Allied operations in the area had been virtually eradicated.

The Japanese had two specific goals for Operation MO. First, the island of Tulagi, which had a good harbor and was reasonably close to Guadalcanal, would be captured and used as a base primarily to observe and support action in the area. Simultaneously, troopships and escorts would move toward Port Moresby—the "MO" in the operation's designation—on the southeastern coast of New Guinea, with aims of capturing that key settlement. Port Moresby was the last bit of the big island still controlled by the Allies. The dotted line that denoted Japanese-controlled territory already ran tantalizingly close, just to the north of the city.

Back at Pearl Harbor, Admiral Chester Nimitz, the Pacific Fleet commander, was not at all in the dark, as the Japanese believed. He had a relatively clear picture of what was about to happen. The Japanese secret naval code had been broken even before the United States entered the war and the Allies had been eavesdropping all along on the preparations for Operation MO.

Nimitz certainly understood the value of Port Moresby. Japanese control that far south threatened even more the Allied convoys that were regularly steaming to and from Australia and gave the enemy the perfect launch base for an eventual invasion of the country. This would be a prime opportunity to try to throw up a roadblock to the empire's southern advance.

The emphasis was on the word "try." Though Nimitz knew what was coming, he was quite aware that he was handicapped in his options to stop it. Only two of his four heavy carriers were anywhere near the region. The other two, USS *Enterprise* and USS *Hornet* (CV-8), were busy in the aftermath of the Doolittle Raid thousands of miles to the north. Nimitz's code breakers had also discovered clear signs of a

Japanese invasion of Midway, making it desirable to keep those two flattops where they were.

Even so, with the heads-up about the looming invasion of Port Moresby and the chance to get a crucial initial victory—and possibly two Japanese aircraft carriers—Nimitz relented. He promptly ordered *Enterprise* and *Hornet* south. Still, there was little hope they could arrive in time to help out in the Coral Sea.

Meanwhile, *Lexington* and *Yorktown,* the two carriers close enough to be of immediate value, along with their accompanying fleet of ships—including the *Neosho*—were directed to meet up with British Rear Admiral Sir John Crace and his three cruisers. Their rendezvous was set for May 1 just off the New Hebrides, the islands that marked the eastern end of the Coral Sea. From there, they were to try to first locate and attack the MO Main Force they knew to be headed for Port Moresby. Secondarily, they were to look for the two Japanese carriers that were expected to be supporting the push with air cover from farther north. The Allied ships hoped to be able to make a surprise assault on them. In addition, the Allied task force was to use their aircraft to locate, engage, and destroy as many elements involved in MO as they could.

The stated goal would be, for the first time, to stop the Japanese advance southward. That made the Port Moresby Main Force—not the big carriers—their primary target and, if they were successful, the enemy invasion force would turn back. The secondary goal would be to inflict enough damage on the big Japanese carriers so that they would not be able to join the force Nimitz knew was coming soon to Midway.

As early as three days after the debacle at Pearl Harbor, Nimitz had been lobbying for reasonable restraint, including being defensively cautious, but also to proceed with aggression where it made sense. In his "Briefed Estimate 10 December 1941" document, which was compiled before the smoke cleared at Pearl Harbor, Nimitz made the case for both seemingly contradictory postures.

The Allies definitely needed to be defensive, especially to prevent a second attack on Pearl Harbor, until more capital ships could be placed into service or salvaged. But they also needed to strike decisively to let the Japanese—as well as the rest of the world, including American citizens—know that the United States still had the capability of, and stomach for, fighting a war.

The admiral described the mission of the Allies, as he saw it, to be "strategically defensive, but an appreciation of the general world situation clearly demands that the action and dispositions required to carry it out must be boldly offensive."

At the same time, Nimitz told his bosses in the Navy as well as members of his staff why there was a need to be prudent: "Our government is more cumbersome [than the Japanese] for purposes of making war. Our Associated Powers in the Pacific are woefully weak, and much weaker today through having lost [the battleships at Pearl Harbor]."

Nimitz knew it would be a tough job. The United States, from the Aleutians of Alaska to the Mexican border south of San Diego, must be protected. At the same time, available warships would need to be quick and aggressive to stem the enemy's Pacific march southward and westward as they conquered more strategic territory and cut the throat of Australia.

So it was that in May 1942 the stage was set for a sea battle that would either stop the Japanese cold—or give the empire yet another victory to add to the long string they boasted already. An Allied defeat in the Coral Sea would provide Japan yet another vital foothold in the region.

Still, only one side was fully aware of the magnitude of the impending clash. Though some had their suspicions, the Japanese did not know that the two U.S. carriers were already in the Coral Sea, preparing to try to stop Operation MO.

That was about the only advantage the Allies had as April flipped over to May.

The upcoming showdown was bringing together an interesting cast of characters.

On the Japanese side, Rear Admiral Chuichi Hara was the colorful commander of the Japanese 5th Carrier Division, including the aircraft carriers *Zuikaku* and *Shokaku*. As noted, it was his carriers, dive-bombers, torpedo aircraft, and many of the same crew members that had played such a major role in the attack on Pearl Harbor. He had been nicknamed "King Kong" by the Japanese people, for both his unusually large frame for someone of his heritage as well as his fiery temper, especially when he imbibed too much alcohol.

Hara had achieved flag rank in his country's navy in a specialty other than carriers and aviation. That required that he quickly bring himself up to speed on the flattops and their aircraft after becoming commander of the carriers in September 1941.

The commander of the Main Force that would support the Invasion Force of Operation MO, including the light carrier *Shoho* and her eighteen aircraft, was Rear Admiral Aritomo Goto. He had already tasted success leading operations at Guam, Wake Island, and Rabaul, the latter of which was now a key command center for the Japanese in the Solomons. By

May 1942 Rabaul was the location of 5th Carrier Division command headquarters, aboard the light cruiser *Kashima*, which was moored there.

Rear Admiral Takeo Takagi, the carrier strike force commander for MO, was a fast riser in the Imperial Japanese Navy. Originally a submarine specialist, he had gained flag rank in the surface navy early in his career. He was promoted to vice admiral, effective May 1, 1942, just as Operation MO was being launched. Unlike many in high-ranking military positions, where a strong ego is typically a necessary trait, Takagi recognized his own limitations. As with so many others in high command, he had little experience in the most important elements of his strike force, the aircraft carriers. Neither did most of the men on his staff.

Takagi willingly delegated carrier operations to Admiral Chuichi Hara, "King Kong."

On the Allied side, the overall commander of Task Force 17—*Yorktown*, *Lexington*, and all the associated warships and support vessels that it included—was Rear Admiral Frank Jack Fletcher. Had it not been for his bad eyesight, Fletcher would likely have been a naval aviator. Most of his experience, though, had been in battleships and cruisers, a ship typically bigger and with more firepower than a destroyer but not nearly as large as a battleship and certainly not the size of a carrier. Fletcher had also spent much time behind desks at various staff positions.

As with many longtime naval officers on both sides, Fletcher knew little about flattops. The first actual fleet carriers were not put into service until the 1920s, and the truly large ones were not deployed until the 1930s. Though the Japanese became the first to launch an air raid off the deck of a ship in 1914, no one had employed carriers in wartime to any great extent until World War II. There had been plenty of practice between the wars but nobody on either side, including Fletcher, had wartime experience.

In the early part of the war, Admiral Fletcher had developed a reputation for being frustratingly conservative. Still, he was generally considered to be a good tactician and leader of men.

No one could question his valor. He had been awarded the Navy Cross for action as a battleship skipper during World War I and, before that, the Medal of Honor for his actions aboard the USS *Florida* (BB-30) during the occupation of Veracruz, Mexico, in April 1914. While under fire, then-Lieutenant Fletcher bravely assisted in the rescue of 350 refugees from the fighting, bringing them aboard the *Florida*, and then overseeing their transportation to safety.

An indicator of Fletcher's cautious side, though, was his dogged insistence on constantly topping off the fuel tanks of his warships while at sea. He maintained that he wanted to be certain that his ships and aircraft would always be prepared with adequate fuel for any engagement. For that reason, he was almost fanatical about making use of and then protecting the tankers attached to his task force.

So it was that this assembled cast of characters steamed ahead toward a crucial showdown. One task force was unaware of the other's existence. The other was fully mindful of the impending conflict even as its foil confidently moved forward with its invasion plans, expecting little resistance, assured of yet another glorious victory for the empire and Emperor Hirohito.

Both fleets were inevitably but frustratingly approaching a historic confrontation, even as storm clouds gathered and the dense tropical haze and squalls obscured each side from the other. As the battle forces assembled, USS *Neosho* calmly and effectively went about her thoroughly unglamorous job, unaware she was about to become an even more important element in the fight that would later be named the Battle of the Coral Sea.

CHAPTER FIVE
Out of Harm's Way

On April 29, 1942, a Japanese force steamed out of Rabaul aimed at Tulagi, the tiny island and harbor town of the same name in the Solomon Islands. The group included a minelayer, two destroyers, several minesweepers, a couple of patrol boats, and, maybe most important, two transports carrying seasoned troops from the 3rd Kure Special Naval Landing Force along with a battle-tested construction unit. Their mission was to capture the port and quickly establish a seaplane base from which Type 97 Flying Boats could scout the Solomons and the Coral Sea. Little resistance was anticipated.

Another mass of Japanese ships, the MO Main Force, was also at sea as April came to a close. Consisting of six vessels, including the light aircraft carrier *Shoho*, four heavy cruisers, and a destroyer, the force had as its primary mission the support of the MO Invasion Force—scheduled to follow them, departing Rabaul on May 4—by providing air cover off the deck of *Shoho* as Port Moresby was captured. Secondarily, *Shoho* would initially also offer air cover for the Tulagi Harbor invasion, about 200 miles to the east, in the unlikely event that it should become necessary.

Finally the whole of New Guinea would belong to the Japanese Empire. Only minimal resistance was expected there, as well.

The Main Force commander, Admiral Goto, understood perfectly that his job did not include seeking out or engaging any possible U.S. warships that might be in the area. Admiral Yamamoto and others already suspected—based on spy reports—that an American carrier, maybe even two, were on the way and would be in the Coral Sea within a week. Still, Goto was to stick to the plan. Without his air cover for the invasion of Port Moresby, land-based Allied aircraft could make the capture of the outpost much more difficult than it should be, if not a complete failure.

On May 1, another component of the vise, the MO Carrier Striking Force, the fleet that included the much bigger IJN aircraft carriers *Shokaku* and *Zuikaku*, left the naval base at Truk, almost 1,200 miles northeast of New Guinea, deliberately taking a roundabout route south and then west into the Coral Sea. Japanese admirals wanted to minimize the possibility of the Allies learning of the presence of the big flattops in the region until after the Tulagi and Port Moresby invasions were under way. No need to attract attention before that mission was accomplished.

Since they would be passing close by Rabaul anyway, the Carrier Striking Force also was asked to perform a rather routine chore. They were to linger in the area long enough to deliver some airplanes to Rabaul. The task should not take more than half a day to launch the aircraft and then wait to confirm they had landed safely.

Once the Carrier Striking Force was in the Coral Sea, and at about the same time as the invasion at Port Moresby was taking place, planes flying off the decks of the two big carriers were to launch vicious surprise strikes against the air bases at Townsville and Charters Towers, on the northeast Australian coast. That would be diversionary, but would also dent any possible air counterattacks if the Allies foolishly tried to halt the assault or retake Port Moresby.

The Carrier Striking Force could not tarry in the Coral Sea, though. Once any response to Operation MO by the Allies had been thwarted, *Shokaku* and *Zuikaku* were to quickly leave the area and steam north, hustling back to Japan. There they would join the other forces that were already gathering for Operation MI, the invasion of Midway, now planned for the first week in June.

The elements of Operation MO were now in motion, and the Japanese were more convinced than ever that it would be yet another major victory for the empire.

True to his reputation, Admiral Frank Fletcher had doggedly insisted on the almost constant refueling of the *Yorktown* and other ships that floated nearby. Captain Phillips and his crew on the *Neosho* were busy around the clock, hooking up, quickly topping off tanks, and moving away. There was no rest for the oiler's tired crew. By the time the floating filling station had given a slurp of gas to everyone, the admiral would send word for it to start the rounds again. Thankfully, although there were passing rainstorms, the seas so far remained relatively calm. That, of course, was subject to change in this part of the world.

All the while, Fletcher and the rest of the fleet were getting constant input from headquarters back in Pearl Harbor. Despite all the pilfered intelligence on what the Japanese were up to, the Allied ships actually in the Coral Sea had so far seen few signs of any additional enemy activity. Fletcher briefly considered moving his task force northward, close enough to Rabaul to launch planes and mount a surprise attack on that key headquarters base. Characteristically, he decided such a raid would be too aggressive and unwise.

Instead, he concluded he should remain out of reach of search planes launched from Rabaul or the Japanese seaplane base at Shortland in the Solomons. Task Force 17 would instead watch for the anticipated enemy invasion vessels in the Coral Sea. He reasoned any force headed to Port Moresby would likely steam down the thousand miles from Rabaul, passing west of but near New Guinea to avoid detection.

Fletcher chose to start that way—northwest—with the hopes someone would spot the Invasion Force well before his own fleet had been seen by the enemy. Then he would launch a surprise attack on the enemy contingent. After all, his first priority was to foil the attempt of the Japanese to capture what little of New Guinea was still in Allied hands. Engaging the main Japanese fleet could wait until that bit of business had been completed.

At that point, though neither side knew it, both the Allied and Japanese carrier fleets—their decks filled with airplanes—were headed almost directly toward each other.

Farther north, the weather was already causing problems. On May 2, while on their way to the Coral Sea, the two big Japanese carriers tried to deliver their nine Zero fighters to the base at Rabaul. Yet Rabaul was socked in by rainfall and the planes were not able to land. Instead the pilots had to fly back to the carriers and wait out the deluge. They tried twice more over the next two days—even losing one of the planes in the process—before finally getting the rest of the small contingent of aircraft on solid ground. By then it would be late in the day on May 4.

Attempting to make a small, routine delivery of aircraft had thrown off the timing of the Carrier Striking Force in its move to the Coral Sea by three days. It also demonstrated just how susceptible the entire MO plan was to any minor difficulties that might occur.

Some historians would later conclude that the mighty IJN had become overconfident. Several incidents over the following few days would give credence to that theory. Yet at the time, Japanese commanders, still unaware of the presence of Fletcher's carrier task force, were only minimally concerned about the frustrating delay while trying to deliver the planes.

That minor task would be completed. Then the carriers could move south, ready to support the next successful thrust of the empire's sword.

Step one in the Japanese plan certainly went well enough. The invasion of Tulagi on May 3 came off just as easily as anticipated.

Admiral Fletcher got word of the invasion late that evening. Surprisingly, news of an enemy success was in this instance welcomed as a good thing—finally, something the Allies knew would be part of the overall plan was actually happening. This, the admiral knew, was only a minor prelude to the coming assault on Port Moresby.

Yet the ever-wary Fletcher had a surprising take on the possibilities. If his planes could attack the new enemy base at Tulagi before it even became operational, it would throw a kink in that segment of the operation. It might even make the enemy hesitate long enough to give the other two American carriers time to get to the Coral Sea. Besides, Task Force 17 could soon be close enough to the newly captured island to launch such a surprise assault.

To the amazement of many on his staff, Fletcher turned the *Yorktown* to the east and increased speed to twenty-seven knots. They would be in position to put airplanes in the air at first light the next morning, on May 4, before the Japanese had even pitched their tents and cranked their bulldozers at Tulagi Harbor.

When Fletcher's aircraft appeared in the sky over the newly captured base at 0820 on the fourth, they were indeed a big surprise to the Japanese. Except for the weapons on the ships of the Invasion Force, the facility was mostly defenseless. No aircraft support was available, either. The light carrier *Shoho*, along with the rest of the MO Main Force—which was supposed to provide any needed cover during the quick, easy taking of the harbor—had immediately turned away the previous day when things had gone so well, moving on to prepare to support the more complicated Port Moresby operation.

Meanwhile, at the time of *Yorktown*'s attack on Tulagi, the MO Carrier Striking Force, with its two big carriers and the 109 airplanes between them, was still busy trying to ferry those nine A6M2 Zero fighter planes through the pesky rainstorms at Rabaul. Thus, they were too far away to send any help, either.

Three separate waves of U.S. dive-bombers and torpedo bombers thundered out of the early-morning sky. Finally, with enemy ships to shoot at, they continued to blast Tulagi throughout most of the day.

A Japanese destroyer was damaged and later beached. Three small minesweepers, four landing barges, and five Type 97 Flying Boat aircraft were destroyed. Eighty-seven Japanese troops were killed. One hundred twenty-four were wounded.

When listed, the inflicted damage sounds impressive, yet the raid's results would, in retrospect, be considered disappointing when taking into account the number of potential targets present, the lack of resistance, and the number of American dive- and torpedo bombers that were pounding away during the attack. Also telling was the fact that the Japanese would continue to hold and strengthen the base on Tulagi for the next three months. It would remain in enemy hands until August 7, 1942, when U.S. forces, mostly the 1st Marine Raiders, retook the island in one day of tough hand-to-hand fighting. Shortly after the Allies regained control of the harbor, Tulagi became the host of a fleet of patrol torpedo (PT) boats, including PT-109, famously commanded by future president John F. Kennedy.

The major result of the *Yorktown*'s attack on Tulagi, though, was that Yamamoto's worries had been confirmed. The Japanese were now alerted that at least one U.S. aircraft carrier was stirring up the waters of the Coral Sea.

Frank Fletcher would have been quite aware that the attack would blow his cover, yet he had shocked everyone by going ahead with it. He had certainly considered the raid at length and discussed the possibilities with his staff and superiors before finally ordering the go-ahead. In the end, he felt the surprise attempt to wipe out the base was worth revealing his presence. It was likely only a matter of hours anyway before the Japanese would know the *Lexington* and the *Yorktown* were on the scene.

Fletcher also would have been aware that it would not be prudent to remain in the area of Tulagi too long after advertising that at least one of the American carriers had shown up. The enemy would quickly come looking for the launchpad of the warplanes that had shot up their new base.

The instant that the last of the Tulagi raid aircraft were safely back on the *Yorktown*'s flight deck, Fletcher ordered a turn and raced away, back to the south and west.

On the morning of May 5, the *Yorktown* rendezvoused with the *Lexington* and the rest of the task force.

Admiral Fletcher's first call was to John Phillips and the *Neosho*. A carrier battle was even more imminent now. After the previous day's target practice at Tulagi, he wanted all ships in his group and each of his airplanes refueled to the tops of their tanks.

Now, more than ever, they had to be ready to fight.

The next day, Wednesday, May 6, as the *Neosho* was yet again fueling the *Yorktown*, seven men were detailed to be transferred over from the carrier to the tanker, using boatswain's chairs and a long strand of rope. These men had been reassigned off the carrier and one of the cruisers, and needed a lift back to Pearl Harbor so that they could move on to new duty elsewhere. The *Neosho*, which was soon to head back to Pearl to refill her storage tanks, would be their taxi, as she often was. The trip might even start before the first shots in the coming showdown were fired.

Among those on the deck of the *Yorktown* awaiting the rope ride over to the oiler was a handsome, young Douglas SBD-3 Dauntless scout plane/dive-bomber pilot named Stanley "Swede" Vejtasa, along with one of his fellow aviators. Both he and his companion had been attached to Scouting Squadron 5, based on the carrier before their reassignment. Vejtasa had deliberately stalled and delayed as long as he could, even after his seabag had already made the trip over the wave tops to the *Neosho*. He was hoping against hope that something would come up at the last minute that would change his orders. Something that would allow him to stay on the carrier and in the cockpit of his plane. He desperately wanted to be a part of the upcoming payback.

"We had shaken hands with our buddies in the squadron and told each of them good-bye," Vejtasa recalled.

He had been primed and was looking forward to engaging the big enemy carriers and the fighters that would try to protect them. Now Vejtasa was on the verge of leaving all that behind. Instead of shooting down enemy planes and sinking their ships, he would be doing his part to win the war by thumbing a ride on a floating gas drum back to Hawaii.

"We didn't want to leave them when we knew we were so near striking a blow against the enemy," he said.

Vejtasa had already had his share of excitement. As one of the pilots who had ripped up the Japanese at Tulagi Harbor two days prior, he was still getting his nerves settled after his harrowing experience in that attack.

His plane had been damaged by enemy fire, and he was forced to blindly limp back to the carrier. Oil leaking from his single engine covered his windshield. Had it not been for another member of his squadron who bravely peeled back and flew alongside him, guiding him, Vejtasa likely would have ended up ditching in the sea with little hope of rescue.

Even then, he made it back to the carrier in the nick of time. Without oil, the engine on his plane seized up only seconds after he had safely landed on the *Yorktown*'s deck and pulled to a stop.

Now, geared up for more combat, Vejtasa reckoned it would take some last-minute reprieve to keep him there where the action would be.

No such luck. The pilot reluctantly allowed the carrier's deck crew to strap him into the boatswain's chair that would ship him over to that corpulent taxicab waiting for him across the water.

Each side was still having trouble finding the other. Despite American land-based Catalina flying boats, a sky full of similar Japanese search planes, plus swarms of carrier-based aircraft from both fleets, no one had yet definitively spotted the ships of the other. In some cases, the planes were simply looking in the wrong places, going by incorrect guesses. The weather was partly to blame, and was getting worse by the hour. Poor communications between various commands and faulty reporting by elements on both sides also were reasons for the frustration.

It would later be determined that at least one U.S. scout plane had come to within twenty miles of the Japanese carriers on May 5. Yet the crew turned back toward its home carrier for refueling, unaware, mere seconds from spotting its objective.

A Japanese flying boat actually spied some elements of Task Force 17, but the pilot reported the wrong location—off by more than fifty miles—as well as the incorrect type, heading, and estimated speed of the ships he saw. Even then, the faulty account was mishandled and delayed in getting to the right people in Rabaul until it was too late to act.

Confusing and conflicting as most of it was, intelligence information started coming in bunches during the day on May 6. General Douglas MacArthur's B-17 bombers chimed in with an exciting and long-anticipated report. They confirmed spotting a light carrier and four other warships heading southwest, passing east of New Guinea. It was Admiral Goto's MO Main Force, making for Port Moresby to support the Invasion Force, which was by then already at sea from Rabaul as well. At the same time, spotter planes were reporting more and more enemy activity throughout the region.

Fletcher and the other commanders in the task force—by this point, with all vessels, including the *Lexington*, combined under the banner of Task Force 17—were convinced that the enemy carrier fleet was nearby. They were correct, but still had no idea how close the *Shokaku* and the *Zuikaku* actually were. The Allies had also confirmed, thanks to the B-17s, that elements of the Invasion Force were where they expected them to be, heading for the passage through the tiny islands east of New Guinea, on the way to Port Moresby.

Finally, things were heating up. The air was electric but calm, as if before an approaching cyclone. Contact and conflict were looming, just as ominous and sure as the tropical thunderstorms that smudged the distant horizon as the sun fell into the sea on May 6.

Frank Fletcher examined the thick stack of reports before him. He had listened to the ideas offered by his staff, who had also been intently studying the swirling fog of confusing and sometimes conflicting intelligence reports. Everything he saw and heard told him he needed to hurry north by northwest. That was where the Invasion Force would soon be steaming through the Jomard Passage, east of New Guinea.

Task Force 17's job was to find and stop the Japanese. The orders Fletcher had received from Admiral Nimitz were as simple as they were vague: "Your task is to assist in checking further advance by the enemy in [the area of New Guinea and the Solomons] by seizing favorable opportunities to destroy ships, shipping, and aircraft."

With no specifics given, it was up to Frank Jack Fletcher to decide how to do the admiral's bidding.

Lexington and *Yorktown* would need to be within air-strike distance of the area south of the Jomard route by daylight if they were to hit the light carrier, which was almost certainly part of the enemy force headed to Port Moresby. Once there, they could launch the attack that would cut that snake into writhing, nonthreatening segments.

That settled it. They would hurry north. But to get to the area by dawn on May 7, Task Force 17 needed to get under way immediately.

By the time of the decision, it had been hours since the *Yorktown* had been refueled. The carrier and the heavy cruiser USS *Astoria* (CA-34) had been the last ships to be topped off by the *Neosho*. With seas building and the weather rapidly deteriorating, the admiral would need to turn the *Yorktown* south to hook up with the *Neosho* and take on fuel. That would cost them far more precious time and distance than they had to spare. Refueling now might well delay by too long their arrival in the area where they needed to be to find, catch, and surprise the MO Invasion Force.

The only other oiler in TF 17, the USS *Tippecanoe,* had only half the capacity of the *Neosho*. She had quickly run dry.

Along with the *Worden*, her escort, she had steamed to the tiny island of Efate in the Vanuatu group to take on more fuel, arriving there on May 4. When aircraft left the *Yorktown* to attack Tulagi, orders came for the smaller tanker to remain in the port for her own protection. And there she would stay, until May 8.

If he had to forgo his usual topping off, Admiral Fletcher decided he would at least be prudent about protecting his now even more vital tanker. That evening, he reluctantly ordered the *Neosho* to leave the fleet and proceed to a point near 16 degrees south latitude and 158 degrees east longitude, about two hundred miles from where the fleet planned to stage its attack on the invading force. The ship was to be escorted by the single-stack destroyer, USS *Sims*, under the command of Lieutenant Commander Wilford Hyman.

If he could not use her, Fletcher wanted to put his tanker as much out of harm's way as he could. She would be down there waiting in an out-of-the-way patch of the Coral Sea. Even so, with the oiler's speed, he could still have her close enough that he could summon her if any of his ships needed to refuel.

As the battle played out, the tanker and her escort were supposed to run back and forth between two turnaround points, dubbed "Rye" and "Corn." They would be available to fuel any ships that might need it by having them show up at one or the other of those locations.

Fletcher and his staff did not know precisely what might happen in the coming action or how long it might take. Such a sea battle was new to all of them. This fight would mostly be between capital ships that might never lay eyes on each other. It could last minutes, or days.

This was to be a far cry from boarding parties armed with

muskets and swords. So very different from dreadnoughts firing booming cannons while lying broadside to one another.

Until it happened, no one really knew what to expect.

Swede Vejtasa was not the only one disenchanted about being sent away from where the action would soon take place. There was a great deal of consternation and disappointment among many of the crew members of the destroyer *Sims,* the *Neosho*'s escort.

The men did not understand why their warship had been chosen to escort the tanker instead of remaining with the task force for the impending showdown with the Japanese. This battle could prove to be historic, but instead of fighting, they would be shadowing an obese, two-thirds-empty replenishment ship floating along way out there by themselves, far from where the momentous clash would be.

Sims crew member Seaman First Class John C. Verton would later report that most of the deck crew saw the escort assignment as "a slap in the face." The *Sims* was, after all, the senior destroyer in the task force. USS *Walke* (DD-416) had originally been picked for the job of babysitting the tanker, but after having trouble with her starboard reduction gear she was dispatched to Brisbane for repairs.

"We figured the captain must be in the doghouse with the admiral," Verton recalled. Why else would their ship be sent off to some backwater pond for such unglamorous duty instead of being where she should be, with the fleet, protecting the flattops when things got going good?

The truth was probably more basic. Early in her commission, the *Sims* had begun to have serious problems with her boiler tubes, and the ship's engineers resorted to some creative fixes to keep her going. Still she had suffered a couple of severe failures since Pearl Harbor, both times requiring that a boiler be taken off-line until the plumbing could be temporarily patched up again. There simply had been no time or opportunity yet to send her back to the mainland, put her in the yard, and fix the problems.

The *Sims* was likely chosen to escort the tanker out of harm's way simply because Admiral Fletcher was concerned about the ship's mechanical reliability in the big battle to come. The destroyer likely would not have to do anything too rigorous while shadowing the oiler, far away from the action. She should be up to that task.

Regardless, many of her enlisted men were disappointed and in a foul mood as they prepared to pull away from the rest of Task Force 17 and the opportunity to finally exact some revenge on the Japanese.

Instead, they led the way—as ordered—so "Fat Girl" could run off and hide in the haze.

Aboard USS *Neosho*, it was all just another day's work. As they steamed away from the fleet and went off duty, Captain Phillips ordered his crew to grab some rest if they could. Those assigned to lookout were to be especially vigilant, or as much as they could be in the darkness and gloom. They needed to be able to spot a submarine periscope or scout plane quickly if they were to duck and dodge.

The tanker might be relegated to the boondocks for a few days but her crew still needed to be watchful. As isolated and distant as they would be from the action, they were still in enemy waters.

Gun crews were reminded of their recent drills and training. Even with the *Sims* running ahead of them, zigging and zagging, there was always a chance some lucky Japanese fly-boy would consider the big tanker enough of a prize to risk dropping a bomb or two on her, or take the opportunity to strafe her broad deck. An I-boat would not hesitate to put a torpedo into her rather sizable haunch, either.

Phillips also sent a most unusual order to his officers. He wanted them to instruct the men as they came off watch to be sure to take freshwater showers and dress in clean clothes.

Over the last few weeks, the men had been forced to use salt water for infrequent bathing since the ship's evaporators were not making enough freshwater to meet all the needs of the vessel. Hygiene ranked last on the list of uses for clean water. It had been a while since anybody—especially the enlisted men—had taken a shower.

Bill Leu was just coming off watch in the engine room when he heard the word that the "old man" had ordered showers and fresh clothes for everybody. Such fastidiousness was not an option. It was an order.

Leu was tired and irritable. They had been grinding steadily, running hard to keep up with all the ships they had to hook up to, constantly refueling the fleet, always in a hurry and under stress, and they had been doing it for weeks already. All the men on board had heard the scuttlebutt about the big impending carrier battle. Everyone was on edge.

"Why I got to take a bath?" Leu questioned his superior officer, annoyed. "I'm dogged out."

The man gave Leu a grim look.

"Why you think, sailor? We're about to be in one hell of a battle. When you get your ass wounded or burned, you're less likely to get an infection if you ain't so dirty and your clothes ain't so filthy."

Leu swallowed hard, turned, and promptly headed for the crew's head to get himself a nice freshwater shower and climb into some newly laundered clothes. As he went, he saw the concerned looks on his shipmates' faces.

Years later he admitted to friends and family members, "We were one bunch of scared sailors."

CHAPTER SIX
Scratch One Flattop

May 7 dawned cloudy and blustery in the area where Task Force 17 was steaming northwestward. The lack of visibility had everyone worried. There were instances in which skittish gunners aboard American ships opened fire on friendly aircraft as they approached and tried to land. Fortunately, no one in TF 17 had been hit so far, but nerves were frayed.

Despite the elements, Admiral Fletcher launched his first wave of attack planes against the Port Moresby Main Force and the carrier *Shoho* at about 0930. It was later in the day than he preferred, and the sun, if he could have seen it, was higher in the sky than he would have liked. Yet at daylight, reports placed the enemy target ships at more than 225 miles away, a bit too far for his planes to fly, engage, and get back home with any margin of error. But with Task Force 17 running north and the Japanese steaming south, they would be within range of Fletcher's airplanes by midmorning.

The sighting of the Japanese Main Force by MacArthur's bombers the previous day had answered many prayers, including those of the young pilot, Swede Vejtasa. Already secured in the boatswain's chair, ready to be sent over to the *Neosho* for the long, boring ride back to Pearl Harbor, his squadron leader sent word to wait, that he wanted Vejtasa and the other pilot, Lieutenant Fritz Faulkner, to remain aboard the *Yorktown*, after all.

With the enemy invasion force now confirmed to be on the move, Task Force 17 would need every able-bodied pilot it could find to go get the Japanese. Vejtasa was only too happy to oblige. He and Faulkner waited impatiently for their seabags to come back over from the tanker, and then they ran below to start getting ready for whatever the admiral wanted them to do.

As he sat through the briefing, Vejtasa learned that he and his fellow pilots would be flying north the next morning as soon as the carrier steamed within range, and they would have the opportunity to stop the Japanese invasion force in its tracks. The young pilot could already feel the adrenaline racing through his veins. It would be impossible to sleep this night.

On the morning of May 7, though, fog and storm clouds were at first disconcerting for Vejtasa and his fellow strike force members, yet the veil of thunderclouds turned out to be a blessing. It effectively hid them not only from each other but also from enemy scout planes all the way to their targets. Just before reaching the spot where they expected to find the elements of the enemy force, the American planes popped out of the soup and into a bright, clear sky.

There below them was the *Shoho*, steaming hard south and bathed in brilliant sunshine. The American planes dived on the unsuspecting target. In mere minutes, the carrier was on fire and billowing smoke. Swede Vejtasa had one of the approximately two dozen direct hits on the ship. The *Shoho* was sunk—the first aircraft carrier lost in the war so far by either side—while only a couple of American aircraft went down.

Half an hour after the attack began, Admiral Fletcher received a cryptic but most welcome message from Lieutenant Commander R. E. Dixon, second in command of the task force's dive-bombers.

"Scratch one flattop," he radioed.

The carriers got busy recovering its victorious aircraft and then turned back south to get into position for the next engagement.

Reports would come later that the remaining elements of Operation MO—now denied air protection from their light carrier—had made a broad turn and were headed back to Rabaul. The Battle of the Coral Sea was, from Admiral Frank Jack Fletcher's perspective, now officially under way, and the Allies could already claim a modicum of victory. They had repelled the huge invasion fleet headed for the south shore of New Guinea.

It was certainly not lost on them that this was the first time in the war that the Japanese had been turned away, denied a major objective.

Still, there was a hell of a lot more battle to go, more airplanes and ships to destroy, and it was going to happen very soon.

A couple of hundred miles away, where the *Neosho* and her escort were trying to make themselves invisible, the weather was also a complicating factor, but for the opposite reason. The morning of May 7 dawned unusually clear and bright down in their area of the Coral Sea. Phillips and his crew would have much preferred clouds and rain. On such a nice, sunny day, any stray Japanese scouts would have little trouble seeing them.

Both the tanker and destroyer skippers knew that most of their task force had been steaming northwestward through the night, away from them, headed for their attack on a key enemy element of the MO operation. With the fleet so far away, it was now less likely that anyone would show up for refueling this day at either of the turnaround points. Still, the oiler would be there if needed.

Phillips could also hope the ruckus Fletcher's aircraft would set off up near New Guinea would draw any attention that might otherwise be directed toward his own ship and her escort.

Meanwhile, Phillips and his crew awaited word on how the raid had turned out, hoping all the while for good news. Either way, they expected to receive orders later in the day for the two ships to rejoin the task force as they went looking next for the big IJN carriers.

Suddenly, their thoughts of the raid and the task force and their hopes for victory were shouted down by a couple of *Neosho*'s lookouts.

Something ominous was spotted on the horizon. Radar quickly confirmed it.

The *Neosho* and the *Sims* had company.

After sinking the Japanese carrier at just after 1100 hours, Vejtasa and his mates next had to locate their mother ships in the midst of a tropical rainstorm. They would also have to get down safely on a pitching, windswept deck. And they would have to do it before they ran out of fuel. They were all able to do so, and then, still tingling from the thrill of the day's success, started preparing for the inevitable next round.

Swede Vejtasa—who had come so close to being a passenger on the *Neosho* instead of a hero in the cockpit of his aircraft—was about to do even more miraculous things.

In amazing action early the next day, May 8, just before the full-scale battle began, he would use his uncanny skill to defend his own plane while taking down three much faster and more maneuverable Japanese Zero fighters, aircraft that had just made the first confirmed sighting of the American task force.

When it came to a dogfight, Vejtasa's Douglas SBD Dauntless, a hundred miles per hour slower and nowhere near as nimble as the Zeroes, was no match for the enemy fighters. Yet somehow Vejtasa prevailed. He and his rear gunner shot down two of the Zeroes. The third crashed into the sea after Vejtasa, in an unbelievable move, clipped the Japanese plane's wing with his own. The mere sight of that amazing maneuver likely was enough to chase away the rest of them.

But the day was just beginning. Welcome word would finally come about 0900 on May 8, reliable reports that the big Japanese carriers had finally been located. He and his fellow pilots would be off as soon as their planes could be refueled.

Just as he had anticipated when he had been abruptly and thankfully redirected from his ride on the *Neosho*, Swede Vejtasa had already taken part in and contributed mightily to something truly historic.

As he roared off the deck of his carrier that morning, headed for the next strike, the pilot was unaware that his giant would-be taxi was now in desperate trouble after making some unexpected history of her own.

CHAPTER SEVEN
Two Specks on the Horizon

Admiral Fletcher had ordered John Phillips and his ship to steam far enough away from the rest of Task Force 17 that the oiler would not attract Japanese scrutiny. Now it was obvious that the *Neosho* had, indeed, drawn some interest. The tanker's radar operator had just confirmed what his lookouts had already reported: Somebody out there in the distance was definitely paying them some mind.

Only an hour after sunrise on Thursday, May 7, two unidentified aircraft buzzed close enough to see the pair of isolated vessels—the *Neosho* and the *Sims*—against the backdrop of the green, white-capped sea below. Still, the planes were far enough away that it was anybody's guess aboard the ships whom those birds belonged to.

The *Neosho*'s executive officer, Lieutenant Commander Francis Firth, stood next to Phillips on the ship's bridge and volunteered an opinion as he peered intently through his binoculars. It was no more than speculation because the XO could hardly make out the two aircraft, let alone discern their markings. Ten miles away at a heading of 020 degrees true, they were little more than gnat-sized specks in a bright sky.

"They could be ours, friendlies," Firth offered.

"Sure. They're likely ours, Fran," Phillips replied, and made a note to that effect for later entry in the deck log. But the skipper was guessing, too. Maybe whistling past the graveyard.

Phillips agreed with Admiral Fletcher that the Japanese likely had bigger targets to pursue. Even if the enemy should accidentally spot the *Neosho*, they would likely not waste bombs and risk their planes on the oiler. In actuality, the bulk of Allied Task Force 17 was not all that far away from the *Neosho* and the *Sims*, a few hundred miles at most, closer at other times.

Surely the Japanese would be more interested in the American aircraft carriers than in John Phillips and his oiler. They would also likely see the task force long before they stumbled upon the *Neosho* and the *Sims* way out there by themselves.

Phillips considered asking his counterpart over on the destroyer, Lieutenant Commander Wilford Hyman, if his crew or radar had managed a better look at the airplanes. But the escort was only a few hundred yards away, still running close ahead of them. Hyman and his bunch could not possibly have seen anything more than Phillips's lookouts. Even if they had, Phillips would know it by now.

A significant amount of seawater broke over the bow of the massive tanker. The seas were moderate, growing rougher. Even so, with still a third of a full load of fuel in her tanks, the heavy fleet oiler was hardly rolling at all as she plowed through the waves.

"Fran, what's our position again?"

"Right where we're supposed to be, Captain. Sixteen degrees south, one fifty-eight east."

That put their ship in her designated box—halfway between "Rye" and "Corn"—in the middle of the Coral Sea, an expanse of water ringed by New Guinea and Guadalcanal to the north and the Great Barrier Reef and northeast coast of Australia hundreds of miles to the southwest.

Phillips looked across the water at the *Sims*. The destroyer was there with them because of the *Neosho*'s minimal weapons. The oiler's deck guns posed some threat to the lightly armored Japanese dive-bombers, but she would not be able to ward off a serious attack by herself. The *Neosho*'s ability to make surprising speed—to bob and weave and dodge bombs, bullets and torpedoes aimed her way—was her only other defense.

That made Lieutenant Commander Hyman and his destroyer an invaluable partner.

The *Neosho* carried 293 men and the *Sims* had 252—husbands, brothers, fathers, sons—and the tanker had an additional five passengers aboard, the men who had come over from *Yorktown* and the heavy cruiser USS *Portland* (CA-33). Each and every one of them wanted to see his home again. Hyman and his crew were there to try to make that wish a reality.

Captain Phillips did not know the *Sims*'s skipper very well, mostly by reputation. By the time Wilford Milton Hyman was on the bridge of his destroyer alongside the *Neosho* in the Coral Sea—he was three months shy of forty-one years old at the time—he had spent half his life in the United States Navy. A native of Colorado, Hyman was the second skipper of the

Sims and had taken command of the destroyer the previous October, two months before Pearl Harbor. USS *Sims* was Hyman's first command.

The ship was named for Rear Admiral William S. Sims, a former naval aide to President Theodore Roosevelt and later secretary of the Navy. Built at Bath Iron Works in Bath, Maine, she was christened by Admiral Sims's widow in April 1939 and commissioned in August.

With a home port on the East Coast when the war started, the *Sims* became part of Task Force 17 nine days after the attack at Pearl Harbor. She pulled out with the carrier *Yorktown* from Norfolk, Virginia, aimed first for the smoldering remains of the base in Hawaii and then on to the war. By mid-January, she was helping the fleet ferry Marines to islands in the South Pacific, and then steamed all over the region, supporting the carriers there.

Before the war, Hyman had served with distinction as gunnery officer aboard two cruisers and another destroyer before he assumed command of the *Sims*. Even as a boy, he had been a crack shot with a rifle. He had developed quite the reputation in the peacetime Navy for his tactical and leadership abilities. With his considerable knowledge and skill as gunnery officer, he was clearly a rising star. This war would give him the chance to ascend rapidly in rank and responsibility. A twenty-year man with a stellar record and a command in which he saw action could suddenly make big leaps in wartime, when the stakes were high.

Captain Phillips continued to squint into his binoculars, trying to see the pair of airplanes better. Nothing. They had now disappeared from sight.

It may have been wishful thinking, but he and his XO assumed for their report that the aircraft were American planes off the *Yorktown* or the *Lexington*. Maybe they were providing a bit of cautionary air cover for the tanker while they searched for the rest of the enemy task force. Maybe, at Admiral Fletcher's urging, they were simply checking *Neosho*'s location and status to reassure the admiral they were still out there, waiting and ready. It would be typical of him.

Phillips and his XO likely knew the aircraft could just as well be off the Japanese carriers, too. One way or the other, out there flying so far from land, they almost had to be somebody's carrier-based aircraft.

Phillips could not help but worry. If those had been Japanese scout planes, and if they decided the *Neosho* was worth the risk and the weapons, it was only a matter of time before his and the destroyer's radarscopes would be pocked with more planes.

Time would certainly tell.

The young pilot in the Japanese torpedo bomber signaled to his partner flying a hundred feet off his left wing, motioning for him to pull away and head back to the welcoming decks of the carrier *Shokaku*.

Their routine, exasperating day had swiftly become a glorious one. He was anxious to share with his commanders what he and his comrades had just seen.

The two aircraft had taken off together from their Imperial Japanese Navy carrier in near darkness, at 0600 hours that morning. Now the fledgling pilot sensed that he and the other two men in his crew, along with the three men in the other aircraft off his left wing, were about to set in motion an important strike for the empire.

The pilot goosed his aircraft to its top cruising speed—about 170 miles per hour—racing back toward the mother ship. There he would land, quickly refuel his plane as he was congratulated by his fellow flyers, and then join the rest of the proud battle force in the certain triumph.

First, though, he had to make his report. His radio operator–gunner—who was no older than the pilot—would need to do his job well. He would have to remain calm, remembering the proper procedures and codes as he radioed back news of their exciting discovery.

"We have found the Allied carrier force," was the message. "At 0722, we observed and have since confirmed an aircraft carrier and an escort cruiser operating alone with no other support vessels." Then he gave the coordinates: 16 degrees south latitude, 158 degrees east longitude. The transmission ended and they immediately received acknowledgment.

The two airplanes' crew members did not hesitate in stating the details of what they were reporting. They likely imagined how wonderful the news would be received by Admiral Shigeyoshi Inoue and his staff back in Rabaul. How exuberant Admiral Hara would be. The young fliers would have been well aware of the frustration that had grown over their inability to locate something as big as an American carrier task force, especially with all the clues the Allies had recently tossed their way. Now he and his mates could finally report such a discovery.

In retrospect, it might have been prudent for them to have flown once again by the ships they had observed down there in the early-morning mist. Maybe buzzed a bit closer for absolute confirmation. But the B5N2s they piloted lacked effective armor, and that might have led to their decision to avoid lingering longer than necessary. They could have been felled by a lucky shot from the cruiser's antiaircraft guns before they could inform the task force of their important discovery. Or planes off the carrier could have zoomed up to challenge them.

At that point, it was more important to finally report the existence and location of the first elements of the fleet—this carrier, a truly worthy target—than for the two scouts to try to get a closer look, let alone launch an attack of their own.

Had there been just a hint of excitement in the otherwise calm voice of the radio operator when he acknowledged the message? He, too, would have been honored to be the one who received and relayed the long-desired report.

The 1,000-horsepower engines hurled the two B5N2s back toward the "Flying Crane," the nickname for the *Shokaku*. Soon scores of dive- and torpedo bombers and fighter escorts would be rolling off those same decks and from the sister carrier the *Zuikaku*. In all, there would be a total of seventy-eight aircraft, almost three-quarters of the planes from the two flattops.

They would catch air, roar away into the hazy skies, and in less than two hours they would be able to strike the next in a series of powerful, victorious blows for the empire.

PART THREE
UNDER ATTACK

Make preparations for abandoning ship and
stand by.

—Captain John Phillips, May 7, 1942

CHAPTER EIGHT
High-Level Attack

A frustrated Rear Admiral Chuichi Hara was as thrilled as his young pilots were when he received their long-awaited report early on the morning of May 7. So were all those surrounding him in the fleet operations center. They could relax more when things were going well, when the admiral's bellowing and table pounding came in response to good news, not to a real or perceived failure by one of them. It had been an exasperating few days, and the admiral had been especially on edge.

First there was the floundering around, trying to get a few airplanes off the decks and delivered to Rabaul. Now his aircraft had been stalking the Allied fleet for better than two days with no success whatsoever. He had already raged at the other commanders in the IJN's 5th Carrier Division Striking Force, berating them for their lack of results as they burned up so much vital fuel and precious time. While his officers were floundering in the Coral Sea, his two carriers should soon be headed north to prepare for the real battle test that was to come at Midway.

Until now, though, no one had seen the Allies, not even warships as massive as an American aircraft carrier, not even in the relatively tight confines of the Coral Sea. The IJN land-based scouts had been a failure as well. It would be a huge tactical advantage for whoever was the first to spot and attack the other side's fleet.

That was why Hara argued vehemently to be allowed to dispatch more scouts off his own carrier decks instead of employing them for useless attacks on bases in Australia.

Sure enough, a pair of young flyers off the *Shokaku* had finally located this morning an enemy carrier and cruiser.

Meanwhile, the MO Invasion Force was well under way and supposed to be off Port Moresby, prepared to go ashore on May 10, only three days away. That invasion would possibly be compromised unless Hara's scouts located the American carrier (or carriers, since intelligence indicated there were now two) and shot down all their airplanes, or sank the carriers, or chased them far away from New Guinea. The mere presence of the Allied task force could thrust a wrench into the gears of Operation MO.

Hara's frustration had only been heightened since the Allies announced their presence by hitting the new base on Tulagi three days before. That attack had confirmed that the Allied fleet was out there, though they had, up until this very morning, somehow managed to remain unseen by the Japanese scouts. After the unexpected assault on Tulagi by American planes, scouts flew the area in which Hara and his staff were certain they would find the enemy carrier. Nothing was seen but wave tops and rain clouds.

Still, the brave and resourceful men on Tulagi had used their experience and training to recover from the attack, to make the base once again operational. Seaplanes that had not been damaged had begun flying reconnaissance missions on May 6, a mere two days after being pounded. They would doubtless locate the Allied ships soon. Thankfully, though, a couple of Hara's carrier-based pilots had beaten them to it, and almost precisely in the area where he now expected the Americans to be.

The scout plane had radioed in the discovery of a carrier and escort. Only a bit later, another aircraft reported seeing an oiler and a destroyer not far from the position of the carrier sighting. That all but confirmed it.

Hara did not hesitate. He growled, pounded the chart table, and immediately sent another attack plane to confirm the reports even as he ordered preparations to get under way for a full attack force to be started in that direction.

Without waiting for the observer to do his job, though, Hara decided to go ahead and send out about eighty aircraft off both his carriers. The launch would include fighters, torpedo bombers, and dive-bombers. They were to surprise the newly discovered enemy ships and sink them. The admiral did not want to risk losing sight of the enemy fleet in the tropical squalls and having to resume the embarrassing, fruitless search.

As plane after plane rolled off the carrier decks into the morning haze and formed up in waves over the open water, Hara likely said a short prayer, thanking the ancestors for the opportunity to continue the successes of the Imperial Japanese Navy. Much was at stake now, and all blessings should surely be invoked.

Divine intervention should not be required, considering the tremendous attack force he now had in the air. It would not hurt to request it, though.

At almost 0930, Chief Petty Officer Robert Dicken was trying to nap in the "goat locker," the chief petty officers' quarters, aboard the destroyer USS *Sims*, but the continual roll of the building seas would not allow him to sleep. The sighting earlier that morning of a couple of mysterious unidentified airplanes had everybody, including Dicken, on edge. He had just come off watch and had precious few hours to unwind. That is, if Captain Hyman and the Japanese would allow him to.

His ship was the lead vessel in her class, the last model of destroyers built prior to the outbreak of the war. Their hulls were longer, extending about ten feet farther than previous versions, to almost 350 feet. They were the first to employ the sophisticated new Mark 37 Gun Fire Control System, offering much quicker aiming solutions and greater accuracy, especially against quick-flying targets such as Japanese dive-bombers and torpedo bombers. The *Sims* had been commissioned on August 1, 1939, so she was not yet three years old. Except for the pesky problems with her plumbing, she had performed well.

The *Sims* was capable of making thirty-five knots, and Dicken was convinced she was doing close to that at the moment, staying well ahead of the *Neosho*'s bow. Dicken would later testify that the ship was doing a consistent zigzag ahead of the big oiler in an attempt to make it more difficult for a Japanese submarine or dive-bomber to hit them square on the chin with a torpedo or thousand-pound bomb.

Dicken finally decided to give up on a nap, go topside, grab a smoke, and enjoy the relative coolness of the tropical morning. He climbed out of the bunk and started up the ladder.

What happened over the next few hours, as it was later related by Chief Dicken and the other men who were there and survived to tell the tale, is not at all clear-cut or precise, nor do the accounts necessarily agree. That should certainly be expected considering the chaos, the violence, and the sheer horror in which the crews of both ships soon found themselves.

The first discrepancy among the eyewitness accounts was over whether or not the *Sims* was zigzagging, as would be expected after having seen aircraft—quite possibly Japanese—in the area earlier in the morning. Afterward, in his official testimony, Chief Dicken reported that they were steering such a course.

"It was very strange," his shipmate, Fireman Second Class Vito Vessia, later offered, disagreeing with the chief's version. "We were going in a straight line. No zig or zag to dodge whatever was being thrown at us."

We do know, though, that a sudden clap of man-made thunder would announce the beginning of the end.

BOOM!

The deafening noise of the unexpected explosion nearly knocked Dicken off the ladder and to the deck.

Then the ship changed course so dramatically that he had to wrap his arms around the ladder once more to keep from falling backward. When he regained his balance and again headed up the ladder, he heard a sound not unlike the rattling of hailstones on metal. The clanging of General Quarters rang out on speakers all over the ship.

The *Sims* suddenly heeled over again, making another abrupt turn. Chief Dicken continued climbing toward daylight beyond the hatch. Now he could hear the firing of one of the guns on his ship. By the time he reached the top deck and neared the bridge, the other guns were already blasting away at something out there on the horizon.

As signalman, Dicken knew he needed to rush to the ship's signal lamp. Somebody appeared to have tossed at least one bomb, which, for all he knew at the moment, had hit them. He needed to use the signal light to make sure this was not one of their own planes, some kid at the stick getting all crazy on them in his excitement. Otherwise, the skipper would continue to try to blow whoever it was out of the sky, friend or foe.

Or, if the *Sims* and her crew were running low on providence this day, the nervous kid in the airplane might get lucky the next time and put a bomb down their stack.

When he got to his station, Chief Dicken began to flash away in the direction of the distant plane, rapidly working the mechanism of the light, hoping and praying that he would see the correct coded response blinking back. Instinct or hunch, he had a feeling that whoever had just dropped that bomb was not friendly at all.

No, that son of a bitch likely had intentions of chopping the *Sims* in two. And of turning the *Neosho* into one titanic blowtorch.

CHAPTER NINE
Déjà Vu

High up on the bridge of the *Sims*, her captain, Lieutenant Commander Wilford Hyman, had just spotted the single aircraft that had come so close to dropping a bomb down one of the hatches of his warship. The captain ordered an immediate hard turn to port to dodge whatever else might get flung his way by the enemy plane, and then another hard zag to starboard to make it even more difficult for the attacker to get a bead on him or the tanker that trailed behind him.

"Left full rudder! Sound General Quarters!" he shouted when the bomb suddenly exploded alongside, too damn close. The first command came before the column of seawater had fully settled back into the brine. Hyman felt the blast as surely as if the bomb had actually struck his ship.

Like Chief Dicken, the destroyer skipper probably wondered if this might be one of his own planes, one that had mistaken them for a Japanese vessel.

There are more discrepancies in the various follow-up accounts here, too, when compared to Dicken's version of events. Vito Vessia and John Verton, both enlisted men, would later maintain that the initial nearby blast did more than startle Hyman.

The explosion was close enough that it damaged the captain's gig, a small boat kept on the bridge reserved for the skipper's use. According to the sailors, it also knocked Hyman to the deck and injured him.

"The bridge talker relayed the message, 'Near miss forward! Captain down!'" Vessia recalled hearing amid the give-and-take on the ship's communication system.

If the captain was thrown to the deck, and if he suffered a head wound, as some in the crew claimed, that injury might explain some of the events that occurred aboard the destroyer for the rest of that awful morning.

Regardless, they were under attack. Everyone agreed on that point.

Hyman had to assume that the plane that had dropped the bomb was Japanese, even if he had not actually seen the meatballs yet. If the plane was responding to a report from the earlier scouts, then there should be more of them out there somewhere, not just a single aircraft. It had come up on them so low and so quickly that they had not had the chance to send recognition signals before the bomb fell. The pilot did not seem inclined to wait for any such formalities.

At some point, Hyman would have to determine why neither radar nor his lookouts had spotted the son of a bitch coming, why they had to feel the concussion and hear the rattle of shrapnel against their hull before they even knew somebody was targeting them. They were, after all, on high alert after an unidentified aircraft had been spotted in the distance only a short time earlier. Some crew members were going on report and would be getting their asses chewed out but good.

The destroyer's skipper would have been able to see that Chief Dicken was already at the signal light, flashing in the direction in which the dive-bomber had roared away. Their attacker now seemed to be drifting back and forth on the distant horizon, matching their course, warily eyeing them from a safe distance, with no response to Dicken's light.

The *Sims* gun crews were in place, still shooting away. Hyman suspected the plane was out of range, but maybe they could get off a fluky shot or the guy would wander in too close. Maybe they could scare him off. The twenty-millimeter and five-inch guns were making lots of noise and smoke.

Fireman Third Class Jones Savage, director of the General Quarters section, later reported that the plane seemed to change course in response to the flash of the guns. Maybe their muscle-flexing was working, despite the fact that quite a few of the *Sims*'s shells appeared to be duds, failing to explode at all. Only after a number of rounds did the fuse settings finally appear to work properly.

Still, they only made for a fireworks show. The enemy pilot—if he was, indeed, Japanese—was probably out there laughing at them.

Whether it was a friendly-fire mistake or a lone enemy attacker, Hyman had to proceed on the notion that if there was one plane, there would certainly be more. He would remain at General Quarters while remaining out in front of the *Neosho*. The tanker had already upped her speed to a good eighteen knots, staying as close on the escort's stern as she could manage.

Then, to the dismay of some of the men on the deck, Hyman ordered them to begin circling the oiler, making a long arc around her. That was an odd maneuver.

Some of the men reportedly shouted loud enough to be heard over the pounding of the guns, openly questioning what their skipper or whoever was now in charge was doing.

"Even the older, experienced sailors began to yell above the fire of the guns," John Verton later recalled. "They were hollering, 'This damn ship better start turning!'"

Somewhere along the way, Captain Hyman ordered the radio operator to report the event as enemy contact by a single aircraft. Then he finally told the gun crews to cease firing. The entire episode had lasted just less than fifteen minutes. The plane had shown no further interest in them other than continuing to ominously loiter out beyond their reach, stalking the two ships. The skipper requested an update from damage control.

"Captain, one casualty," one of his officers reported. A man at the number-two gun mount had been struck on a shoulder by a fragment from the bomb. He had a nasty cut but would get some stitches from a corpsman and be okay, back at his gun if needed.

All hands at number-one and number-two gun mounts reported significant hearing loss from the barrage. Men working in the ship's fire room had heard shrapnel from the bomb clattering against the port hull, but there was no apparent damage. Number-one gun had a blistered barrel after only fifteen minutes of firing.

As far as damage to the destroyer or other casualties, there was nothing in the official incident report about the captain's gig being smashed, or of the captain having suffered a head injury.

Regardless, it had been a close call, and there could be plenty more fire and brimstone where that came from.

Over on the bridge of the *Neosho*, John Phillips stood wide-eyed as he witnessed the sudden explosion that tore open the sea so near the *Sims*. He, too, had been surprised by how quickly and unexpectedly the plane had appeared, made a pass over the *Sims*, and let loose its single bomb. It had been a close drop, no more than a hundred feet away from the destroyer.

Captain Phillips, as Hyman likely was, was mightily concerned that his own radar and lookouts had not spotted the single attacker in time for some kind of response.

Fifteen nervous minutes passed after the near hit on the *Sims*. The guns on the destroyer went silent.

The sky was bright, hazy, empty. Every so often one of the lookouts could still make out the dot that was the sneaky bomber. He had not gone away. Though they could see him in the clouds only occasionally, he was still lurking out there, keeping pace with the destroyer and oiler. It had to be a carrier-based craft. No land-based plane would have the fuel to fool around out there so long. It was impossible to see if he was carrying any more bombs. If the one he dropped was one of the big 800-kilogram models, then that was all he had. Why was he still there?

Twenty more minutes passed.

No sign of other airplanes. No indication that the single aircraft was coming back for more, if he had anything else left. The *Sims* had long since stopped firing her guns and wasting ammo. There was no longer any conjecture about whether or not the plane was friend or foe. He was one of the emperor's boys.

Both ships were eerily quiet. Men remained at battle stations, but there was no chatter, none of the usual kibitzing common during drills. They all seemed to be holding their breath, waiting for whatever came next. The usual throbbing heartbeat of the ships' engines, their bows hissing as they cut through seawater, provided the only background sound.

A palpable sense of déjà vu arose among many of the sailors on the tanker. Phillips and most in his crew had been in a similar situation before, at Pearl Harbor. This time, though, he and his ship might be the primary target, not an assemblage of nearby battleships. Going by previous experience, he figured his men would fight valiantly and effectively, and with the help of the *Sims*, they should be able to repel any reasonable attack. Hopefully they could do so without significant damage to either vessel.

The Japanese would not commit any major force simply to knock off an oiler. Not with the *Lexington* and the *Yorktown* out there, primed for the real sea battle to come. The enemy also would not want to give Task Force 17 any indication of where the Japanese carriers were located. Launching a sizable attack on the oiler and escort would do just that.

Unbeknownst to any of the players, though, Captain Phillips's workaday ship was by this time playing an inadvertent role in the bigger scenario, one that would affect the outcome of the Battle of the Coral Sea.

One of the *Neosho* crew members passed along to Captain Phillips a report that had just been received from the destroyer.

"Sir, the *Sims* lookouts report aircraft, coming our way, 025 degrees true. At least ten of them. Maybe fifteen."

The captain reached for his binoculars and looked to the northeast. He saw them at once.

A squadron of planes, decked out with red-circle markings, was speeding closer, growing ominously larger by the second.

It was 1005 on May 7, and the sky overhead was about to get very crowded.

CHAPTER TEN
Look-see

Lieutenant Commander Kakuichi Takahashi, the commander of the *Shokaku* air group carrier attack planes, led the first wave of ten fighters directly toward the two targets. The American ships were easy to see as they steamed in open waters directly ahead, near the position where the previous Japanese scouts had reported them to be.

As they drew closer, Takahashi and the others in the group could easily see this was no aircraft carrier, no cruiser escort. Instead, the larger vessel appeared to be an oiler. It was a big enough ship, to be sure, one that might easily be mistaken for a light carrier. That was especially true if there was poor visibility, or if the report was from someone with limited experience or too strong a desire to please his superiors.

Takahashi ordered his formation into a sweeping turn to the west, keeping their distance from the escort, now clearly identified as a destroyer, but certainly a warship with some sharp teeth. Meanwhile, they continued to look for other elements of the American fleet, including the major prize, the carrier. He instructed the other seventy or so planes coming behind them to do the same, slowing, peeling off to one side or the other.

No doubt Takahashi had to reach deep for the courage to radio back the details of what they had discovered. He knew only too well how his commander would take the news of the mistaken sighting. He would have much preferred to face the fire from the American destroyer's guns than endure the ire of Admiral Chuichi Hara.

With his eyes still scanning the avocado-hued sea 10,000 feet below his fuselage, with the oiler and escort still a dozen miles away, barely in the periphery of his vision, Takahashi reluctantly made his report.

Hara was just as livid as his air group commander had anticipated. Yet Takahashi's news was not the only upsetting dispatch that had just hit his desk.

His strike force—about half of the aircraft at his disposal—was now far to the south of the fleet and they were reporting only an oiler where an aircraft carrier was supposed to be. No sign at all so far of any more of the American fleet in the area. The single bomber that had gone ahead of the attack force had also reported the same disappointing information. He had even swept low enough to not only confirm what he saw, but to drop his bomb near the escort, coming close to hitting the apparently unaware destroyer before pulling away. He was keeping the oiler in sight while he, too, continued to look for the rest of the American ships.

As if to mock him and his folly, the flabbergasted admiral's staff was now telling him that the young scout pilots were no longer so certain that what they had seen out there was an aircraft carrier. Yes, through the thick water vapor and blinding rays of early-morning daylight and from the significant distance from which they had been required to make the sighting, it could possibly have been some other large vessel, maybe even one of the Americans' big tankers.

All Admiral Hara knew was that a significant part of his battle assets were circling an illusion, searching for still more ghosts, and they were doing so more than a hundred miles south of his task force. What if someone finally spotted the real American fleet now, somewhere else in some distant portion of the Coral Sea? What if the oiler had been sent far from the fleet for protection? What if it was merely a decoy?

Even before the admiral could explode, another piece of news, even more disturbing, was brought to him. A floatplane, part of the Operation MO Main Force, searching near Rossel Island, east of the south end of the Jomard Passage, had spotted something unmistakable. Unlike previous bogus reports, this one—of what had been seen, with precise coordinates of where it was located—was undeniably accurate.

It was an Allied force that included one *Saratoga*-class aircraft carrier, another carrier of unknown class, and various support vessels. Far worse, even as the floatplane watched, the final planes of an unmistakable air strike force were rolling skyward, one after the other, launching off the carriers' decks. They appeared to be forming up and flying northward toward the MO Main Force and the light carrier *Shoho*.

Precisely as he had feared, an apoplectic Admiral Hara now knew that his planes were off on a fruitless chase just when he needed them the most. Woefully out of position to go to the rescue of Goto's MO Main Force, he could not simply rush north while he had more than six dozen planes in the air to the south, with no other place to land.

Seething, he recalled Takahashi and his aircraft.

Even if the strike force headed back immediately, by the time they returned and the carriers recovered all those airplanes one at a time, and then refueled and prepared them to fly again, it would be much too late in the day to locate and launch a full-force attack on not one but two American carriers. Even if he did have enough daylight, the Americans would have moved. He would have to find them again.

He had lost the opportunity this day to sink the enemy ships with most of their planes still aboard, or to send the carriers to the ocean floor and deny the returning American aircraft a place to land.

The very opportunity for which he and his counterparts had been working had just been squandered, thanks to a series of ridiculous blunders.

By the time Takahashi confirmed receipt of the recall to the base ship, he had already sent several squads of his planes down to circle, form up, and make preparations to sink the oiler and destroyer. The rest of the attack force continued to scan the sea for any signs of the main fleet. Then, before he gave up and returned to the *Shokaku*, the air commander made one request that he felt was practical, necessary.

Hara immediately approved it, apparently without comment.

There was no point in taking an attack force to the sky without at least trying to sink—if they had the time and opportunity—any available and worthy enemy targets they encountered along the way.

After all, the huge air attack force would not be required

to make a detour at all. Foolish mission or not, they were already in the neighborhood.

Why not try to salvage something of value out of this colossal debacle?

The radar operator and lookouts on the *Sims* first spotted the dozen or so enemy aircraft at 1005. Wilford Hyman made certain Captain Phillips over on the *Neosho* knew what was coming. The oiler's own lookouts had not yet spied the newcomers. The aircraft were approaching from just east of due north, and as binoculars by the dozen from both ships now pointed in the direction of their new visitors, the planes veered away, angling toward the western horizon, maintaining their distance and altitude until they were out of sight of lookouts, if not radar. Then they circled, still maintaining their aloofness, like a pack of prowling wolves.

Both Phillips and Hyman were perplexed. Not relieved, but curious about what the planes were up to. Why didn't they just come on in and make a fight of it? Or go on about their business, continuing their hunt for the main fleet?

"These planes made no attempt to attack, but flew parallel to the course of this vessel on the port side at high altitude, well out of gun range, and disappeared to the northeastward," Phillips would later relate.

Out of range or not, Wilford Hyman instructed the gun crews on the *Sims* to again fire some shots in the general direction of the airplanes. It was more for bluster than from any hope of actually hitting anything.

Maybe it worked. After reappearing for a few minutes far out on the western horizon, this time headed back to the northeast, the planes were soon erased by the altocumulus clouds and the usual tropical ocean spray.

Less than twenty minutes later, another group of seven or so planes appeared, heading toward the oiler and escort from a bearing of ten degrees. There was a suggestion from someone that these may have been the same guys, circling back around for yet another look-see. Surely, once they were certain the *Neosho* was not the *Yorktown* or the *Lexington*, they would fly on back to whatever Jap carrier had launched them.

Regardless, the *Sims* opened fire once again as soon as the aircraft appeared to be flirting with the range of her guns.

By now trailing well behind the destroyer, John Phillips had ordered his own gunnery crews to commence throwing up some flak as well.

"These planes flew parallel to this vessel on the port side, crossed the bow, and disappeared to the northeastward, having made no attempt to attack either the *Sims* or the *Neosho*," Phillips later recounted. These aircraft had taken the same tack as the first bunch earlier in the day, looking hard but not seeming the slightest bit interested in coming any closer or wasting any more bombs or torpedoes.

Maybe the fireworks display was working. Or maybe the two ships were simply not a tasty enough morsel for the Japanese to try to skewer.

Both captains kept their crews at General Quarters. Everyone remained on alert. They continued to steam a hopefully unpredictable course at near top speed.

Once more, except for the building clouds, towering high, hinting of storms later in the day, the sky was empty from horizon to horizon.

Then, at 1023, first the radar and seconds later the younger, sharper-eyed lookouts reported yet another group of ten aircraft. They were approaching, this time from the southeast, 140 degrees true, the opposite direction from the first two flocks. They were likely one of the original units. After flying a big, broad half circle—probably looking for the task force to which the tanker and escort were attached—this latest ominous drove was now coming in from the opposite compass point.

Almost immediately, John Phillips noticed that three of the planes were twin-engine aircraft. The rest were single-engine. Judging from their altitude and alignment, they seemed determined this time to do far more than simply take a look-see. The men on the decks of the two ships could already hear the deep-throated grumble of the aircraft engines.

And, God Almighty, they were coming fast.

CHAPTER ELEVEN
Hard Aport!

Neither John Phillips nor Wilford Hyman was under any illusions about the intent of the enemy bombers this time. As the two ships continued to zigzag, the ten planes made a descending turn even as another group of ten planes suddenly showed up following the first, boring in from nearly the same heading. By this time the *Neosho* was almost a mile behind the *Sims*. The escort had gotten farther and farther away and seemed to be steaming an almost straight course, according to sailors on the destroyer's deck.

The first group of enemy planes lined up for what appeared to be a direct attack on the destroyer. Both ships resumed firing, again trying to sway the risk-versus-reward equation.

Phillips dictated a rapid-fire series of notes even as he watched the planes from the time of their reappearance and as the attack unfolded.

1024: Changed course to 242 (degrees) T.

1025: Changed course to 207 (degrees) T; commenced firing with 3"/50 caliber guns. Again observed what were assumed to be white flares from planes.

What Phillips was actually seeing was star shells, flarelike loads that could be set to explode at a predetermined distance either to illuminate the area or help gauge distance of a target. Always seeking greater accuracy, the old sure-shot Wilford Hyman had ordered his gunnery crews on the *Sims* to load every tenth shell with star shell to help home in on the attackers.

1033: Changed course to 243 (degrees) T.

1034: Group of ten planes approached from 140 (degrees) T, of which three planes (twin-engined bombers) broke off and commenced horizontal bombing attack, others proceeded to eastward.

1035: Three bombers dropped three bombs simultaneously.

The men surrounding Phillips on the *Neosho*'s bridge were wondering why their skipper suddenly began steaming a straight course, 243 degrees. If there was ever a time to dodge and parry, this was it.

Yet the captain remained quiet as he continued to peer through his binoculars, watching as the three Japanese bombers roared directly at them at attack altitude. Then, the instant he saw bombs drop from the belly of each plane, Phillips yelled his order.

"Hard aport! Hard aport!"

Two of the bombs landed precisely where the *Neosho* would have been had she not swerved so abruptly. Still, that was barely twenty-five yards to their starboard side, close enough that the resulting geyser of water soaked the ship's deck and gave some of the gun crews a seawater shower. The third explosion was farther away, but still only about a hundred yards.

Bill Leu's General Quarters station was a different one after Pearl Harbor. He was now belowdecks, working in number-one magazine, passing up ammunition rather than toiling on the top deck. Now he and two shipmates could only guess what was going on above. They could hear enough on the J-V phones, the ship's intercom system, to determine that they were now under air attack.

"Here comes three! Three off our bow!" came the breathless report.

Leu and his buddies could only do what they were supposed to do, what they had trained for. They kept sending up shells. The two near misses exploded just twenty-five yards from where the men worked, almost deafening them, giving them quite a jolt.

"I was on the starboard side where I was standing," Leu later recalled. "The cork plaster came down and there was this real loud noise. I [staggered to] one side and the guy on the other side went [stumbling] over there. The guy that was on the phone, he was laughing. We were scared. We were all scared. And somebody yelled, 'Are you guys still alive down there?' I said 'Yes, we are, but I'm sure scared.' He laughed and said, 'So are we.'"

Just before the planes appeared with clear intent of attacking them, the ship's exec, Francis Firth, was down in the mess hall. With enemy planes buzzing around up there all morning, he wanted to make certain their five passengers from the *Yorktown* and the *Portland* had been properly briefed. Though they were hitchhikers, unwittingly caught aboard the *Neosho*, they, too, had assigned stations they were supposed to man and specific duties to perform while they were at General Quarters.

Or, heaven forbid, what they would do should they be ordered into an abandon-ship situation.

Firth was about finished with his briefing when he heard the first squawks on the J-V about rapidly approaching bombers. He immediately sent his passengers off to their proper spots and dashed to his own battle station. He arrived at battle II on the ship's port side, just forward of gun number four, just in time to see the three bombs fall off to starboard and hear the excited voices from crew members below who were not sure what had happened.

He interrupted the chatter on the phones to inquire if there were casualties or if anyone had damage to report. Nothing serious. Just some electrical fittings that had been shaken loose in the engine room. They were quickly reset.

From his duty station Firth could see the *Sims*, out a good mile away, and it was clear that she, too, was getting some unwanted attention. He saw the guns on the destroyer launching shells, star shells, and smoke, even as the vessel appeared to sway from side to side.

Of course, his own skipper had just made a nifty move of his own, especially for such a bulky vessel. Had he not done so, at least two of those bombs would have likely hit the *Neosho* square on.

Firth could imagine what the result might have been had that happened, considering all that incendiary fuel sloshing around in the massive tanks below his feet.

The *Sims* had the undivided attention of at least ten other Japanese bombers, zooming all around her.

Captain Hyman would certainly have been pleased with the response so far of both his ship and the crew. They had managed to duck and deflect just enough so that only one bomb came anywhere near them during the assault.

That one did no damage to the ship, though one of her twenty-millimeter guns had jammed during all the firing, leaving them with three working twenty-millimeter weapons. A couple of the other guns had seriously blistered barrels, which could cause problems should there be a more prolonged assault.

For the time being, all twenty or so planes had broken off the attack and moved away from the two ships. Had they scared the enemy off with their deck guns? Had the Japs simply decided they were not worth any more of their time and trouble?

As they stood on their respective bridges, Hyman and Phillips did not even attempt to guess. They kept their crews ready, waiting for whatever the next few hours held in store. They continued to maintain top speed—with the engineer on the *Sims* keeping a close eye on the shaky boiler tubes—all the while stirring up foam in their wakes.

They were listening, too, for any news about the Allied fleet, whether or not the American carriers had sent planes up north to meet the enemy invasion force or if they had by now encountered the Japanese carrier task force. All the while, Phillips fully expected to get the order any moment to hurry back from "Rye" and "Corn" and get busy refueling the fleet.

Maybe that was why the bombers had given up so easily, why an hour passed with no sign of returning enemy attackers. Maybe they had been summoned back to launch the long-anticipated attack on the Allied fleet, or to attempt to repel an assault from the Allies that might already be under way.

All was quiet again. Many prayers were sent up, asking that it remain so.

Radar was not hearing the prayers. The scope on the *Sims* continued to show blips that were enemy planes, flying beyond the sight of those watching for them through their binoculars.

Those distant craft seemed to be searching for something else out there, and it was not the *Neosho* and the *Sims*. The Japanese bomber pilots would by now know precisely what those two vessels were. The wish was that the enemy planes would soon fly on to where the real battle was and leave the *Neosho* and her escort alone.

Admiral Hara fumed. He had summoned Takahashi to return at 1100. The planes had already launched an initial attack on the misidentified vessels. Now they would certainly quickly sink them and come back.

Yet that was not his primary concern. Even as a significant portion of his air fleet was pounding a replenishment ship and destroyer—overkill, if there had ever been such a thing—word was coming that the Americans were now conducting their own attack on Admiral Goto's MO Main Force, and specifically on the *Shoho*.

Over the next half hour, updates confirmed that the light carrier had taken direct hits, that she was on fire, that she was sinking fast with great loss of life, almost certainly more than six hundred men.

Hara knew he would have to act with urgency now. The taking of Port Moresby and trying to get into position to provide air cover for the invasion force were no longer the primary goals. The American carriers were. Based on the number of planes that had hit the *Shoho*, he now knew for certain that there were two flattops out there somewhere.

He had already sent scout planes into the air with emphatic orders to sweep to the south and west. They were to once and for all locate the big Allied carriers. At the same time, he commanded that all attack aircraft, including those that would return from sinking the "mistakes," were to be prepared for an immediate assault, even at dusk if the enemy carriers should be found soon enough.

Mistakes. Weather. Incompetence. Lackadaisical attitude. Wrong assumptions.

All had led to the loss of what had once been a true and overwhelming advantage. Hara was already hearing it from his boss, Admiral Inoue, the commander of the 4th Fleet.

Admiral Hara, in his usual style, let his aides and subcommanders know that he intended to regain that squandered advantage and to do so with unbridled viciousness.

Frank Jack Fletcher was just as frustrated as his enemy counterpart. He still had not located the main Japanese carriers, and had now completely lost any element of surprise. The Japs could count—they would now know there were two Allied carriers operating in Task Force 17.

Still, one side would eventually spot the other and have the upper hand, at least for a brief window of time.

Fletcher was, however, more than happy to have taken down the smaller flattop, a major notch on his gun stock. It was the first bit of really good news to report back to Pearl Harbor in months.

The timing—whether by luck, happenstance, or skill—had been perfect. Wave after wave of attack planes had been more than Fletcher needed to send to finish off the light carrier, yet the admiral wanted to be sure he sank the enemy ship, not just damaged her. As his attack progressed, no accurate sightings of the big carriers were reported, so he had not been required to postpone an attack on them while he recovered his aircraft. Still, his instincts told him the Japanese were close. If only he could determine where, which direction.

Like his enemy counterpart, Fletcher considered going ahead and launching a sundown attack toward where he assumed the Japanese fleet would be, or to hit what was left of the invasion force again, erasing more warships. He was aware by now that the force had turned away and plans for invading the New Guinea port had either changed or been delayed.

He quickly dismissed both ideas. The weather in the area of the American fleet was getting even worse. Many of his pilots had had a fruitful but tiring day. With seas building and skies darkening, recovering them would be a tense, dangerous, and time-consuming chore. Actually finding the big IJN carriers in the rain and diminishing daylight would be a pull of the slot machine lever at best.

No, he did not trust his gut that much. He would wait until early on the morning of the next day, May 8. Get reports from more scout planes. Gauge the weather, the sea state. Have a rested crew and a deck full of prepared aircraft.

Maybe even start his big oiler, the *Neosho*, back toward the task force during the night so that he could top off his carriers' fuel tanks.

Thankfully there had been no reports of damage after the oiler radioed—in the midst of all the excitement of the *Shoho* attack—that she had attracted a brief, nasty, but unsuccessful air assault. No word of a follow-up attack. No distress signals from her or the *Sims*, either, so he could assume all was well out there.

Of course, Admiral Fletcher had no idea what was really happening with his oiler and her escort. No idea, either, that the following morning would bring some of the most remarkable series of coincidences in the annals of war.

His carrier aircraft would spot the MO Carrier Striking Force at almost the exact moment that Japanese planes off those flattops would finally sight the American carriers.

Almost precisely one hour later, air strikes would depart simultaneously from the decks of both sides' carriers.

Then, within a quarter hour of each other, each side would launch attacks on the other's big ships.

The skirmishes were over. The maddening, unsuccessful probing was done. The Battle of the Coral Sea was finally ramping up.

Once it started, the primary clash in history's first all-carrier-based battle would last only about two hours.

The *Neosho*'s horrific ordeal, however, would last much, much longer.

CHAPTER TWELVE
"Abandon the Bridge"

The Japanese attack planes still painted distant but ominous blips on the radar operator's scope aboard USS *Sims*. They were still out there, but well beyond what the lookouts could see. Wilford Hyman continually updated John Phillips over on the *Neosho*.

So far, no news was good news. Still, why did they not fly on and look for more bomb-worthy targets like the *Lexington* and the *Yorktown* and the true trophies of Task Force 17?

Meanwhile, Phillips instructed his communications officer, William G. Driscoll, a young Navy Reserve lieutenant, to periodically check with the ship's navigator and then radio back to the fleet their position and the nature of the aircraft contacts. Admiral Fletcher would certainly be interested in the activity of the enemy planes, and especially to learn that they were carrier-based aircraft. That would give him and his staff a good idea of where to concentrate the search for the big Japanese flattops.

Phillips briefly studied his communications officer's face as he reminded him about sending out the periodic contact reports. Frankly, he had his doubts about the man's suitability for leadership, and it was not because he was a naval reservist. He had already had at least one heart-to-heart chat with Driscoll about his general attitude. In that conversation, Phillips informed Driscoll that he was stubborn and uncooperative. He pointedly told the man that he had to "quit being a weakling and leaning too much on the enlisted men." The captain still had serious concerns about how the young officer would perform if things really got dicey.

From his previous wartime service, Phillips had experience in judging a man's mettle by the look in his eyes, the expression on his face, how quickly he jumped to do what needed to be done without being told twice. During the initial attack that morning, Driscoll had appeared to be on the threshold of panic. It would not instill confidence in the rest of the crew if one of the officers appeared to be terrorized, not in control of himself or the situation.

Now, in the aftermath of the near misses, Driscoll seemed reasonably calm. Phillips remembered that Driscoll had been an asset and performed his duties well during their unmooring and dash across Pearl Harbor on the morning of December 7. That action was enough to test the competence of any officer. Driscoll certainly had it in him. There was no new reason—other than the look in the man's eyes—to suspect the officer would not be able to do what he had been asked if this situation worsened.

Still, that was more than enough to give the captain some doubt.

Meanwhile, the ship's navigator, Henry K. Bradford, another Navy Reserve lieutenant, was busily plotting a fix of the sun and the dim orb of the planet Venus. His hands shook as he slowly, carefully entered the numbers in his navigation workbook. The previous attack had been especially nerve-racking for him, and he knew there could possibly be worse to come.

Bradford looked again at the numbers, making certain they were legible for Bill Driscoll so that he could radio them back to the task force. The fleet would need to be sure of the *Neosho*'s location if the Japanese came back and sank them. Rescue would need to come quickly. There was talk of sharks in the waters here. Of swift currents that could grab a life raft and carry it to Borneo—an island populated by vicious, notorious headhunters—in a matter of days. The tropical sun would have survivors already cooked to medium rare by then.

"Latitude 16 (degrees) 25 (minutes) S; Longitude 157 (degrees) 31 (minutes) E."

Confident he had written down his plot clearly, Bradford motioned to Driscoll to come over and take a look while he stood by. He wanted to make sure the communications officer had no questions.

Accuracy in reporting their position was now more crucial than ever.

Just before noon, an hour and a half after the initial air attack on the *Neosho* and the *Sims*, the radar scope on the destroyer was suddenly flecked with growing blips.

Signalman Robert Dicken, still at his post on the destroyer's bridge, saw the long string of approaching aircraft at almost the same moment that the radar report rang out. He began frantically blinking his light in that direction, using the day's authentication codes.

No recognition code flashed back from any of the aircraft. Dicken was not surprised. He immediately shouted out his report of "No response!"

Without hesitation, Captain Hyman ordered his destroyer's gunnery crews to begin firing the five-inch guns as well as the remaining working twenty-millimeter antiaircraft weapons. He also sent his vessel to flank speed—the fastest speed of which a ship is capable—and a turn to port to put the *Sims* on the port quarter of the *Neosho*, the ship he was bound to protect at all costs. With the guns firing furiously, no one could hear the roar of the approaching planes. There was little doubt about their intentions, though.

Later official reports would place the number at twenty-four attackers in this wave. Men on deck as well as on the bridge aboard the *Sims* heard the excited bridge talker report "at least fifty airplanes." At any rate, the Japanese soon broke up their orderly formation and began to attack the destroyer individually. In a matter of moments, they seemed to be coming at the *Sims* from all directions of the compass.

Now there was absolutely no doubt about their intent.

From the bridge of the *Neosho*, John Phillips could easily identify and count the approaching attackers.

"Mr. Driscoll, get our position from the navigator and report to task force commander our position at 1205. Inform them that we are under attack by twenty-four dive bombers, certainly carrier based." The comm officer stood there, wide-eyed, mouth agape, staring at the approaching planes, not moving, not even acknowledging his skipper. "Mr. Driscoll, you get that?"

"Got it, Captain," he replied weakly, and turned away.

Phillips had no time to watch Driscoll to see if he appeared to be doing what he was told. The captain was feverishly casting about other orders. Speed, course, commence firing, watch the *Sims*, and don't, for God's sakes, collide with her.

Within seconds, the first of three waves of bombers took a sharp dive in tandem from about 15,000 feet, screaming toward the *Neosho* from her stern. Just as it appeared some of them were going to crash right onto her long, flat deck, they pulled up, each releasing bombs at almost point-blank range.

The big ship swerved as geysers erupted from the sea all around her, some mere feet away. Amazingly, none of the bombs hit her. Phillips and his men were making all the right moves so far.

Meanwhile, out ahead of the *Neosho* and Phillips, the *Sims* kept blasting away. One shell caught a Japanese bomber directly, and the aircraft exploded into pieces in midair, what was left of it raining down into the deep. Most shells, though, missed. Tracers from the ship's twenty-millimeter guns seemed to pass right through the airplanes, the bullets apparently not fazing them at all.

Still, that was all she could do. Get enough hits to scare them off. Convince the Japs they were not worth the risk of losses.

Keep shooting. Keep praying.

Quickly, with no time for either ship's crew members to catch a breath, a second wave of dive-bombers approached the *Neosho*. Again they roared across her length from stern to bow. Diving sharply, just before they would have crashed into the sea adjacent to the big vessel, they abruptly pulled up, their deadly bombs falling away from beneath them.

Once more, miraculously, none of those bombs hit home. It was as if the big oiler had some kind of protective shield around her, deflecting the ordnance. One bomb did fall so close, it rattled the deck plates and shook the ship hard. Men had to grab something solid to keep from falling.

"Captain, the gyro compass is not working," someone shouted. The near miss had apparently broken the instrument.

"Steer by the magnetic compass," Phillips quickly responded. No big deal. They were course-plotting wildly and randomly anyway, attempting to be as much of a moving target as they could. Dashing and darting had worked on both waves of bombers so far. The unexpected speed and agility of such a big ship seemed to have thrown off the Japs' aim. The ships' antiaircraft fire appeared to have made them skittish, too.

But even in the frenzy on the bridge, Phillips could see that three or four of the last group of attackers had peeled away from the formation after dropping their bombs, likely five-hundred-pounders. They formed up and quickly zoomed in on the *Sims* this time. They were probably still carrying sixty-kilogram bombs under their wings.

This was all taking place in clear view of many of the *Neosho* crew members at their battle stations on the upper decks. It was all happening close enough for them to witness the fury of the attack as it was now directed at the destroyer. Those not too busy in the gunnery crews looked on in horror as a bomb fell in the water just to the port side of the *Sims*, amidships, maybe missing, maybe not. From that distance it was hard to tell.

Then, only a second or two later, another bomb hit home and set off a big explosion in the ship's forward engine room. The men on the oiler's deck could clearly hear the deep-throated boom. Flames, smoke, and debris formed a column

150 feet into the midday sky. A man, maybe a lookout, was thrown overboard, his arms waving in terror as he flew into the air and then fell back downward, swallowed up by the sea.

An instant later, a third bomb plunged through the after upper-deck house—the structure in which the ship's torpedoes were stored—and on into the after engine room, setting off another thunderous blast. The fourth plane's bomb appeared to hit, also solidly, somewhere near the number-four gun at the destroyer's stern.

The *Neosho* crew could discern no more tracers from the after twenty-millimeter gun, and now both guns number three and four were silenced.

Men had died there. That was plain to see.

So was the fact that their escort—and by far the *Neosho*'s best defense from the zooming enemy dive-bombers—might well be mortally wounded and on the verge of sinking.

In the midst of the chaos aboard the doomed destroyer, Robert Dicken had his own clear view of the destruction all around him. He could hear the terrible back-and-forth rattling away on the ship's communication circuit, a mishmash of panic, coolness, damage reports, and appeals for help. To add to the pandemonium, the general alarm sounded continually with a loud, obnoxious growl until someone finally located and threw the electrical breaker to stifle it.

Four bombs, three hits. Only the first bomb to fall had been a near miss.

The *Sims* had suffered severe damage. The deck was brutally buckled just forward of the afterdeck house, ripped from port to starboard with twisted beams poking up oddly from the rift. The radar antenna had fallen across one of the motor whaleboats on deck. Both were broken. Fires raged in the upper-deck house as the men who were able moved to try to contain them. Neither of the five-inch guns astern was firing.

Vito Vessia was at his duty station in the after fire room. His boss ordered him to hurry topside and close off the fuel oil stop on the port side before it spilled enough oil to cause and feed a massive fire. Vessia was horrified by what he saw as he ran.

"It was a mess," he recalled. "I could look into the forward engine room from the top deck. There was nothing but split-apart machinery and partially dismembered men I had just talked to a few hours before."

Machinist's Mate Second Class Vincent Canole was on duty belowdecks on the *Sims*. He later described hearing the pinging and rattling of bullets hitting topside and striking the ship's hull as the Japanese pilots—the ones who had already dropped their complement of bombs—now strafed the damaged and dying destroyer with their wing machine guns.

Inside the pilothouse on the bridge, where Dicken stood, everything was a shambles. The chart table was torn loose, glass from instruments littered the floor, and the quick-acting watertight doors—the main exit from the area—had jammed shut. Similar doors elsewhere on the ship were wedged closed as well, blocking men from being able to find a quicker route to the upper decks, away from the smoke and fire and in-rushing seawater below.

And many of them were trying to do just that, scrambling away from the hellish blazes and trying to find breathable air. The general alarm that had been sounding since the first hit was the one that was supposed to signal a gas attack. That fed rumors already flying about that the captain had issued the order to abandon ship. So far, no such order had been given, but the destroyer was clearly in bad enough shape that abandoning ship was understandable.

Worse, the ship was now dead in the water, all power lost. Then, remarkably, the auxiliary diesel generator coughed to life, urged to resurrection by a few dedicated sailors. At least it was supplying power for some of the ship's electrical systems, those whose cables had not been severed and ripped loose from their panels.

Someone reported that six of the ship's eight Carley life rafts had been blown to bits when the after engine room went up. Depending on how many of the ship's more than 250 crewmen had survived, there likely would not be enough rafts left to hold them all if they did have to go over the side.

Thankfully, guns one and two were still booming away. But as Dicken watched, the barrel on the five-incher at number one mount—which had already been smoking heavily—suddenly burst into flames. The gunnery crew did not miss a beat. They kept pounding away until the last dive-bomber was clearly out of range, even as hungry flames swirled and licked upward and around the length of the barrel.

At least two of their attackers had been shot down, and the remaining gunners kept trying to up the total. The intense barrage of fire from the *Sims* guns convinced the planes attacking the *Neosho* to drop their bombs from a much higher altitude, affecting their aim considerably.

Belowdecks, Vito Vessia had been lucky to survive when the final five-hundred-pound bomb plummeted into the after engine room. A large piece of machinery had stood between him and the bomb's blast, effectively shielding him, but the concussion threw him through gratings and he ended up in the bilges. When he struggled to his feet, he regained his balance and headed toward what light he could see through the thick, choking smoke. Once topside, he saw immediately the results of the strafing runs by the enemy pilots. "It was grue-some," he remembered. "All the fire room gang were dead, laying there like limp rags on the deck."

Vincent Canole was even more fortunate, though he likely did not think so at the time. The detonation of the final bomb to strike the *Sims* propelled him through the resulting hole in the ship's deck. Before he even knew what had happened, he realized he was in open air, flying just above the wave tops. Still reeling from the stunning blast and before he could even dread the impact, he was underwater. He struggled to swim to the surface, frantically pulling himself toward daylight. When his head finally cleared the surface and he sucked in a deep draft of smoky air, he grasped that he was a shockingly far distance from the ship, looking back at her in disbelief as she burned. Canole desperately searched around in all directions for something to grab hold of, for crewmates.

And, dear God, for shark fins.

Captain Hyman took in all he could see from the bridge and made quick notes of the damage reports now coming in like an avalanche, doubtless trying to get a bead on just how dire their situation was. He knew a number of his crew had been killed and both engine rooms had been damaged. Still, he fully intended to do all he could to save the ship and crew, keep her afloat, and not only prepare for any follow-up assault on his vessel but to do everything in his power to continue to protect the big tanker.

In his later recollections for investigators, Dicken still did not say anything about his captain having suffered a head wound, or that he seemed in any way disoriented. Yet some of the enlisted men speculated that the skipper's injury may have kept him from fully comprehending his ship's dismal circumstances. They felt he should have ordered an evacuation of the ship sooner. In so doing, he might have saved the lives of more crew members.

"From the bridge, the damage was not as apparent as it was from down there on the deck," Robert Dicken would recall. "And certainly not below, where things were a mess. The captain, though . . . he was not going down easily."

Many of the destroyer's crew members were reluctant to give up the ship for lost. The boat's chief engineer, Ensign Lionel Tachna, though wounded, was still at his station in one of the engine rooms. He called up to the captain to assure him that he and the crew were doing all they could to get the engines working again.

The ship still had steam. The three big boilers so far held fast. The notoriously problematic plumbing, too. They would somehow get the ship back under power.

Amazingly, the men at the forward five-inch gun continued firing away. Somehow the ship's gun crews had managed by then to down an estimated six enemy planes, and the men in the lone remaining gun mount were still trying to take down more of their attackers or at least frighten them away.

Wilford Hyman considered the smoke, fire, and mayhem on his ship. The *Sims* was beginning to sink from the stern. He took a quick look through the glasses to make certain no other planes were coming their way. The attackers apparently figured the destroyer was done for, or they were out of weapons. Some had flown away. Others were now concentrating on the oiler.

Hyman took a glance over to the *Neosho*. As he watched, a shot from the *Sims*'s gunners hit a Japanese target, and the pilot somehow managed to steer his crashing plane directly onto the deck of the *Neosho*, into the area around that ship's number-four gun enclosure. Flames immediately raced across the big ship's deck, and thick black smoke swirled up, blotting out the midday sun.

Hyman knew that the oiler's crew was well drilled on firefighting, yet he knew all too well that if fire reached the remaining fuel they carried—and especially its fumes—it would get very hot very fast.

"Engineer, give me an honest assessment on the engines," Hyman called down to Ensign Trachna.

"Captain, looks like it would take a miracle," was the discouraging report.

"Then we can make better use of our time and efforts."

Hyman had finally come to a reluctant decision—as much as he wanted to stay afloat, the *Sims* was likely done for. Resolved, his priorities changed. First, he needed to make sure they did not blow up any surviving crew members still aboard. They needed to get rid of anything that could explode.

Next, they would make the ship as light as they could to try to postpone the inevitable sinking. Then they needed to lower lifeboats into the water and pack as many men into them as possible. Since there would not be enough boats or life rafts to carry the entire crew, those who could not fit would be ordered to don life vests. Some men would have to stay afloat until they were rescued.

The captain was also determined to control the fires raging at the destroyer's stern. For that, he would need men in a whaleboat to work their way around to that quadrant of the ship, somehow climb back aboard, and try to put it out.

Along the way, they could also pray that the *Neosho* would

still be around to pick up survivors—and hope that the fleet was aware of their position and circumstances so that help could quickly find them if the *Neosho* lost power or sank.

"Quartermaster, you stay here with me," Hyman ordered. "Everyone else, abandon the bridge and await orders."

The men glanced at each other for a quick moment, surprised their skipper was giving up, after all, but they did as ordered. Since the doors were jammed, they had to climb one at a time down the high, vertical ladder at the rear of the structure.

According to Chief Dicken's later report, Wilford Hyman spoke quickly then, issuing commands calmly but succinctly. He wanted the engineer—if able—to come topside with as many of his engine men and other crew members who were able to make it. Forget about trying to get an engine going. Once Tachna got there, he was to try to jettison as many torpedoes as he could. That would eliminate one potential explosion hazard. Yet it would be difficult to do. The second bomb had damaged the number two torpedo mount. That left only two more.

With that task complete, Tachna was to organize a party to fight even harder to put out the blaze in the torpedo deckhouse from the area of the deck just forward of the flames. That space, the captain believed, was another impending blast area.

Yet another party was organized and told to get busy jettisoning anything heavy or loose, but especially the barrel-like depth charges strapped to their deck.

Vito Vessia heard an order from the captain to dismantle the five-inch-gun mounts and get them over the side. Vessia shook his head, assuming the captain's earlier injury had made him irrational. The gun mounts were far too heavy for the few remaining crew members to move, even if they could get them apart. Besides, what the hell good would it do? Would it even slow their plunge to the bottom by a second? The order was simply ignored by the few who heard it.

The only two remaining life rafts were put over the side. Men also lowered the port motorized whaleboat, only to watch wide-eyed as it immediately filled with seawater and sank.

The ship's other whaleboat had six men assigned to her with instructions to get it into the water, but they discovered a big hole had been punched through its bottom by a piece of shrapnel. The men were ordered to somehow make it seaworthy, then to shove the boat through the tangle of rigging on the deck and over the side. There was no time or means to lower it properly, and with the destroyer's tilt to the stern so pronounced now, it was not that much of a drop from the deck to the sea.

Once in the water and unmanned, the heavy seas pulled the empty boat away from the ship. According to Vito Vessia's later account, he quickly volunteered to go after it. Except for the two life rafts, the whaleboat appeared to be the only other sizable thing off the *Sims* that could hold enough survivors to make a difference.

A junior officer gave him the reluctant okay and Vessia dived into the oil-covered sea. Thankfully, he was a strong swimmer. He reached the boat only to find its control panel smashed and the patched hole in the side leaking badly. Still, he managed to climb in, get the motor started, and turn back toward the listing ship. Along the way, he picked up a half dozen men who had been blown into the water. One of those was Vincent Canole, the machinist's mate who had been tossed into the sea through a hole in the destroyer's hull.

• • •

Chief Dicken's account of the whaleboat launching varies from Vessia's. Dicken reported that as Vessia and the other men were lowering the lone remaining motorized whaleboat into the water, Captain Hyman had another thought.

"Get Signalman Dicken down to the whaleboat," the captain ordered. According to Dicken's account, two men had ridden the boat over the side. Both were firemen, members of the black gang, and knew nothing at all about handling a small craft; they were clearly in danger of allowing it to drift out of sight. "Tell Dicken he is in charge. Give him the gist of what we need him and his men to do to fight the fire back there [at the destroyer's stern]."

By the time Dicken got the order, the whaleboat had already drifted a considerable distance from the ship. Dicken and four sailors climbed down some rigging, dived into the Coral Sea, and swam out to the boat as fast as they could, hoping all the while that the explosions had scared away any curious sharks.

When he was pulled aboard, Chief Dicken saw the men had stuffed the hole in the boat's bottom with life jackets. The repair job was not working very well, and each man was busy bailing water. No telling how long the makeshift patch would hold.

At least the boat's diesel motor worked when they cranked it up.

Dicken later reported that he took the tiller and steered around the lee side of the ship, pointing the boat's sharp-nosed bow aft to see what they could do to knock down the roaring fire back there.

In addition, the captain wanted them to attempt to flood the ship's magazine, again in an effort to prevent all the ammunition stored there from exploding and blowing what was left of the *Sims* sky-high before she could sink on her own.

Controlling the fire would be next to impossible. Flooding the magazine would be a monumental task, too, but they were bound to at least try. The deck between the main deckhouse and the ship's machine shop was already awash. At first, the men in the boat thought that might make it a little less difficult for them to get back aboard the ship, yet the seas had been building, and if they drew close at the wrong instant, they would certainly risk colliding with the vessel as the waves tossed them about.

Then, Dicken reported, he was surprised to see a large number of men already in the water. Captain Hyman had apparently given the order to abandon ship, to try to swim to the two life rafts that had been thrown overboard or to the lone whaleboat. Both Dicken and Vessia later reported seeing about two dozen men climbing into one of the bobbing life rafts. The other raft, apparently empty, had drifted almost out of sight.

Back aboard the *Sims*, the captain finally instructed his quartermaster to leave the bridge. Yet Hyman remained where he was, apparently determined to stay aboard until every man was in the whaleboat, the raft, or the water. There they could make for the *Neosho*, should she survive, or be rescued by a ship from the fleet. Help was likely already en route.

"The last I saw of the commanding officer," Dicken recalled, "he was standing on the bridge. He showed an example of courage throughout the entire engagement."

When the men in the whaleboat team realized they could not put out the fire, they motored back around to take on more survivors. The ship's midsection was clearly buckling, and an ominous rumbling erupted from the bowels of the vessel.

Several wounded men were passed down to them from the ship's listing deck. Vessia also maintained later that this was actually the point when Robert Dicken came aboard the whaleboat. He also reported that Dicken passed out from exhaustion as soon as he was on board.

Meanwhile, John Verton was ordered to climb down and try to make it to the raft that was already occupied by a couple of dozen men. As he climbed over the railing, following the gunnery officer's orders, Captain Hyman yelled down at him from the bridge, "Hey, sailor! Where are you going? I have not given the order to abandon ship!" He ordered Verton back on deck, and instructed him to free some injured—but, to Verton's eyes, already dead—men who had been trapped beneath a tangle of damaged steel and rigging.

As he obeyed the order and tried to cut the mess loose, Verton glanced up and saw the raft he had been aiming to swim to. Filled with men, the vessel was quickly drifting away into the distance. The next time he looked up, the raft was nothing more than a dot on the horizon. Much later, Verton learned how lucky he was that he had not made it to that raft.

Now, however, the seaman was convinced that his ride to rescue was gone. The other raft was nowhere to be seen. He was making no progress moving the mangled rigging, and, besides, there was no sense in "rescuing" shipmates who were gone to Glory already.

All the while, the deck was breaking apart beneath his feet. The horrible growling of the ship's infrastructure was an obvious death knell. Without further hesitation, Verton ran and leaped over the side of his vessel.

Once in the sea, he swiftly swam away, then paused to

look back. He witnessed an awful scene: his ship was seemingly breaking in two, like a toy smashed by giant, unseen hands. Verton could see Captain Hyman, still on the bridge, calmly riding her down.

One of the last men off the ship was Machinist's Mate Second Class Edward Munch. He later recalled standing at the edge of the deck, silently weighing his options, wondering whether his best hope would be to stay aboard or to take his chances with the sharks and the formidable, building waves. Realizing how difficult it was simply to keep his balance on the destroyer's listing deck, he made his decision.

Seconds before he dived, he spotted an unsecured depth charge and took time to lash it down. If that thing got overboard, somehow armed itself, and blew up amid him and his shipmates, it would do far more damage than even the teeth of a hungry shark. Certain the depth-charge barrel was not going to follow him overboard, Munch jumped over the side.

Hyman, Vessia, Verton, and Munch were not the only ones who showed remarkable courage that day. Despite the viciousness of the attack and the odds against them, the men of the *Sims* demonstrated exceptional bravery. Chief Dicken later stated, "I never saw any sign of panic. Everyone was on their [sic] stations doing their job and the whole ship worked as a well-organized unit until the end." He added, "Discipline was excellent."

The whaleboat crew, their hopeless task at the stern now abandoned, stopped to pick up a few more of the swimmers they passed. Then they began looking for still more, as well as for the life rafts. The men did all they could do, wrestling wet, exhausted, oil-soaked, wounded, and scared men into the whaleboat.

Just then, the occupants of the leaky whaleboat heard a

rolling explosion from somewhere deep inside the destroyer. All assumed it was the ship's boilers letting go, but the firemen said no, that the last they heard, there was zero pressure in the boilers. Still, something had blown up deep inside the *Sims*, doing fatal damage.

Another enormous blast rang out, maybe torpedoes or depth charges. The whaleboat was steered away from the ship at top speed, the sailors wary of flying debris, or worried the sinking ship would suck them down with her all the way to the bottom.

John Verton was still swimming as hard as he could, trying to put distance between himself and the inevitable oily whirlpool of the sinking destroyer. Looking back, he was amazed to see that even as the *Sims* broke up and began quickly sinking, the men in the forward gun enclosure were still stubbornly firing, shooting blindly, but still shooting, even though there were no longer any enemy aircraft overhead. The gun was completely submerged when the final round broke the surface and flew skyward.

Another massive explosion erupted from inside the ship, likely from the magazine. Though he had managed to swim several hundred yards away, the shock wave from the blast ripped off Verton's shirt and forced the contents of his intestines out his rectum and mouth. He choked, coughed, spat, all while trying to tread water and keep his head above the surface.

"I prayed I would die before the sharks found me," Verton remembered. "I was sure I was the only survivor after the explosion. The water was filled with bodies but they were all dead. Some were decapitated and bobbed up when I swam up to them."

The men in the whaleboat were stunned when they heard something they would never forget—a terrible, painful groan coming from the dying *Sims*. An excruciating wail emanated from somewhere deep in the proud ship's substructure.

The sailors looked back in shock as the rear of the destroyer seemed to tilt upward and forward at an odd, impossible angle, the stern rising up out of the sea, revealing her dead, motionless screws. Ahead, through the smoke, they could see the bow flipped up even as the middle of the vessel plunged absurdly downward.

The USS *Sims* was breaking in half.

CHAPTER THIRTEEN
Courageous Tenacity

The scene seemingly played out in slow motion as John Phillips looked on from aboard the *Neosho*. A Japanese dive-bomber took a hit from a gun on the *Sims*—or one from his own ship . . . it was difficult to tell with so much ammunition being spat into the air—and a part of the plane's wing and tail section went spinning away. The plane was going down, likely into the sea, a mere hundred yards from the *Neosho*'s port side.

Somehow, the airplane's pilot willed the damn thing to not crash into the water. Keeping it airborne, he fought what must have been a furiously bucking stick and goosed the throttle to make the damaged bird fly just a bit farther. Instead of hitting the surface of the sea, he deliberately crashed it directly into the *Neosho*, hurtling into the area of the ship's number-four gun enclosure. Fire instantly spread in all directions, fed by the plane's aviation gasoline, enveloping the port side of the ship, racing aft, looking ravenously for more fuel. A collection of life rafts hanging there—eight or nine—provided energy for the insatiable flames.

The captain ordered a crew to rush to the area and get to work putting out the flash fire. Enough volatile fuel was still held in the storage tanks belowdecks to set off a catastrophic inferno.

Next Phillips tried to raise on the communication system his XO, Francis Firth, who would have been close to where the suicide pilot had crashed his plane. He wanted to get a damage report from him, but what he wanted most was to see if his second in command was okay, even as another wave of Japanese planes approached purposefully from the north. They were already setting up for another stern-to-bow run.

No word from Firth. He was either hurt or busy. Maybe both. Maybe now out of the picture.

Phillips had no time to consider the possibilities. The skipper turned his attention to continuing to order the zigs and zags, to encourage his gun crews to keep firing away, to keep track of damage reports and what his other officers were doing.

So far, the top-speed erratic course and the constant antiaircraft fire were their salvation. There had been no direct hits yet on the big vessel with one big, destructive exception: the plane that had hurtled onto the deck even as they continued to try to keep the ship headed crosswind.

The gun crews—at least the ones that were left—blasted away at the ducking and diving targets. Phillips would later say he was certain his gunnery crews on the *Neosho* shot down three dive-bombers. The American ships' steady fire had forced the attackers to drop their bombs from a higher altitude, leading to many near misses. Bone-rattling near misses that still did some damage, but nothing like direct hits would have.

"The greatest majority of the planes diving on the *Neosho* were forced to deliver their attacks at a high altitude," Phillips would later report. "Only three or four dove to within a few hundred feet of the masts."

Maybe so. But then, for the next eighteen minutes—with the sinking *Sims* able to offer less and less and, ultimately, no fire cover—the enemy pilots were able to zero in on the big oiler, no matter the drunken course in which she was steaming or the shells hurled into the air by her persistent guns.

Throughout the rest of the attack, despite the number of bombs falling mostly harmlessly into the sea, seven of them ultimately hit the tanker, each doing horrible destruction to ship and crew. There were simply too many airplanes dropping too many fireworks.

Damage reports came quickly and furiously from various stations on the ship, most delivered in panicked or pained voices.

The first direct hit fell on the port side of the main deck, gouging out a fifteen-foot-long section of the ship.

The next ripped into the stack deck's starboard side and continued downward at an angle, on through the ship's store and bunker tank compartment. Its blast destroyed the pump room, ruptured an oil tank, and sent murky liquid gushing all over the engine room. The oil immediately caught fire, and thick, black smoke quickly filled the compartment.

"Oh, God!" someone cried out on the J-V. "We took a hit on the forward gun group. Two men . . . Christ . . . one of them had his head . . . Jesus."

One near miss, a fragmentation bomb, sent deadly shrapnel hissing through the air, ripping apart the men in the machine-gun position, decapitating one sailor in view of many crew members, tearing apart another man who had been standing on the flying bridge, only a few feet from the captain. Blood speckled Phillips's face.

Another bomb struck the ship's port side, buckling the main deck like some massive tectonic force.

Still another, an armor-piercing weapon—as most of them had been so far—nosedived through the deck and into the fire room, just above the engine room, before exploding. Every man there died instantly. Steam hissed from fractured pipes, creating a deadly, boiling fog.

Three more bombs knocked enormous holes in the fuel-storage tanks but, miraculously, did not immediately ignite the fumes or flammable oil held there. As far as anyone could tell, the bombs continued right on through the hull and back into the sea, leaving a hole but no fire. The *Neosho* still clung to a bit of her seemingly blessed existence.

Nevertheless, it was clear that the big tanker was now in serious trouble.

"Despite any courageous tenacity on the part of the gun crews, it was quite obvious that if a pilot desired to carry his bomb home, he could not be stopped," Phillips later wrote.

His ship would soon be no longer able to move through the water to avoid her attackers. The boilers could not hold steam pressure, and the turbines, and thus the screws, had stopped. The massive ship would drift to a standstill, her wake a curling tail of churned foam stretched out behind her.

The electrical system was out. Damage reports confirmed that fires raged in several areas of the *Neosho*, she was taking on water uncontrollably, and men were being cooked alive by escaping steam in some of the compartments below.

Just as disturbing, there was word that some of the crew members, terrified by what they had seen when the *Sims* was so savagely attacked, and broke in half, and sank out of sight in mere minutes, had already panicked. Many had begun to jump overboard. Even more worrisome, some had apparently cast loose over the side the rest of the *Neosho*'s now-scarce life rafts. Empty, they would soon drift too far away to be of any use to survivors, whether the men were in the water yet or not.

Phillips listened to the communications flooding in—fact, rumor, and undetermined veracity—and began to assay the best course of action. Just then, a young messenger showed up on the bridge with word from Francis Firth.

The XO was hurt badly, with a head injury and serious burns. But he was conscious, had taken charge, and was ready to do whatever the captain ordered.

Captain Phillips quickly made his decision. He would tell his exec to spread the word to prepare to abandon ship in case it came to that, but he was to wait for his command to do so. He gave the messenger his instructions for Firth and sent him on his way.

Even if he was second in command, Francis Firth was not really aware of much that was going on aboard his ship in the wake of the vicious attack. At least not beyond the area where he was standing when the apocalypse erupted. He had been at his General Quarters station at battle II on the port side, close enough to gun four that he could hear the young gunners inside the mount whooping and yelling as they launched shells toward the attacking enemy dive-bombers.

Then, out of the corner of his eye, he saw one of the Japanese planes take a hit. He could not tell if the shot had come from the *Sims* or the *Neosho*, but it appeared the enemy pilot and his gunner were about to take a fiery bath in the Coral Sea. Somehow, though, the mangled aircraft, afire and missing parts, managed to stay in the air, to climb improbably for a moment, and then to whirl at a cockeyed, flaming angle directly toward the *Neosho*.

It came in straight at the nearby gun mount as if drawn by some invisible cable.

Firth did not even have time to run. Instinctively, he took two big steps forward, shoved three sailors out of the way of the quickly spreading flames, and then jumped over them, shielding the men with his body.

Electrician's Mate Third Class Edward Flaherty, one of the passengers taken on board from the *Portland*, witnessed the astonishing act. When the first attack had broken up Firth's briefing for him and the other hitchhikers, he had followed Firth up to the XO's position, to be of help in any way he could. Though Flaherty was burned, too, he was impressed by Firth's actions.

"The lieutenant commander was a little fellow," Flaherty later recounted. "When that plane hit, he threw himself at three or four boys back there, knocking them down and trying to shield them from the flaming gas. It was actually funny to see this little officer trying to protect those men, but he did it. They don't make them any braver."

In his dive to the deck, Firth hit his head on something hard enough to knock him out cold. The XO never knew how long he was unconscious, but as the fog in his aching head cleared, he realized he was lying prone on a blazing deck. He felt blistering pain. Both his arms and his face had been badly burned. Through his woozy headache, he sat up and quickly checked the rest of his body.

No other obvious damage. But he was deaf. He could hear none of the explosions or gunfire around him. He felt the shock wave of a bomb explosion, felt the ship shudder, but heard nothing.

He glanced over toward the number-four gun mount. It was no longer firing, now wrapped with burning, smoking metal, the remains of the enemy plane. What was left of the Japanese pilot or gunner lay in a bloody, lifeless heap against a bulkhead, where he had been ejected on impact. Hopefully the sailors inside the gun mount were okay and could get the weapon back into service.

Slowly, Firth climbed to his feet, so dizzy he had to lean against something to stay erect. He could feel the heat, smell the smoke. Then his hearing seemed to be returning, only to be assaulted by the thundering din all around him. The XO picked up a communications handset but it was dead.

He spotted a young seaman standing nearby, dazed, doing nothing, but apparently not injured.

"Sailor, I need you to go to the bridge and give the captain a message," Firth yelled, to be heard over the clamor. "Tell the captain that his exec is okay. Tell him I don't have any working communications here but I am waiting for his orders." The sailor stared blankly at the officer. Firth's face was one angry blister; his uniform blouse was blackened and still smoking. "Understand, sailor? Now, hurry!"

The seaman saluted, turned, and disappeared at a run.

Firth looked around, tried to take in the mayhem, the chaos. Despite the searing pain, the dizziness, the disorientation, he knew he should take charge, do something.

He flagged down a corpsman and directed him to a couple of sailors who were clearly in bad shape.

"Sir, you better let me look at you first," the doc told Firth. "You got some bad . . ."

"No, do as I say. Help those guys. I'm okay."

"But . . ."

"Do as I say!"

Firth actually did not feel so good at that moment, yet he did not have time to sit down and have salve smeared on his burns or get them bandaged. Those other men required the medic's assistance far more than he did.

The XO knew that his first chore was to see what he could do to bring some order into what had become bedlam on the rubble-covered, listing deck of USS *Neosho*.

That was what he would do while he awaited the orders of his captain.

CHAPTER FOURTEEN
Snipes and Bilge Rats

Like most of the other "snipes"—the firemen, engine men, boiler men, machinist's mates, and pipe fitters whose duty was mostly within the bowels of the ship—Bill Leu could witness none of the action going on topside. His battle station had him working away in the number one magazine. He knew, of course, that his ship was under one hell of an attack. Number-one gun fired continuously as he and his two buddies working next to him furiously sent up ammunition, three boxes at a time, without rest.

Leu also knew they were taking some damn hard hits. When bombs blew at the stern or amidships, the ship shook and shuddered and knocked them around a bit, but as he would later declare, that first near miss during the initial attack had been the hardest blow he had felt so far.

The next one? That could be the one that fell right on top of them. At least they would die doing their jobs, though.

As Leu reached for another shell box, somebody came running through, yelling, "Captain says 'Abandon ship!' Captain says 'Abandon ship!' We're sinking! Everybody overboard! If we don't blow up, we're going down!"

Leu could smell smoke, hear panicked shouts, feel the impact of each bomb hit and some near misses. He was not surprised by such an order.

He looked up at the gun mount above them. The guys up there would quickly be out of ammo if they ran. The gun would be useless.

But if the captain had ordered them to go, he had no choice. He was required to go overboard even if he was not wearing a life belt. Some sorry so-and-so had stolen his. Leu knew who it was, but retribution would have to wait. Life belt or no, he would have to get off his big, doomed ship, the only home he had known since joining the Navy.

Leu punched his nearest buddy on the shoulder and shouted to be heard over the uproar.

"Let's go!"

Another "snipe," Harold Bratt, would have had no choice when it came to either staying below or going topside and into the sea. He would not have been able to hear any order from the captain to abandon ship.

A machinist's mate, Bratt was in charge of the watch and battle station working in the after engine room, making sure they had all the steam power they needed to keep the *Neosho* at flank speed as they tried to dodge the enemy bombers. Their compartment was directly below the ship's fire room.

When the bomb tore through the deck and exploded above them, he and the four men on watch with him were knocked down hard, momentarily dazed by the force of the jarring blast.

Bratt knew at once that their situation was dire. There were only two ways out of the engine room: up vertical ladders, one fore and one aft, that led through hatches in the floor of the fire room above them. But the men suspected that would now mean opening a hatch through the floor of hell.

They could hear the hissing and whistling of high-pressure steam—450 pounds per square inch and 750 degrees hot—disgorging into the compartment above. Everybody up there was dead, if not from the bomb's blast, then from the searing fog.

They could now feel the decided slant of the deck beneath their feet, and the shudder of more direct hits, or near misses. It made no difference. The ship was still getting pounded by an overwhelming enemy, and they would certainly soon be sinking like an anvil.

"Boys, we are going to stay right here for a bit," Bratt finally told his four shipmates. Coming from a senior man, his suggestion was supposed to be followed. A lantern in one hand and a gas mask in the other, he shone the light in each man's face. Some actually were "boys," mere teenagers. "Look, we'll sure as hell get boiled alive if we try to go through that steam up there." He motioned with the lantern toward the ceiling of their compartment, the floor of the fire room.

Beneath oil and sweat, one man's face in the lantern light was angry, defiant, terrified. "The hell I'll stay here!" the man growled. "I'm taking my chances gettin' out of this tomb. I'm not going to drown down here like some damn bilge rat."

"Look, the boilers are likely ruptured and losing pressure pretty fast, so if we just give it a few more . . ."

Another man abruptly shoved Bratt hard, catching him off guard, pushing him out of the way, toppling him backward into the bilges.

"I'm going up, too," the sailor growled. "We can run through the fire room quick enough. We'll be okay."

The second man kicked Bratt hard in the shoulder and roughly snatched the lantern and gas mask from his hands. Then he and the other sailor ran for the forward ladder that would take them to the compartment above.

"Men, wait!" Bratt tried to shout, but the impact of the fall had knocked the breath from him. It was difficult to draw in air. He figured he must have broken some ribs when the fleeing sailor shoved him backward into the bilges. "You got to stay . . ."

But they were already up the ladder, opening the hatch cover, ignoring the hot steam that swept down around them like a deadly, clutching mist.

Meanwhile, one of the remaining men had found a flashlight. He shone it toward Bratt, who was trying to scramble back to his feet.

"Look at that," the man said, pointing, shining the light where Bratt had just been lying. Seawater was already rising at their feet, getting deeper by the second. At that rate, the engine room would be full in a short while. "Maybe them boys made the right move, Chief. Maybe we ought to . . ."

Bratt winced and tried to suck in enough of the smoky air to be able to talk, to sound confident as he gritted his teeth and tried to reason with them.

"I'm telling you, boys. There is no way they can make it through all that steam and fire up there." The hatch cover slammed shut above their heads with a metallic clang, punctuating Bratt's prediction. "You hear all that hissing and whistling. That steam is still filling up the compartment and there's no way a man could get through there right now. Look, here's what we'll do."

Bratt told the men to find all the wiping rags they could and wrap them around any exposed skin. When the time was right, they would put on gas masks to protect their faces and lungs. Still, they would wait patiently. Wait and try not to watch the seawater as it crept up to the soles of their shoes, to their ankles, to their knees, to their midthighs.

Forty-five minutes after the bomb had hit the fire room, with the water up to their chests and climbing faster, Bratt finally decided they could wait no longer.

"Stay together," he told them. "Hold hands. If a man goes down, the other two pick him up and keep moving. Whatever you do, keep moving."

They climbed up the after ladder to the escape hatch. The first man had to use one of the wiping rags to push up the hatch cover. It was too hot for him to touch with a bare hand.

The upper compartment was still thick with steam and the floor was slick with dampness. Condensation covered their masks. By memory, they worked their way quickly through the room, trying not to touch any scorching surface, knowing it would leave a blister. They could feel the roasting deck through their shoe soles, so hot it burned the pads of their feet.

Halfway across the compartment, they stumbled on something on the floor. All three men lifted their masks just enough to see what it was and how to make their way around it.

All three later wished they had never done so.

There, on the floor of the fire room, were the cooked bodies of the two men who had ignored Harold Bratt's advice and insisted on pursuing their own course of action. Their faces were blurred by sagging skin, their features erased by the superhot vapor.

The three survivors hurried around the bodies of their shipmates, toward cooler, clearer air.

• • •

The second direct hit—the one that sliced right through the stack deck and blew up in the pump room—also touched off a serious fire when it passed through and went on to put a hole in an oil tank. Thick black liquid spilled onto the ship's two main pumps and doused two men working there. Covered in hot oil, they could not see enough to get out of the way.

Machinist's Mate Second Class Wayne Simmons was on duty in the pump room when the bomb fell. Though well out of the bomb's path, he quickly ran to the two men in trouble and, despite the fire and smoke, helped them stagger away blindly from the pumps and get to relative safety.

Common sense told Simmons he should join the other crewmen and get clear of the compartment. Smoke was everywhere and the fire would certainly spread. Yet he knew that if someone did not man the throttle of the remaining working feed pump, then water would not get to the boilers. No water in the boilers, no steam. No steam, the ship would coast to a halt and be an even easier target for the Japanese dive-bombers.

Though it was not his assigned battle station, Simmons ignored the danger, tried to control his breathing so as not to suck in too much greasy smoke, and took over the throttle.

As his captain would later say in his incident report, "In spite of heavy black oil smoke filling the space, Simmons remained at the operating feed pump throttle station until a bomb explosion in the fire room ruptured steam lines and cut off steam supply to all machinery. Simmons's quick action, fearlessness, courage, and devotion to duty resulted in the maintenance of feed water supply to all the ship's boilers then steaming under full power conditions right up to the moment when the bomb explosion in the fire room totally disabled the boilers and main steam lines."

Later, all Wayne Simmons ever said about his amazing and tenacious act was that he was simply doing what he was supposed to do.

Chief Watertender Oscar Vernon Peterson had been at his battle station in the crew's mess when the attack started. He and his men stood by, ready to go to work to fix anything the Japanese bombs might break.

Their primary responsibility was to tend the fires that heated the boilers and the maze of pipes that took steam to the turbines. He and his crew would be called upon to repair any breaks in the ship's steam lines to keep the vessel under power. If damage to the lines was too serious, the men were to shut off the four main steam line bulkhead stop valves, saving steam pressure while preventing more damage to the ship's systems or injury to the crew. Then Peterson and his men would work to patch up the destruction.

They heard the first bombs, the near miss, and then the one that destroyed the pump room. The compartment quaked and the noise was painful, but so far everything in their area was okay. No damage to report.

In an awful instant, that all changed.

The bomb that settled in the fire room—just on the other side of the bulkhead from where the men waited—blasted away the massive iron door between the fire room and the crew's mess. Men were sent flying. Some were seriously hurt by iron fragments, or crushed when they were flung against the far bulkhead. Steam immediately filled the compartment.

Oscar Peterson found himself on his back, a painful searing sensation all over his body. Something was cooking him. His hands and face burned ferociously. When he rubbed his cheeks, flesh came loose.

Somehow, he managed to cover his face and pull himself to his feet. He was sure his arm was broken. It felt as if a million needles were pricking both arms and his face.

But he had a job to do.

Peterson knew the blast had torn loose steam pipes, scalding him and his men. What he did not know was that the boiler casings had also been ruptured. Steam was escaping all over the adjacent compartment, spilling through the doorway into the crew's mess.

The turbines required steam, and his job was to get the pipes—main and auxiliary—shut off before they lost all their pressure. To do that, he would somehow have to close off the bulkhead stop valves and halt the escape of deadly steam.

To reach the valves, he would need to work his way through the fire room trunk, a tight crawl space that ran above the two forward boilers.

Peterson considered his horribly scalded forearms and hands, seeing exposed pink flesh where hair and suntanned skin had once been. He was not sure he could make it, but none of the other men were in any shape to attempt it.

He knew he would have to try.

Ignoring the agonizing pain as he pulled on a pair of work gloves, he waited a few minutes for the steam to dissipate. It wouldn't do anybody any good if he got himself broiled to death in the trunk halfway there.

His experience and intuition told him the moment when it might just be possible to make it through that strip of hell. Injured men still conscious watched helplessly as Peterson crawled into the trunk and began to inch his way agonizingly slowly toward the first of the valves.

More bombs rocked the *Neosho*, but those were the least of Peterson's problems. Anything he touched, even through the thick gloves, or with his knees through the cloth of his work pants, burned him badly.

After a while, he could no longer feel his hands. The air itself was scalding and seemed to melt away skin, but his nerves had simply given up, shutting down.

Somehow Peterson made it. The pain came rushing back as he struggled to crank closed each of the four valves, one after the other.

By the time he was pulled from the fire room trunk by some of the other men, he had suffered horrible burns, his skin hanging from his face, arms and hands, stretched and torn by the steam. Thankfully, he was soon unconscious.

But he had done it. He had closed the valves, preserved the precious steam pressure so that they could remain operational for the moment. He had saved lives.

Saved lives by giving his own.

Peterson would succumb to his injuries several days later, even as rescue appeared to be close at hand.

Meanwhile, on the ship's bridge, Captain Phillips was hearing snippets of reports, news of the bravery and steadfastness of his men as they risked their lives to save the ship and each other. Crew members were working miracles to stomp out fires and stop steam from spewing away. Sailors continued to man their guns, waiting for the next wave of bombers to show up on the horizon, even as the ship had begun her ominous lean to starboard.

But why was he also hearing of other men rushing about in panic? He was now receiving reports of officers losing control of their charges. Of some officers losing control of themselves.

And, dear God, why was he actually seeing men jumping

overboard into the waves, abandoning ship like mindless, wild-eyed lemmings?

There had been no order to abandon ship. He needed every man to help keep the *Neosho* afloat. Yet from the bridge he could see that the sea was already full of men floating amid the oil, swimming away from the ship.

What in hell was going on?

CHAPTER FIFTEEN
"Prepare to Abandon Ship"

At about 1230, when it appeared the dive-bombers had finally decided to leave them alone, Captain Phillips ordered that two motorized whaleboats be put into the water to pick up those who had jumped into the sea. He needed them on board to help fight fires, to try to save the ship and get her back under power. Some of the men in the water were severely wounded, many with awful burns. With the seas and current running as they were, the men might soon drift out of sight, and the *Neosho*'s remaining crew would be unable to get them back aboard before nightfall.

Why had some men wildly tossed into the sea what few life rafts they had left and dived in after them? Phillips wondered. With a number of rafts destroyed in the suicide crash, they were now alarmingly scarce. There had certainly been no orders from the bridge to set adrift the few they had remaining, or to abandon ship.

Phillips was certain he had been clear when he sent the runner back with the message for his executive officer.

"Tell Lieutenant Commander Firth to make preparations for abandoning ship and stand by," he had told the young sailor. He repeated it precisely, and asked the sailor for confirmation.

Had he not also made it clear to Henry Bradford, his navigator, who was at the time of the attack acting as officer of the deck? Had he not explicitly said that the crew was to *make preparations* for abandoning ship and then *stand by*?

Yet, during the confusion of the attack, Bradford had left the bridge without requesting permission. Phillips later learned that his OOD had gone directly to the nearest railing and proceeded to jump overboard.

Had Phillips not been clear when he instructed his gunnery officer, Lieutenant Commander Thomas Brown, to get word to the three-inch guns that they were to prepare—clearly "to prepare"—to abandon ship and stand by for orders? The gunnery officer did precisely as he was told, instructing his assistant gunnery officer, Ensign Robert N. Hargis, to communicate word for word that exact message to the gun crews.

Hargis never did.

Meanwhile, Thomas Brown, with no planes to shoot at by that time and thus no gun crews to oversee, got busy assisting the captain in the absence of his injured executive officer. Brown immediately began directing boat crews, relaying orders, and helping to gather classified materials for destruction should it become apparent that they were going down. Phillips was not surprised at Brown's abilities and willingness to stand in and help. Brown had been one of the officers the captain commended highly after the events at Pearl Harbor.

Then Phillips heard that Ensign Hargis had lost control of

the raft to which he was assigned—the last raft they had—and that panicked crewmen had thrown it into the sea, jumping in after it. Meanwhile, Hargis was now doing all he could to get himself into whaleboat number two and lower it into the water by himself.

Others, not Hargis, were assigned to that job and had drilled repeatedly on the operation.

"Where is Ensign Hargis supposed to be?" Phillips asked the gunnery officer.

"He's assigned to life raft number four," Brown answered immediately. He did not even have to check his duty roster.

Phillips lowered his binoculars.

"Then why in hell do I see him lowering the whaleboat? And why is he the only man in it?"

"I have no idea, Captain."

Phillips angrily sent Lieutenant Commander Brown down to stop Hargis, to tell him to get a couple more men in the whaleboat with him, get in the water, and try to pick up as many survivors there as he could manage. At the same time, he was to gather up all the life rafts they could reach—occupied or not—lash them together, and tow them back to the ship so that they could be properly loaded in an orderly fashion should they actually need to abandon ship.

If the *Neosho* did sink—and Phillips had not yet decided that was inevitable—they would need every raft they could retrieve, and more. He still did not know how many men had been killed, or how many survivors might be coming over from the *Sims* now that the destroyer had gone deep.

Still, the captain kept asking himself questions. What had gone wrong? Why were some of his men jumping ship? Why were some of his officers losing control of the situation?

Most important, what could they do to get men back

aboard? How could they douse the fires, stop the escaping steam, minister to the wounded, and do whatever they had to do to save the *Neosho*?

Or at least keep her afloat until help arrived.

Seaman Bill Leu was stunned when he reached the top of the ladder from below and saw the mayhem on the deck of his ship. Smoke billowed from where the plane had crashed into the area around the stack deck. More flames were visible toward the stern, in the area impacted by the other hits. He had already taken notice that the deck beneath his feet had begun to tilt.

A buddy ran past Leu to the rail and, without hesitation, leaped over the side. Before he could talk himself out of it, Leu followed him into the sea.

Oil coated the water in every direction. Leu could see smoke and flames on the surface, and tried to put as much seawater as he could between himself, the oil fires and the sinking ship.

The effort of swimming through the thick oil while trying to keep his head above the surprisingly big waves soon had Leu completely tuckered out. He wished he had that life jacket, the one that son of a bitch had stolen from beneath his bunk.

"I was out there swimming and having a hard time and no life jacket," Leu later recalled. "I thought, 'Well, what the hell? I might as well just end this.'"

He stopped swimming and allowed the next wave to claim him. The situation seemingly hopeless; he fully intended to drown himself before fire or a voracious shark got him instead. But then, underwater, as his last breath escaped his heaving chest, Leu had a change of heart. When he popped to the surface, he was well clear of the slick of sticky, cloying oil. And next to him, treading water, was one of his best buddies.

"Bill, that you?" With Leu's face covered in oil, it was a miracle the other fellow even recognized him. "Hold on, Bill. Hold on. I'll help you."

The sailor instructed Leu to grab onto his life vest and they both swam farther away from the ship. Just as they were growing weary, swallowing seawater, in danger of going down together, they were suddenly shaded from the relentless sun—a motorized whaleboat was almost on top of them. Soon Leu was one of about forty men who had been tugged aboard a craft designed to safely carry half that number. But at least he was out of the sea. At least he was no longer swallowing salt water and anticipating the jolt of a shark's teeth.

At least he was still alive.

Captain Phillips would later learn that some of his men became terrified when they overheard the words "abandon ship" and spread the false order to get overboard. While most of his officers were performing admirably, a few were clearly in a panic. That was enough to send enlisted men over the side, assuming from their officers' demeanor that the ship was going down at any minute. After all, many had just watched in horror as the *Sims* quickly broke up and sank.

Now, with the attack in a long lull, Phillips, in consultation with his officers, set their priorities. While sailors and life rafts were being recovered from the sea, the captain ordered his crew to do whatever they could to restore power to the ship, get the turbines turning, and maybe even get the vessel under way if at all possible. No one could predict if additional waves of attackers might show up on the horizon at any moment to finish what the others had started.

Fires still burned throughout the ship, while steam continued to hiss from ruptured piping and cracked boilers. The men who remained aboard were doing their jobs, but desperately needed help.

Phillips considered all the information at hand. The *Neosho* was in clear danger of sinking. She was taking on water in several places still to be determined. There was a good possibility of fire reaching the storage tanks and the fumes and gasoline they held. The deck was buckled badly, indicating serious damage to the ship's superstructure. With the pressure of seawater and the sheer weight of the ship herself, that would likely continue to get worse.

Engineering Officer Lieutenant Louis Verbrugge, who had stayed in the main engine room until the flames in the bunker tank grew too intense, finally confirmed that they had lost all steam power. Though his crew would continue to assess damage and repair what equipment and systems that they could, it would be unlikely they could get the engines going again.

Phillips ordered Verbrugge to check the status of a few more whaleboats, the ones hanging from davits on the starboard side of the ship. If they could be reached and if they appeared to still be shipshape, he was to get men into them and get them launched to assist the other two rescue boats. The engineer soon delivered bad news on that front. Because of the list of the ship, the seas were already breaking heavily over that side of the vessel, and he simply would not be able to get to the boats. They were, in fact, underwater, unreachable, and even possibly damaged beyond repair.

Phillips received confirmation that the ship's medical officer had been killed. Pharmacist's Mate Robert Hoag and Pharmacist's Mate First Class William J. Ward were now working their way around the ship, treating the wounded. On the deck of a listing ship, smoke, oil, and dust everywhere, the two men would have to take special care to clean wounds thoroughly and bandage them up as best they could to prevent infection. Especially the horrific burns they were seeing on so many of the men.

Surveying his mangled vessel and suffering crew, Phillips finally decided to do exactly what he ordered Francis Firth to do a half hour earlier—prepare to abandon ship, then do just that if it was clear they were going down. Meanwhile, they would try to remain afloat until help came. While the deck continued to tilt more noticeably, it did not appear that they had settled any deeper in the last few minutes. Their two-thirds-empty gasoline storage tanks might just be keeping them buoyant long enough for support to arrive.

Help was almost certainly already on the way. The communications officer had made certain the radio operator reported the attack and their exact position to the task force even while they were being bombed. If they did have to abandon the ship, it would only be a matter of hours before someone would come to their aid. Certainly by the next day.

There were other practical tasks to do, including some specific measures to try to keep the *Neosho* off the bottom.

Orders had already been given orders to immediately destroy all classified material, including codebooks, a process that had begun even as the attack raged. Now Phillips made sure all papers in his possession were dropped into a barrel and burned, along with every other piece of sensitive documentation. Paper floats. Even if the ship went down, the enemy could easily fish top secret materials out of the sea.

The captain made certain that the radio operator got word to continue sending messages in plain language, letting the task force know of their situation and last known coordinates. The auxiliary generator was the only power source now, and the radio seemed to be acting up—the antenna might have been damaged—so the *Neosho*'s transmissions were not being acknowledged. Of course, the task force may have been busy with their own pyrotechnics by then. The radioman— not the chief radioman, who had left his position and jumped overboard—kept pounding away on his key at regular intervals, sending the latitude and longitude the navigator had provided him.

Besides the threat of yet another wave of attackers, Phillips's biggest concern was the increasing list to starboard. He stationed a man at the inclinometer to report the number on the gauge every quarter hour, even if there was no difference. There was a change, though, with every update. The list was increasing at an alarming rate, eventually to more than thirty degrees, with the ship's starboard rail completely underwater. The pair of precious whaleboats that hung there were now even deeper. If the angle continued to grow, the big tanker might simply flip over, possibly without enough warning to allow them to get off and away from the capsized ship.

Meanwhile, the seas were growing rougher. Five-foot waves crashed over the low side of the ship. Phillips ordered that the valves to the wing tanks—numbers five, six, and eight—be opened, allowing seawater to flood in and counter the heaviness to the other side of the ship. He desperately wanted to open valves three, four, and seven as well, but they had been damaged in the attack and were inoperable.

The captain and his de facto executive officer, Thomas Brown, had been too busy to check on how the two whaleboat crews were doing in their efforts to get men back aboard the ship. The boats and rafts were by then too far away to see clearly through binoculars, effectively hidden behind the growing swells.

Once Phillips and Brown received reports concerning the rafts from those on the deck, both officers were perplexed by what they heard.

Apparently, Ensign Robert Hargis and Lieutenant Bradford, who eventually took charge of the other motorized boat, had worked diligently to pick up fellow sailors floating in life vests or clinging to debris among a watery battlefield of dead bodies. Getting farther and farther from their ship, the whaleboats were eventually closer to the drifting rafts than to the *Neosho*. Both Hargis and Bradford knew they would lose valuable time and fuel ferrying all the way to their ship and back. Instead of bringing the survivors to the *Neosho*, the two men had transported most of their exhausted, oil-covered passengers to the rafts.

They also figured it would be easier to get injured men onto rafts than to deliver them safely to the tilting deck of the tanker in rough seas. It seemed a better idea to let them ride out the few hours until rescue on the rafts, rather than risk losing them trying to get them back aboard a ship that was on fire and slowly sinking.

There was legitimate concern, too, about overloading the pair of whaleboats, which were designed to hold only about two dozen men. They could easily capsize and sink in what was quickly becoming a treacherous sea. Winds were now blowing at force 5 to 6 and were expected to increase. They were also afraid they might collide with the *Neosho* if they approached top-heavy. Hargis and Bradford made the decision to ignore the captain's orders and place most of the men they pulled from the water onto the seven remaining life rafts as long as there was room for them.

If the captain had a problem with it, the two junior officers would take the heat later. Right now, they had to get tired and injured men away from the teeth of hungry sharks and out of the churning sea.

Finally, they did have to bring some men back to the ship. The rafts were simply too full for safety by then. Running low on fuel and with night approaching, the men who rode the two boats back to *Neosho*, including Bill Leu, Ensign Hargis, and Lieutenant Bradford, volunteered to return to their doomed ship, fully aware the tanker was sinking. They felt that doing anything else would place the lives of those on the rafts in danger. Though both whaleboats were carrying far more men than was safe—many of them badly injured and burned—they worked mightily to get them transferred onto the decks of the listing oiler before it grew too dark.

Yet neither motorized whaleboat had towed a single raft back with them. Seven rafts, each filled with men, floated out there in the inky distance. Now the survivors were either on the *Neosho*—which was in danger of sinking—or out there in the gloom on those seven life rafts. Some aboard "Fat Girl" were of the opinion that the men on the rafts were the lucky ones, in a far safer place than were their shipmates on the tipping tanker.

The sun was quickly dropping into the sea. Darkness was coming abruptly, as it always did in this part of the world, and especially as they approached what passed for a Southern Hemisphere "winter." There was no way now that the boats could get out there and bring back any of the rafts before nightfall.

Besides, there was a real possibility that the *Neosho* would not make it through the night. They might need the two whaleboats at any time to get some of the more than a hundred men off the ship.

Even if the rafts continued to drift away from them during the night, pushed along by the trade winds, they would not be too far away for their rescuers to quickly find them. The ship or ships would likely be there at first light. They would swiftly locate the rafts.

The *Neosho*? By dawn she could be nothing more than a debris field in the midst of an oil slick in the middle of the Coral Sea.

Captain Phillips thanked the boat crews—including Henry Bradford and Robert Hargis—for their backbreaking work and sent them off to get some dry clothes, food, and rest. He would deal later with his two officers and their serious failure of leadership that afternoon during the assault. He would also discuss with Hargis his refusal to follow direct orders to bring the rafts back to the ship. From what he was hearing, though, Phillips was now of the opinion that the officers had done all they could to save lives once they were on the whaleboats in the water. In retrospect, they had also probably made the correct decision to put most of the men on the rafts for the night.

Several times, Phillips attempted to locate the rafts off in the distance in the waning light of day. No matter how hard he tried, he could no longer make them out. Riding low on towering waves, they were difficult enough to see, but their greenish color camouflaged them perfectly against the seawater.

Now, more than five hours since the attack ended, most of the fires aboard the tanker had been controlled. Smoke still rose from the ship and the remaining flames could yet find new fuel. The exhausted damage-control parties were watching the situation. As darkness fell, the captain decided it was time to take stock.

"Mr. Brown, call muster and let's see if we can get a count," Phillips ordered.

He wanted to determine how many men had died. How many were missing. How many were able-bodied and available to help with a quick transfer off the ship if it came to that. How many might be healthy enough to tread water until the rescue ship came.

Mostly, though, he wanted to get an idea of how many of his crew might be out there in the blue-black darkness, drifting helplessly on that loose flotilla of life rafts.

PART FOUR
ADRIFT

Water, water, every where,
And all the boards did shrink;
Water, water, every where,
Nor any drop to drink.

—Samuel Taylor Coleridge,
"The Rime of the Ancient Mariner"

CHAPTER SIXTEEN
Long Odds and a Tenacious Corpsman

Jackie Rolston's back felt as if somebody were repeatedly stabbing him with a knife and cruelly twisting it. He shifted his weight as best he could, trying not to disturb the men around him in the packed life raft. Some were in much worse shape than he was. When he moved, though, his leg hurt like hell. He had taken a couple of bullets in his calf and some shrapnel in the back during the attack on the *Neosho*.

"You doin' okay, Jackie?" asked Grove Hough, his buddy not just from the tanker but from back home, from before the war.

"Hell, he's just goldbrickin'," came another voice from somewhere else in the darkness. Ken Bright, another shipmate from Rolston's home state, from the area of Smithville, Missouri.

"Aw, I'll be all right," Rolston responded. "I just wish I had myself a fishing pole and a worm. I'm gettin' hungry."

How could three young men, all friends from the same area of Missouri, end up drifting along together in a life raft somewhere on the other side of the world, in the Coral Sea?

Four of them had been serving together on the *Neosho*, four friends who all went down to Kansas City and enlisted in the Navy at the same time, the very day after Pearl Harbor. Enlisted and sent away to duty together on the same newly constructed replenishment ship, the USS *Neosho*.

Jackie Rolston had been seventeen years old when his parents signed the papers for him to enlist. Though he was their only child, the Rolstons saw the determination in their son's young eyes. Besides, many families decided the Navy was a better deal than a draft ticket into the Army.

Rolston and his friends were thrilled to be serving together, going off to fight the Japs as a Show-Me State quartet. All four men considered it a good omen when they first learned their assignment was on a ship named after a river that wound through the flat land close to their homes in far western Missouri.

Jackie turned eighteen on April 3, 1942, just over a month prior to the day the three of them ended up stranded in the Coral Sea on the other side of the planet.

The fourth Missouri amigo? His name was Noel Craven. He had grown up over on East Eighth Street in Smithville. Now he lay still—dead, as far as Rolston knew—covered by a blanket, back on the listing deck of the oiler.

"Jackie, did you see Noel? Was it bad? Did he suffer?" Bright asked.

Ken and Grove could not see Jackie's face in the starlight as he pondered Bright's question, remembering the awful scene he had witnessed only a few hours before. Rolston was manning an antiaircraft gun toward the stern of the tanker as dive-bombers swept down in relentless, well-coordinated waves, one after the other. Noel Craven was at the same mount, helping feed the gun. The gunnery crews had been doing a good job, their efforts keeping the Japs high and away each time the pilots dropped their bombs. Most drops were bone-jarring near misses. Jackie was certain he had hit a plane, sending the aircraft spinning into the drink.

Then one near miss turned out to be a fragmentation bomb. When it blew, it flung hot metal like a murderous hailstorm. Noel was cut down immediately, chopped up horribly by the deadly spray of the bomb's debris. Bleeding badly, he lay so very, very still on the deck. It took a moment for Rolston to feel pain and realize that he, too, had caught some shrapnel in his back. That some hot, ricocheting bullets from one of the planes' strafing runs had peppered his leg.

Rolston was in shock, from his wounds as much as from seeing his longtime buddy go down so viciously. Unsure what to do next, he heard men screaming something as they ran past his position.

Finally he understood. They were telling him what to do, at the top of their lungs.

"We're sinking! Abandon ship!"

"Captain's orders! Every man for himself! Get overboard! We're going down!"

Rolston hobbled away from the gun. It may have been the way he was standing on his bad leg, or it could have been his imagination, but he thought he could detect a pronounced tilt to the ship's deck. More men raced past him, waving their arms and yelling in terror.

"Better get in the water, get away from the ship! She'll pull us all down with her when she goes!"

"She's gonna blow up! Get overboard! She's gonna blow!"

Dizzy and nauseated, Rolston leaned against a bulkhead for a moment, getting his bearings. From out of nowhere, one of the pharmacist's mates ran up to him—he did not notice if it was Hoag or Ward—and told him to sit down while he put some sulfa powder and waterproof bandages on his injuries. Meanwhile, Rolston could see men frantically shoving empty life rafts over the side. An officer—Rolston's assistant gunnery officer, Ensign Hargis—stood by, watching them for a long moment as if shocked to inaction by what was happening. The officer did not give orders or do anything to try to stop the crewmen from tossing the irreplaceable rafts into the sea.

Then, as if shaken awake from a nightmare, Ensign Hargis abruptly turned and ran off toward one of the boats, the ones with the distinctive double-pointed bow that they called "motorized whaleboats."

When the corpsman finished his hasty bandaging, Rolston got back to his feet. He watched as Hargis wrenched the boat over the side, trying to launch it all by himself.

Rolston made up his mind. If the captain had ordered them to abandon ship, he was bound to follow the order. If his assistant gunnery officer was trying to get a boat in the water, there was no doubt. If the *Neosho* was sinking, Rolston was not interested in going down with her. It was clear he could do nothing for Noel, lying there on the deck in what was now a shockingly large puddle of blood. His buddy was surely gone.

Rolston checked his life belt, hesitated for just a moment, and then went over the side. He hit the surprisingly cold water hard. After he opened his eyes, he was thrilled to be on the surface, facing upward toward the sky. And amazed at who he saw the first thing.

Again, the first sailors who swam past were his Missouri

buddies, Ken Bright and Grove Hough. They helped him kick away from the ship, treading as far as they could from the doomed vessel. He looked back at the *Neosho* as he swam, at where Noel had taken his last breath. Smoke and fire surged from the stack deck and on back to the stern. There were columns of smoke climbing upward from the area of the poop deck. Men were jumping over the edge in desperation.

Rolston and his buddies eventually lost track of how long they had been in the water. They were looking all around for one of the life rafts so they could swim for it. Once clear of the thick oil near the ship—some of it aflame—they did not even have to try hard to put distance between themselves and the burning vessel. The current, wind, and waves took them away. Before long the massive tanker was little more than a dot on the horizon, a shimmering, smoking orb bobbing in the far distance, visible only when the waves took the swimmers high.

Occasionally they could hear men screaming. Rolston imagined sharks biting off their legs and swallowing the rest of them whole in the next gulp.

Others who swam nearby said the screams came from the worst of the wounded men, hurting when they were conscious, crying out for help. Or men simply too frightened to do anything else but shriek.

Where the hell were those rafts that Jackie had seen being thrown overboard?

The seawater might have been cold initially, but it warmed up quickly. The sun was soon fiercely hot. They tried to orient their bodies away from it so that it would not blister their faces, but then it only cooked their necks. Some men became seasick, riding up and down, up and down from wave top to deep trough. Even with seawater all around them, they were desperately thirsty. Nobody had thought to grab a canteen. They had gone over the side in too great a hurry.

Later in the afternoon, they heard a voice hailing them. It came from somewhere behind and above them. With the sun in his eyes when he turned, it was hard for Rolston to see who or what it was. Then he could make out the whaleboat. The gunnery officer he had seen launching it earlier was now at the tiller.

"Boys, see if you can climb in," the man said. "We'll take you over to the life rafts and you can get out of the water. That'll be a better place to wait until we get rescued."

The boat seemed full already, packed with hurt men, drenched men, men covered in black oil and dark blood. Every one of them had a slack face and hollow eyes. But they shuffled aside to make room for three more shipmates. There would be reports later of uninjured men who voluntarily jumped back into the sea to make room on the two whaleboats so those who were hurt could be transported to the rafts. Or of others who later rode back on the whaleboats to the fated ship to make room for more survivors.

Ken Bright and Grove Hough scrambled into the crowded boat with a little help from the others, then dragged Jackie in behind them. The boat motored off, heading away from the ship.

Before long, the three Missourians were lying in the bottom of a Carley raft with eight or ten other men. That was about all the thing was supposed to hold. How many more would Hargis try to pile onto it?

In an hour, darkness came suddenly, as if someone had flipped a switch. That was when Ken Bright decided to ask the question about how their friend had died.

"I didn't see Noel get hit, but I saw him lying there and . . . ," Rolston said, his answer trailing off. He studied the eerie streaks of phosphorescence in the water, the amazing intensity of the new, twinkling stars overhead.

"Okay," Bright said. "That's all we need to know."

Unbeknownst to Rolston, Noel Craven was still alive when Jack followed what he believed to be the order to abandon ship. Craven would hold on for two more days, until the night of May 9, before he passed away. He would be buried at sea on the tenth.

The men in the raft were quiet for a bit, listening to the waves slapping against the sides, gazing in the far darkness for some sign of the *Neosho*. Their heavily damaged ship had been completely out of sight since long before the sun had set, her position marked only by a persistent column of black smoke on the horizon.

At least she had not sunk yet, as far as they knew. That was amazing to those who had made it to the safety of the raft. They had been told she was going down quickly and to get overboard if they expected to save themselves. She was clearly one tough ship!

As the winds subsided and the seas calmed just a bit, they could hear men on the other rafts, talking or screaming or crying in agony. Others called out for help, as if their rescue ship could hear them already. A few, the more seriously wounded, moaned, cried out for their mothers, begged for morphine. Then it was quiet again for a while.

Once or twice, their raft bumped into one of the others in the black night and they recognized someone they knew by his voice. Then there would be a happy reunion, each man glad to see his friend had made it off the ship to safety. Eventually they would drift away, and it would be eerily quiet once more.

"Reckon there's a canteen of water anywhere on this dinghy?" one of their raft mates asked.

"Or a ham sandwich," another inquired. "With lettuce and mustard."

The men laughed softly. Everyone knew there was no water or food. Despite their hunger and thirst, they figured they could make it until morning. Help would be there with hot coffee and a Danish and fried eggs and bacon.

"I'd settle for a cup of water and a crust of bread," someone said.

"Long as it's rye," another added.

Only a couple of them laughed.

They had all seen horrible things that day. Things they were trying to forget. Now it was going to be at least one long night of bad dreams accompanied by the cries and whimpers of suffering men. The Japanese bombs had kept coming, getting closer, and then finally struck them dead on. Shipmates had been killed in terrible ways right before their eyes.

Guilty feelings stirred among the men huddling together in the raft. They had made it through the ordeal that day while many of their friends had been selected by fate to die. Men they knew remained stuck over there on that burning, sinking shell of a tanker. Likely some of their shipmates were still swimming out in the expanse of sea between them and the *Neosho*, too.

As they discussed the circumstances, the survivors in the rafts convinced each other that they were the lucky ones, even if they did have to do without food and water for one long, rough night. They were safe and dry on the rafts.

Nothing could be worse than going down with a burning

ship, or treading water all night in darkness, with sharks and sting rays and sea snakes.

Nothing.

The men from USS *Sims* who made it to their lone whaleboat had watched in stunned disbelief as their destroyer broke in two and sank. It seemed to take only a few seconds until she was gone, swallowed whole by the sea. Then they realized they had no time to ponder the impossibility of such a thing happening. Their shipmates remained in the water.

John Verton was among them, still swimming but praying for a quick death. He could hardly breathe; his throat and mouth were burning from the digestive fluids he had vomited up. His gut from stomach to rectum was wrenched by terrible spasms.

"While in the water, I prayed to die and thought I was lucky to have bought life insurance [before I shipped out]," he later said.

Then, as he floated to the top of a crowning wave, he saw the whaleboat in the distance. He waved and yelled as best he could, hoping they would see him.

The leaky whaleboat moved from one floating body to the next, no longer pulling in survivors. Mostly corpses or pieces of corpses bobbed around them. Several times they saw men floating on their backs, appearing to be okay, drifting, held up by their life vests, only to discover they were nothing more than torsos, the rest of their bodies gone, burned, blown or eaten away, their insides trailing like the tatters of a ripped flag.

As they did their grisly work, they scanned the horizon for the two floating life rafts, the ones from the destroyer and the men aboard that they had seen earlier. The accounts of both Robert Dicken and Vito Vessia agreed that there might have been more than twenty survivors in the one raft the last time they saw it. There could be more by now. If they saw them, they could go tie them to the whaleboat and keep them from drifting too far away from their last reported position to be found by a rescue ship.

Then, in the distance, they spotted movement in the water. Somebody was waving at them. They turned the boat and hurried that way.

Vito Vessia recognized the oily, filthy man long before they reached him. John Verton had been a friend since their first days on the *Sims*.

They could smell him even before they reached down to tug him aboard. Even in such dire circumstances, they kidded their rescued shipmate about how badly he reeked after the explosion had emptied the contents of his guts out his mouth.

"We pulled him into the boat and almost immediately we wanted to throw him back over the side," Vessia would later joke.

An hour and a half after the *Sims* disappeared, Dicken and Vessia were finding only dead men. As their boat took on water faster than they could bail it out, the motor began to run rough, spitting and choking. They took a quick count of the survivors. Fifteen men, a couple of them in bad shape who might not make it until dawn. How many men had been on the *Sims*? About 250? Only the 15 sailors in the whaleboat had made it off, plus 20 or so who were presumed safe somewhere out there on one of the two drifting life rafts.

By late afternoon, they turned the leaking boat's bow toward the distant tanker. At least she was still on the surface.

They had no idea what kind of shape the *Neosho* might be in by now. All had heard the enemy planes diving on her and caught the rumbling thunder when some of their bombs hit home. Some had even seen the suicide plane hit her deck. They half expected to find nothing left but a burning oil slick on the surface of the sea where she had been swallowed up.

Now, though, they could see she was still afloat, albeit with lots of smoke swirling upward from her stern. Even from this distance, she appeared to be sitting oddly in the water, her decks, masts, and stack tilted. She looked to be heavily damaged. Still, there was no other place to go. Not sure how long their boat could stay afloat and under power or how long it might be before rescue came, either Vessia or Dicken—whichever one was actually in control of the little vessel—twisted the throttle and made for what was left of the *Neosho.*

Any port in a storm.

Despite the aching in his back and legs, Jackie Rolston had just about found sleep. Suddenly he felt the raft tilt, heard splashing and a disembodied voice. Someone had swum up to the raft in the dark and was pulling himself up to look inside. Shimmering phosphorescence on the surface of the water gave the swimmer an odd, otherworldly appearance.

"Anybody here burned?" the shadow asked, his words more a breathless gasp than real speech. "Anybody hurt?"

"Two guys over here in pretty bad shape," one raft rider answered.

The visitor climbed into the raft and fell exhausted onto the only open spot in its floor. He was wheezing, gasping to catch his breath.

"I'm Pharmacist's Mate Tucker," he announced after finally filling his lungs with fresh air. His voice carried a strong Southern accent. "I got a little bit of tannic acid in this bottle to treat the burns. Not much else in the way of medicine left, I don't reckon, and my light's about to peter out. I'll get to the burns first."

Tucker squirmed through the maze of arms and legs to the seriously burned men and went to work on their wounds even as his light flickered and grew dimmer and dimmer.

"I'm going to try to get over to another couple of rafts while the light's working," he told them. "And while I still got some of this burn salve left."

"You sure, Tucker?" a man asked him. "You ain't looking too spry. Maybe you better stay here, wait 'til daylight."

"Naw. I figure I better get the worst of the burns covered or the infection'll set in. We'll be all right. Help'll be here tomorrow but it'll likely be too late for them that's got all the skin burnt off. God bless y'all."

Tucker rolled off the raft and back into the sea. They could hear him swimming for a bit. Then it was mostly noiseless again.

Pharmacist's Mate Third Class Henry Warren Tucker had been in the water all afternoon, swimming from whaleboat to life raft and back, treating all kinds of wounds but especially the nasty burns.

Edward Flaherty, the passenger off *Portland* who had observed Francis Firth's act of bravery during the suicide plane's crash, and who had suffered burns when the aircraft hurtled into *Neosho*'s gun mount, also witnessed the corpsman's courageous work. Despite his own injuries, Flaherty joined one of the whaleboat crews, helping to pull men from the water and deposit them on the rafts. That was where Flaherty saw firsthand the remarkable efforts of the young pharmacist's mate from York, Alabama.

"I wouldn't be here and neither would a lot of others,"

Flaherty later related to a newspaper reporter. "If it wasn't for that pharmacist's mate who jumped overboard with his shirt loaded with tannic acid, then swam to the life rafts and whaleboats to spread the stuff over our burns. The doctors in Australia said many of us would have died [from infections] if it wasn't for that tannic acid."

Others who, like Flaherty, returned to the *Neosho* on the whaleboats told the same story. Sadly, Tucker would ultimately be declared missing, assumed lost while trying to save the lives of others. Later that year, he was posthumously awarded the Navy Cross. The citation noted that his "valorous actions enhance and sustain the finest traditions of the United States Naval Service."

The destroyer USS *Tucker* (DD-875) would be named in his honor.

CHAPTER SEVENTEEN
Help on the Way

John Phillips had no way of knowing if his ship would remain afloat throughout the long night ahead. He ordered all men to come topside, and to bring up the wounded. They would spend the night on the deck. With the pronounced list, continued flooding, and portentous groans from the ship's innards, he wanted to be sure his men could get into the water quickly if forced to abandon ship. One good thing about the sudden arrival of twilight: the Japanese airplanes would not be back to finish them off. At least not for the next ten hours.

Sailors lay at all angles across the deck as the pharmacist's mates moved among them, attending to wounds. Even so, several of them died. They would have to be buried at sea come daylight.

Phillips and his officers decided to keep many of the more seriously wounded men in the two whaleboats overnight, floating about a hundred yards away but tethered securely to the ship. Those were the men who would not have been able to survive in the water, men too injured to swim, too delirious to keep their faces out of the sea.

A chief from the *Sims* had motored up near the *Neosho* in the late afternoon and remained about 250 yards away, awaiting instructions. Phillips ordered that he be signaled to approach and formally be placed under his command. It turned out that there were fifteen men in the boat. Some of the uninjured were brought over to the *Neosho* to help out, while several badly wounded men on the tanker's deck were transferred to the destroyer's whaleboat to spend the night.

Some brave members of the *Neosho* crew made quick, dangerous trips below, gleaning food, water, blankets, cots, mattresses, medicine, lights, batteries, life belts, and anything else they might need to make the night more bearable or to survive in the sea should the ship go down. Some of the scavengers said quick prayers before disappearing down the ladders. From the way the ship was leaning, with seawater rushing in and waves rocking the helpless vessel, they judged she could capsize or sink at any minute. Anyone belowdecks risked being taken down with her into the deep before he could climb out. What's more, fires still burned below, filling the lower compartments with dense, deadly smoke and fumes. With limited electrical power, there was no way to vent the noxious and explosive vapors outside the ship.

Each of the twenty-six gasoline storage tanks was a potential firebomb. So far, the carbon dioxide fire-extinguishing system had not been utilized. There was no way to know if it would still function, or to calculate how much fuel still remained in the damaged, leaking tanks. In a couple of the tanks, seawater was diluting the fuel. The others, as far as anyone could tell, were undamaged, and the flammable mixture they held would still be at full potency.

Meanwhile, there was nothing else for the crew to do but to get some sleep, help their shipmates who were in pain, and wait for a command to abandon ship. Lights were kept at a minimum to save auxiliary power and not attract unwanted attention from enemy surface ships or submarines. Except for the *Neosho*'s constant rocking, it was a pleasant tropical evening, with a plethora of stars arrayed overhead. The angle of the deck made it a bit difficult to get into a relaxed sleeping position, but it was far better than treading water.

The men passing the night in the three whaleboats nearby were even less comfy, but equally thankful to be alive. Bill Leu was one of them. There was no room for the men to lie down in the cramped boat, except for some of the the most badly wounded, so he sat on a bench all night gripping the sides of the vessel as it heaved in the choppy waters. Leu and the rest of the men on the whaleboats had the same thoughts as those who remained on the damaged, sinking tanker.

They had survived a vicious enemy attack. Now the war was over for many of their friends. Some had died horribly. More of them likely would not make it, even if help came soon. Others were so severely wounded that they would probably go home for the duration. All the wounded were hurting, suffering.

Why had some survived unscathed? What turn of fate made them the lucky ones? Why were some buddies killed or maimed while others came through the ordeal just fine?

On *Neosho*'s listing deck, aboard whaleboats and rafts, sleepless sailors talked quietly of home. They wondered if they would have shore leave once they got plucked off the tanker

and were awaiting their new assignment. Others angrily plotted revenge against the Nips.

Some snored fitfully. Some cried out in pain.

Some died in their sleep.

None of the survivors of the *Neosho* and the *Sims*—not the
men sleeping or hurting on her decks, not the men in the
whaleboats, not the men on the drifting life rafts, not even
the captain of the doomed tanker—had any idea that attack
planes from their task force had finally found that long-awaited
initial Allied victory. While the oiler and destroyer were getting pounded by mistake, almost 400 miles away members of
TF 17 were lighting up that smaller Japanese aircraft carrier.

Meanwhile, none of the stranded sailors knew for sure
that the *Neosho*'s radio reports of the attack and the details of
their position had been received by the fleet. In fact, they had.

At first, based on the information sent from the *Neosho*,
the assumption was made that the tanker and her escort had
survived a brief attack by three planes, and all was well.

That assessment later changed. At about 1600 on May 7,
reports from the *Neosho*'s radioman, transmitted by auxiliary
power, brought the news weakly amid static that their escort
had been sunk and the oiler was heavily damaged and likely
sinking.

Thankfully, the radio operator gave what he believed was
the precise position of the impaired ship, the coordinates that
had been ascertained by the *Neosho*'s navigator.

As Captain Phillips and every other man in the crew anticipated, Admiral Fletcher immediately ordered a ship—the
destroyer USS *Monaghan* (DD-354) under the command of
Lieutenant Commander William P. Burford—to race to that
location to look for and rescue any survivors.

Prior to those orders, the *Monaghan* had been screening the *Lexington*. Earlier in the day, she had been tasked with radioing back to Pearl Harbor the wonderful news of the sinking of the enemy carrier *Shoho*. The *Monaghan* was dispatched a good distance away from and south of the fleet to make the broadcast. That was to maintain radio silence, to not give the enemy any possible indication of where the bulk of the fleet was now located.

That excursion southward by the *Monaghan* was the first bit of good luck in the ordeal for the survivors of the *Neosho* and the *Sims*. The point to which the destroyer had been sent to make the radio transmission fortuitously put the rescue ship much closer to the two ships' last reported position.

The *Monaghan* would easily be able to get to that very spot in the Coral Sea—the coordinates reported by the tanker's radio operator—and be in position to rescue survivors by daylight the next morning.

Using what little light he could manage, Captain Phillips studied the results of the muster earlier in the evening. They were heartbreaking.

There was no way to know how accurate the tally was, but it appeared that of the 20 officers and 267 enlisted men who had been aboard the *Neosho* at sunrise on May 7, they now had 16 officers and 91 men either on deck or in the nearby whaleboats. One officer and 19 men were known to be dead. That left 4 officers and 156 men still missing. (Phillips's count was actually off by 2 men. There were 158 officers and men unaccounted for.)

Phillips knew many of those missing would be in the rafts, yet those rafts could not accommodate 160 men. Maybe a hundred, 120, tops, and in pitching seas that could be hazardous. That meant the other men were either dead in the water, dead somewhere belowdecks, where damage control parties could not yet reach, or—and the thought was likely painful for the captain—alive, maybe severely wounded, and floating helplessly in the darkness in the Coral Sea.

Fifteen survivors had arrived from the *Sims*. The destroyer's chief reported seeing as many as twenty men on one of that vessel's life rafts, but felt that the rest of the crew was dead. They had searched a long time for survivors in the water and found none. The *Sims* had carried more than 250 men. It appeared 35 or so had survived, with only 15 now accounted for.

Hundreds of families would soon be receiving bad news.

Phillips and his officers discussed what they would do to assure that the rescue operations the next day would go smoothly. Everyone aboard had trained repeatedly for such an eventuality. Still, they certainly did not want to lose any more men when deliverance was finally so close at hand.

They also reviewed plans for a quick exit into the water, off the *Neosho*'s decks, if they saw she was not going to stay afloat during the night. There was no more room in the motor launches. If the ship was still floating at dawn, they would attempt to free the other two whaleboats, now well underwater on the starboard side. The only option for the men still aboard the *Neosho* was to quickly get everyone into the water, strapped to something that would float if he did not have a life vest.

A crew member had wrestled a mattress from somewhere belowdecks and brought it to the bridge for the skipper. It smelled mightily of oil and smoke. Captain Phillips had one more notion in mind before he lay down. He jotted down a note for the incident report he expected to compose soon after their rescue.

One recommendation he would include in that report was

"that the words 'Abandon Ship' be deleted from all preliminary orders given . . . that the words 'Abandon Ship' be used only when it is desired to accomplish just that."

That unfortunate mistaken command was still eating at the skipper. The memories of the resulting panic, the image of sailors jumping overboard, the thoughts of them now out there in the darkness in the sea or on rafts made sleep difficult to come by for Phillips throughout that long night.

They would continue to do so for the rest of his days.

PART FIVE
SEARCH AND RESCUE

But out of that silence from the battle's crash and roar rose new sounds more appalling still; a strange ventriloquism of which you could not locate the source, a smothered moan, a wail so far and deep and wide, as if a thousand discords were flowing together into a key note—weird, unearthly, terrible to hear and bear, yet startling with its nearness. The writhing concord broken by cries for help, some begging for a drop of water, some calling on God for pity, and some on friendly hands to finish what the enemy had so horribly begun.

—Colonel Joshua Lawrence Chamberlain recalling the aftermath of the first day of fighting at Fredericksburg, the American Civil War

CHAPTER EIGHTEEN
Unwitting Decoys

When the sun came up on May 8, the sky above Task Force 17 was almost perfectly clear for the first time since the fleet had moved into the Coral Sea. Admiral Fletcher's ships could now be easily seen by any enemy scouts in the area. Yet if the Japanese MO Carrier Striking Force, with its two big flattops the *Zuikaku* and the *Shokaku*, was nearby, they would be just as easy to spot. That is, if the Allied planes could locate them before the inevitable late-morning rainstorms began to boil up with the heat of the day.

At about 0820, each side finally found the other. Within an hour, strike forces rolled off the decks of all four flattops, each aimed primarily at the other's carriers but ready to take on escorts, airplanes, and other assets.

Thirty-nine planes off the *Yorktown* struck first, at 1100. As they hit the *Shokaku* with two 1,000-pound bombs—and missed with everything else—her sister, the *Zuikaku*, quickly found the relative cover of a convenient rainsquall. A follow-up attack on the *Shokaku* by planes off the *Lexington* was less successful, though one more 1,000-pounder did hit home. The second wave of Allied planes had been scattered by the same weather the *Zuikaku* was so effectively employing and were unable to manage a productive assault.

The *Zuikaku* was not hit at all. Admiral Hara determined, however, that the *Shokaku* had suffered too much damage to her flight deck to land planes. Still under power, she was ordered out of the area under escort of two destroyers.

Meanwhile, Lieutenant Commander Kakuichi Takahashi's planes were airborne, scanning the seas for the Allied fleet. They found their elusive targets in the area where they had been sighted earlier in the morning. The IJN aircraft attacked at almost the same moment their own carriers were being bombed by American planes.

Despite heroic efforts by the *Lexington*'s captain and crew to avoid torpedoes and bombs from the Japanese assault force, two torpedoes struck her in crucial spots. Subsequent attacks did even more damage, but miraculously it appeared the big ship could still float and would live to fight another day. The *Yorktown* was also under attack but, while she did take one bomb hit, she was not as badly damaged as her sister carrier.

It seemed neither side had struck a lasting, significant blow against the other. The initial action in the long-anticipated battle appeared to have ultimately been anticlimactic.

Then, later that afternoon, a massive explosion ripped through the *Lexington*. It was subsequently determined that one of the two torpedoes had struck in the area of the ship's aviation fuel tanks—filled with the gasoline she had taken on two days before from the *Neosho*—leaving cracks in the seams. That structural failure allowed explosive vapors to escape.

When those vapors finally reached the ship's motor generators, they set off an immense blast, which ignited raging fires. Two more devastating explosions over the next two hours rocked the vessel.

Unable to control the fires and fearful of even more explosions and loss of life, the captain ordered that the ship be abandoned. He was confident the carrier was doomed. Getting men off the burning carrier would allow the survivors a better chance to be rescued. The smoking hulk could also be scuttled before the sun went down. With all survivors removed, the ship was sunk, using torpedoes from American destroyers. That would eliminate the chance of her falling into enemy hands as well as becoming a menace to navigation. One-fourth of the American carrier fleet in the Pacific was now gone. 216 crewmen had perished.

With the loss of the *Lexington* and damage to the *Yorktown,* the initial tally now seemed to confirm that the Japanese had prevailed in the historic, long-delayed carrier battle. One IJN light carrier was sunk and another Japanese carrier damaged but still under power. Conversely, one of the Americans' big flattops was now on the bottom of the Coral Sea.

In retrospect, the showdown would eventually be declared a tactical draw but a strategic win for the Allies. That determination would hinge on the *Yorktown* and what she and her crew did at Midway, a battle that would occur less than a month away.

The *Shokaku* proved to be too heavily damaged to join the invasion force at Midway. In the five days of action in the Coral Sea, many IJN planes, pilots, ships' crew members, and support vessels had been lost as well. So many of *Zuikaku*'s air group were lost that she was effectively out of action for the next two months, including for Operation MI.

By contrast, the *Yorktown* would be quickly repaired and available for action at Midway. That alone turned out to be enough to tip the next close battle of near-equal-strength fleets in the Allies' favor.

Operation MO had been scrubbed. For the first time, the Japanese expansion southward had been stopped cold, turned away. That would prove to be a serious tactical blow, as well as have a major effect on the morale of both sides.

After the long-anticipated carrier battle was over and Admiral Fletcher had learned that all elements of the Japanese Port Moresby invasion force had retreated, he made a quick decision. He would immediately move his remaining carrier and the rest of TF 17 out of the battle area at high speed while he had the chance. He was well aware that one of the IJN carriers could still launch its remaining aircraft once it was refueled and came back south. With the Allies losing a carrier, a destroyer, and possibly its only big replenishment vessel, the Japanese would certainly push the attack. Fletcher felt it better to get his remaining flattop repaired and equipped to fight the enemy another day, when he had more help. And he needed to get to another ready supply of fuel for his ships and planes if the *Neosho* had to undergo repairs or was lost.

The *Yorktown* and the other elements of TF 17 raced toward Pearl Harbor.

Meanwhile, Admiral Yamamoto did indeed order the refueled but limping task force to look for the *Yorktown* and try to put her where the *Lexington* now rested. By then, however, the American carrier force was long gone, nowhere to be found, despite another frustrating search by the IJN.

On May 11, the Japanese fleet gave up looking for the American carrier and turned back north, toward Tokyo Bay and the repair yards.

The Coral Sea represented a series of lost opportunities for the Japanese. Coincidences. Wrong decisions. Mistakes. Weather. Overconfidence.

Their losses of the light carrier, aircraft, escort vessels, and other assets—along with enough damage to keep two of their big carriers out of action—were a major setback. The Americans, who had their own share of lost opportunities for all the same reasons, felt they had learned much in the momentous battle. Now they believed they knew more about surviving and conducting such a different type of naval clash.

Military scholars would long consider what might have happened had the Japanese spotted the Allied task force first, earlier, and especially if they had found the Americans on May 7, as had almost happened. Such a discovery would have given them a full day's advantage, the chance for a surprise attack a day before the Americans finally located the MO Carrier Striking Force. The battle—without the simultaneous attacks by each side—might well have played out differently. It might also have come in time to usurp the Allies' successful attack on the MO Invasion Force.

What key event occurred on May 7? At one point, on the day before the carrier battle, a Japanese attack force—consisting of almost eighty fighter planes, torpedo bombers, and dive-bombers—was a mere fifty miles away from Task Force 17. With top speeds of 235 to 275 miles per hour, the Japanese "Kate" and "Val" dive- and torpedo bombers could have quickly approached and attacked the Allies.

That enemy attack force, however, missed sighting the American fleet. The Japanese pilots were of a single purpose: to speed to the last known position and attack what they believed to be an American carrier and escort, the two ships spotted earlier in the day by a young scout pilot.

Ships that actually ended up being a tanker named *Neosho* and the destroyer *Sims*.

Two vessels that had unwittingly become decoys helped turn the outcome of the following day's primary battle.

Two vessels whose surviving crew members had no idea on the morning of May 8 of what was going on, or what their unintended role had been in that epic battle taking place only about 200 miles away.

Stanley "Swede" Vejtasa would be awarded two Navy Crosses for his actions in the Coral Sea, including the attack on Tulagi, the sinking of the *Shoho*, and the remarkable skirmish early on May 8 against enemy Zero fighter planes. When the fighting ceased at the end of the day on May 8, though, Vejtasa heard some vague but disheartening news. It dulled his exhilaration over the actions in which he had played such a big part.

The oiler *Neosho*, on which he had come so close to being a passenger, had reportedly come under attack the day before. It had been at about the same time that he and the others had been on their way to intercept *Shoho* and send her to the bottom.

When he heard the news, Vejtasa exchanged glances with the other pilot, his buddy, who had also been stopped just short of transferring over to their giant "hackney cab." They could only shake their heads.

Coincidence? Providence? Pure dumb luck?

Regardless, Swede Vejtasa had been spared from whatever the vagaries of war now held in store for the *Neosho* and her crew.

Lieutenant Commander William P. Burford would certainly have been familiar with USS *Sims* and USS *Neosho*, even before he was ordered to take his destroyer, the *Monaghan*, down to rescue survivors off both vessels. Wilford Hyman was a fellow destroyer skipper, attached to the same task force, while the *Neosho* had always been a welcome sight when she sidled up next to Burford's ship and refilled her fuel tanks.

But Burford had been familiar with the *Neosho* long before they both floated in the Coral Sea as part of Task Force 17. Burford and the *Monaghan* had been at Pearl Harbor on the morning of December 7.

The destroyer had been on "ready watch" that day, meaning she was the designated ship in the harbor to remain under steam and have a full complement of crew members aboard, ready to race out and rescue a ship in trouble or hurry to help any vessel that might spot something suspicious in the harbor or in the sea around Oahu.

Ready watch was scheduled to end at 0800 that morning. Many crew members had already gathered, most outfitted in their best dress whites, intending to go ashore or over to one of the battleships for church services when they were off duty. They never got the chance.

Four minutes before the first Japanese bomber appeared from the north, ten minutes before ready watch would be over, Burford received an excited call from Bill Outerbridge, skipper on their sister destroyer USS *Ward* (DD-139). He wanted Burford and the *Monaghan* to come help him launch an attack on a mysterious, unauthorized submarine that they caught trying to enter the mouth of the harbor. But just as the *Monaghan* was getting under way and heading out to cross the harbor, Burford got detoured.

First came the stunning ambush by the Japanese warplanes that filled the Hawaiian sky. They required return fire from the *Monaghan*'s guns. Next, as the destroyer steamed around

Ford Island, USS *Arizona* blew up. As Machinist's Mate Julius Finnern, a crewman aboard the *Monaghan*, later described it, "You could have heard that explosion all the way to Nebraska."

They were further rerouted when a lookout spied a midget submarine, which promptly proceeded to launch a torpedo at the destroyer. Burford and the crew of *Monaghan* returned the favor by ramming and then depth-charging the two-man sub. In the process of going to top speed to hit the submersible vessel, the destroyer ran aground and had to be towed out. The gunnery crews kept firing away through the entire ordeal.

Now, after running across the Coral Sea during the night, the destroyer captain had his ship closing in on where the oiler and escort had come under attack. Just before dawn on May 8, they arrived at the given coordinates. Burford had little idea of what to expect to see when the sun came up. Communications from Pearl Harbor had confirmed that the *Sims* had been sunk, with apparently few survivors, and that the oiler had been heavily damaged and might be sinking. Yet that report had come the previous afternoon, almost eighteen hours earlier. Burford fully expected the *Neosho* to be gone, too.

What he did not anticipate was what he actually saw in the first light from an early-morning sun, rising in an unusually clear sky.

Nothing. Nothing at all.

No damaged tanker. No debris. No survivors in the water. No life rafts. No oil slick.

The last was truly surprising. A tanker damaged badly enough to sink would certainly leave some kind of oil slick.

Yes, the seas were choppy, but it would take days for the waves to break up a slick from a ship like the *Neosho*.

Burford asked his navigator for a confirmation of their position.

"Sixteen degrees, twenty-five minutes, one fifty-seven degrees, thirty-one minutes," he reported, double-checking his notes.

"Thank you," Burford responded. They were precisely where they were supposed to be.

But there was no sign anywhere of a large oiler ever having been there.

CHAPTER NINETEEN
Going to Work

Daylight revealed to John Phillips and his officers just how serious their situation really was. Now they could fully see the frightening tilt of the ship. They could confirm that the starboard rail was well underwater. It was clear they were still settling, that seawater continued to rush in and would inevitably drag them down. The continued buckling of the deck plates and the groaning noise they made were cruel but graphic measures of how their circumstances were worsening by the minute. Though the fires were mostly out, smoke still rose from the stack deck and from open hatches toward the stern. Everything smelled of smoke and oil, making it hard to take a deep breath. During the night, the oil in the sea all around the *Neosho* had sloshed across the deck, covering it with thick goo, painting the already miserable men black.

Most discouraging, though, were the faces of the men who had spent the night out on the open deck. They were all covered with oil, their clothes greasy and blackened from smoke and soot, their eyes distant, glassy, and red-rimmed. Their spirits had already been claimed by terror and exhaustion. Every structure, line, rigging, or deck plate was slippery with oil. Merely walking across the skewed deck without falling was a chore. Helping a wounded man to find shade or a toilet was almost impossible. Some simply vomited, urinated, and defecated on the already filthy deck, adding to the mess and contamination.

When the whaleboats drew near to take on food and water, the men who had spent the night in them looked even more haggard and defeated than those on the ship's deck. Two of the wounded in the *Sims* boat had died during the night. They were brought over to the *Neosho* for burial later, along with those who passed away on the tanker's decks the day before and overnight.

Work parties continued to risk their lives resuming their trips below to search through as many compartments as possible, looking for more supplies as well as other bodies. Those men who had died down there deserved a quick, decent burial, too.

With daybreak came wind and sun. Soon the wind was gusting to force five to six once again. For a seaworthy vessel, such a choppy sea and blustering wind would have been no issue. But for a sinking hulk, riding low in the water, and for the three motor launches—two of them with patched holes in their bottoms and taking on seawater—it was downright treacherous.

On the deck of the tanker, despondent men measured the increasingly dire condition of their ship by how many more deck plates were askew. On the boats, weary men continued to bail constantly to keep them from foundering.

The sun, bearing down from a beautiful, clear blue sky, quickly became yet another problem. Sailors tried to move the injured around on the slippery deck into the shade, yet as the ship moved with the building waves, that shade migrated quickly from one section of the deck to another. For the men in the boats, there was no place to hide from the searing tropical rays.

The *Neosho*'s crew still had food, water, blankets, bandages, mattresses, and medicine, but stocks on deck soon diminished. Brave men again went back down the ladders to the lower compartments to look for more, hurrying back each time in case the next shift of the ship was all it took to finally take her down.

Lieutenant Louis Verbrugge, the engineer, spent most of his time below, certainly risking his life, working his way through every space he could manage. He was trying to see if he and his men could stop the flooding, or otherwise give them a better chance of keeping the *Neosho* on the surface, just in case their rescuers were delayed a day or so. Though he reported often to the captain, always confidently and positively, he found there was simply nothing he or his snipes could do.

Fran Firth was also a positive force, consistently upbeat and positive. Though the XO had horrible burns on his arms, face, and body, he stayed with the captain. Phillips later noted that he could not imagine the agony Firth must have been experiencing, but the exec never complained. Lieutenant Commander Tom Brown was another one with a positive attitude when dealing with the crew. The captain would later formally commend these two officers and others for helping maintain both by deed and demeanor what little positive mood there was among the wretched men aboard the wounded vessel.

Before it became too hot, Phillips organized a burial party. Two more sailors had died during the night, one from the *Neosho*, one from the *Sims*, along with those who had been killed during the attack and whose bodies could be recovered. Each was wrapped in whatever they could find and had a weight tied to anchor the body. Neither Captain Phillips nor anyone else knew the full name of the man from the *Sims*. It was Allen Clark, a yeoman, but everyone who knew him had gone down with the destroyer, were out on the rafts, or were in the whaleboats. After a brief ceremony conducted by the captain, the bodies were dropped over the side. They sank immediately. No bugler was available to play taps, and, considering the situation, Phillips dispensed with the typical three-volley rifle salute.

When he looked back into the faces of the crew members who had gathered for the burial, the captain knew at once that the ceremony had not given them the closure or encouragement he had hoped for. If anything, the men looked even more defeated. Still, there was no way they could keep the bodies on the ship in the tropical heat, even if rescue was expected to come soon.

The captain's next order did not help the mood of the crew, either. It did, however, put many of them to work. That was a good thing, because they would not have time to dwell on the sad ceremony or their own mounting discomfort and fears.

There was growing concern that they were running low on uncontaminated water. Seeping oil could quickly ruin what they had left. Phillips sent a party below to check the tanks, make sure the water was clean, and then find any and all receptacles they could. They were to fill each with the freshwater, being especially careful not to taint it as they worked in their filthy clothes. Then they were to bring the water containers to the deck and align them along the high port side, away from sloshing seawater and leaky oil.

The men were even more depressed when their captain told them that the freshwater would be used only for drinking. No one knew how long it would have to last. Everyone was covered with oil and hoped to be able to wash some of it off. Their hair was thick with the nasty stuff. Some tried to bathe in seawater. Even with soap, the ocean water would only bead up and roll off their skin. If they drifted through a rain shower, each man was to try to catch as much of the precious liquid as he could in whatever was handy.

In an effort to get better organized, the officers formed other formal work parties, one to go below and bring up food, another to look for clothes to replace the oil-sodden garments the burned and wounded men wore, and another to make themselves available to help the corpsmen as they tended to the injured.

Watches were designated. Senior men became the work party leaders. Officers oversaw the groups.

Phillips recognized the importance of not only keeping his men occupied, but also maintaining order, discipline, structure, and accountability. It was a difficult thing to do. Many sailors had seen the *Sims* break in half and sink within mere minutes. Had watched as friends were ripped and blown apart or cooked in clouds of steam. Had witnessed and heard wounded shipmates suffering during the night. Had seen others die and be buried at sea. Had wondered about shipmates who had gone over the side and were now out of sight somewhere out there in the life rafts. Or about those who had not been picked up and had, instead, drowned or been eaten by sharks.

By midmorning, Phillips and his officers had decided to get

the more seriously injured men out of the whaleboats and back onto the *Neosho*. They figured those wounded would be more comfortable on the hulk and out of the blistering sun. They could also get better attention from the pharmacist's mates and quicker access to medicine, clean clothes, and somewhat cleaner blankets. Moving the wounded required another work party and no small risk for all involved.

The captain occasionally gazed through his binoculars at the horizon. It was not so much to see if the Japanese planes or ships were coming. By now, he assumed the enemy knew the oiler was done for and were employing all their assets to find the Allied fleet. No need for them to waste bombs, bullets, or torpedoes on a ship that was clearly dying. He searched for the rafts with all those men aboard. He had not seen them since shortly after the end of the previous day's attack. They would be difficult to find, even from the air. He could only pray some ship or plane would spot them. Bad as it was on the oiler, it would be much worse on those rafts by now, with no shade, no water, no food, no medicine.

He scanned for signs of changing weather. A blue-sky morning could quickly revert to raging storms out here. It would not take much of a squall to tip them on over and dump them all into the sea.

The main object of his search, though, was the ships and aircraft that were certainly on the way to locate and rescue them. He had fully expected friendly vessels to be sitting there at first light, waiting, ready to take them off the *Neosho*.

Realistically, it could take time for any help to arrive, Phillips knew. He likely considered occurrences that could delay the arrival of help. By now, one fleet may have sighted the other. The battle could be raging to their north and he would never know it.

There was even the possibility that the Allied fleet no longer existed. The enemy could well have destroyed them all.

A few days? A week?

Some of the wounded would not last that long. Some would likely not make it through another night. There would be more burials at sea. They would begin to run out of water and food. They were already rationing food. They continued searching in compartments not already flooded for more food and supplies without risking the lives of the work parties any more than necessary.

Confident as he was of rescue, Phillips decided to hedge his bets. By the early afternoon, on the stifling-hot bridge, he assembled his officers.

"First, get me a detail to transfer over supplies of food and water to the whaleboats," he told them. Curious looks appeared on a few oil-smeared faces. "If the ship shows signs she's about to go down, we'll need to get as many men into the boats as we can as quickly as we can, and we'll need food and water if we want to make it to Australia. If it comes to that, it's better we use the time to transfer men, not stores."

Grim nods all around.

"Secondly, let's bring the *Sims* whaleboat in and see if we can fix that hole in its side. I hear it's leaking faster than the men can bail. We'll need it to be more seaworthy than it is now if we lose the ship."

"What else, Captain?"

"Don't alarm anybody, but get a work party and start stripping any good pieces of wood wherever they can find it. Anything that will float. Lash it together and try to make some rafts. We won't all fit into those whaleboats. And even if we drift closer to the life rafts, we have to figure they are full of men already. We just need to be able to float for a day or so if our rescue ship is delayed. We should also consider the possibility of making for Australia if nobody shows up before we lose the ship. Any questions?"

"Captain, I've been thinking some more about the port motor launch," said Verbrugge, the engineer. He was reluctant to give up on any task, about the most determined man Phillips had ever seen. Now he was talking about the only other boat available, the port motor launch. Both Verbrugge and Phillips had previously not considered using it because of the lack of power to get it off its hooks and into the water, especially now that the list of the ship put the boat high above the sea, dangling at a cockeyed angle.

Verbrugge and the captain had also already dismissed once and for all trying to get to the other whaleboat and the motor launch on the starboard side. The sea had been breaking over them since the day before. Not only were they likely damaged beyond use, but it would be next to impossible to get to them, launch them, and put them to work.

"What are you thinking?" Phillips asked.

"The port launch is okay, no damage that I can see," Verbrugge said. "The problem is she's still swinging on her davits. We don't have any power, so we have no way to launch something that big and heavy. But let me think about it and see what I can come up with."

"We'll all think about it. Now, let's get to work, and maybe our rescuers will be along soon and make it all moot."

Captain Burford and his crew on the destroyer *Monaghan* spent all morning crisscrossing the wide stretch of green-colored sea. They spotted neither debris nor oil, nothing at all to indicate a couple of ships had so recently been sunk there. Two ships do not go down without leaving plenty of signs floating on the surface for days afterward.

Burford and his officers had already considered the possibility that they were looking in the wrong place, that the coordinates they had were somehow incorrect. Or that the hulk of the *Neosho* quickly drifted away from where the attack had occurred. The seas and currents were sufficient to have done that. But in which direction?

Meanwhile, word came that the fleet had come under a massive air attack. The *Lexington* and the *Yorktown* had launched their own planes after locating the Japanese fleet, and the fight was on.

Yet the *Monaghan* was 200 miles away, doing rescue duty, and could be of no help from there. The Australian destroyers and cruisers that had been made a part of the task force were now hundreds of miles north, watching for any sign of the Port Moresby Invasion Force. USS *Farragut* (DD-348) had been sent to join the Australians the previous day. With the *Sims* gone and USS *Walke* in the repair yard in Canberra, Task Force 17 was left with only nine destroyers to protect the carriers and the rest of the fleet.

Burford reluctantly responded to an order to turn the *Monaghan* around and head back north to rejoin the task force. He was happy to learn that the search for the *Sims* and *Neosho* survivors was not being dropped. PBYs stationed at Nouméa on the New Caledonian island of Grand Terre— hundreds of miles away—had been alerted. The long-range flying boats would concentrate on looking for survivors in the general area of the last known coordinates, even as they searched for submarines, warships, and any other signs of enemy activity. At a top speed approaching two hundred miles per hour, they could cover plenty of ocean.

Additionally, Commander Leonard B. Austin, Destroyer Division 7, announced that he would take one of his tin cans, the USS *Henley* (DD-391)—which was also based in Nouméa—and get under way first thing in the morning on May 9 to go take a look to see if he could find the survivors of the oiler and escort. Austin had instructed the *Henley*'s captain, Commander Robert Hall Smith, that they were to head at all due speed for the position where the attack by the Japanese had reportedly taken place.

The *Henley* had a long distance to travel, and would possibly encounter enemy vessels along the route. Out there all by themselves, Austin, Hall, and the crew would necessarily have to steer a zigzag course and keep an eye out for the Japanese for the entire route. "All due speed" would not be nearly as fast as any of them would have preferred.

The PBYs would be the best hope for those who might have survived the destruction of their ships. Stranded crew members would just have to continue to hold it together until the planes found them and a rescue ship could steam across enemy-controlled seas to get to them.

Commander Austin and everyone else involved in the search for survivors of the *Neosho* and the *Sims* were certainly aware of one hard, cold fact: If the men were in the water or on life rafts, the odds of finding anyone alive were growing longer and longer with every passing hour.

CHAPTER TWENTY
Sixty-Four Miles

The sun was unbearably hot but there was no place to find shade on the raft. Men pulled their shirts over their faces, but that left their bellies or backs exposed, so even more skin was sunburned. The sun was relentless, even before midmorning on May 8, their second day adrift.

They were already too thirsty to be hungry. That was a small blessing.

The *Neosho* was still nowhere to be seen. No more smoke was rising in the distance as the sun came up that morning. Had she sunk? Or had the crew extinguished the fires and she was out there, still on the surface, just out of sight over the horizon? But which horizon? The elements were disorienting, and no one had a compass. They could only hope the crew had gotten their ship back under power and they might appear any minute, looking for them.

That would be the answer to their prayers. The current

was too strong and they were already too weak to use the paddles they had on the rafts to try to get to the oiler, even if they knew in which direction she might be.

Jack Rolston was still amazed that good luck had put him in the same raft as his buddies, Grove and Kenny. They spent most of the morning trying to keep each other's spirits up, talking about their adventures or favorite hangouts back home or spinning sea stories. They eventually ran dry of those tales, though.

Later, the sun was high overhead, so it must have been near noontime. Four of the rafts had drifted relatively close to each other and somebody suggested that they tie themselves together. It would make it easier for them to be spotted from the air or from a ship. They would lash together with the others, too, if they spotted them, but they had scattered during the night and were now nowhere to be seen.

Someone even went to the trouble to count the men in the four rafts. Sixty-eight, mostly enlisted men but a couple of officers among them, too. Neither officer seemed especially interested in taking charge. Apparently rank had been left behind when they jumped off the *Neosho*.

Some survivors were hurt pretty badly. Others, like Jackie Rolston, who had been less seriously burned or wounded, looked to be able to make it a day or two, until help arrived. Some were seasick. All were tired, hungry, and awfully thirsty.

"I was just thinking," one of the men said. "Remember that Charlie Chaplin picture, the one where he was so hungry he ate that shoe?" Some remembered it and grunted wearily. "I was just wondering if my shoe might taste anything like a pork chop."

Nobody laughed. It was too damn hot to laugh.

"I reckon you better keep that shoe," Seaman Second

Class William Smith finally answered. "One of these rainstorms pops up, you best fill both of them up with water to drink."

The first sailor simply nodded and put his face between his legs, trying to keep the sun off his cheeks and forehead. His ears and the back of his neck were bloodred and covered with ugly, running blisters.

With the sun overhead, it was difficult to tell, but the lashed-together rafts with sixty-eight men aboard seemed to be drifting westward.

Westward, where the nearest land was more than five hundred miles away.

By midafternoon, John Phillips began to worry that if help did not show up soon, it might be too late in the day, too dangerous to try to move men off the *Neosho*'s oil-slick deck in the darkness. Of course, nightfall would also preclude their being spotted from the air. By now, that was the most likely scenario. The PBYs out of Nouméa, about three hundred miles to their southeast, would be looking for them, even if nobody else was.

Certainly the fleet now knew their plight. Even if the radio messages had gone unheard, TF 17 would be aware that the *Neosho* and the *Sims* were in trouble if no one had heard from them in more than twenty-four hours. If nothing else, the *Neosho*'s cargo of fuel meant enough to Admiral Fletcher and the fleet that they would come looking for them.

As the long, hot day stretched on with no stacks appearing on the horizon, it began to look more and more as if they would have to spend another night on the ship. The *Neosho* had so far been stubborn, refusing to die, no matter how badly damaged she was. Still, when the captain observed the ship's condition, when he saw the wash of the sea over her starboard side, and as he took note of the alarming buckling of the deck plates, he had to wonder if she could stay afloat through another long, rough evening. Men still making gleaning trips belowdecks also reported some more worrisome news: Compartments that had been dry earlier in the day were now flooded. Food, blankets, and other necessities were being ruined.

Phillips again assembled his remaining officers.

"We need to get anything heavy on the starboard side overboard," he told them. "We have to make her lighter or a good wave will finish us."

By far the heaviest movable object on that side of the ship was the anchor. With no power to lower it, the only solution was to break the iron chain and send the anchor plummeting to the bottom. Yet with no cutting torch, the only way to break it was to use a wedge and sledgehammer.

That chore proved to be not only backbreaking, especially on the slanting deck, but ultimately impossible. By design, the heavy chain would resist almost any effort to break it.

Someone suggested simply running out the chain in the hope that it would tear itself loose when it reached its end. That did not work, either. The anchor remained in place, but the heavy chain now stretched downward into the sea, only adding to the drag on the ship's starboard side. Trying to improve their plight, they had actually made the situation worse.

A dejected and exhausted work crew reported their failure. Captain Phillips thanked them and sent them off for food and water. He would have to give the project more thought.

The captain checked with the radio operator and with Bill Driscoll, his communications officer. The radioman was supposed to be sending a terse message, including their last position, in plain language, using the auxiliary transmitter and whatever was left of the antenna. With limited fuel for the auxiliary power, Phillips and Driscoll both knew they had to be careful how often they fired it up to use the transmitter. When they did, the operator used partial transmission power to broadcast his chirping message.

Phillips was still concerned about Driscoll, not sure his instructions about regularly radioing their coordinates were being followed. He made a note to emphasize once again their importance to the young officer.

Though sundown was quickly approaching, it remained agonizingly hot on the *Neosho*'s deck. Men were wilting. Everyone sought shade. That included John Phillips.

The inside of the bridge was just as torrid, but at least he could avoid the rays of the tropical sun for a few minutes. As he sat there, he began reviewing the notes of his officers over the last forty-eight hours. He was already composing in his head the incident report he would be required to write should they survive this ordeal. It was especially important in a case in which a skipper lost his ship that such a recap be complete and accurate. There would be review panels, multiple reports, eager second-guessing, continual speculation—both reasonable and unreasonable—and far more questions than anyone could possibly answer. Future skippers could learn from what happened to the *Neosho*, from what did not work as well as from what did.

As he checked facts for his notes, the captain's eye fell on the navigator's precise handwriting in the pages of his workbook. Then he noticed the position Henry Bradford had determined the previous day by shooting the sun and the planet Venus. The geographic position where they were located just after the initial attack and before the main one. The position they had been reporting for a day and a half, whether anyone was receiving their dits and dahs or not.

"16 degrees, 25 minutes south, 157 degrees 31 minutes east."

Idly and for no particular reason other than to keep himself occupied and distracted from the oppressive heat and humidity, Phillips replotted where they had been just before noon on May 7, using the same observations the navigator had.

The captain's heart missed a beat.

No. It could not be.

He reran the plot again, twice.

The navigator's position was wrong by about sixty-four miles. God only knew how far and fast they had drifted since. That likely put them even farther away from where they had been telling TF 17 they should be, where any rescue ships and planes would have been concentrating their search. They had wasted their time while the powerless tanker drifted even farther away.

The captain's first impulse was to summon the young lieutenant and verbally reprimand him. But what good would that do? The man had not made the error on purpose, Phillips would later note. Even the details of the potentially lethal mistake that ended up in the captain's eventual recap of the incident would be relatively mild and straightforward: "In a lull in the engagement, acting in his capacity as Navigator, plotted a fix in the sun and Venus in an incorrect manner, and entered the result in his Navigation Work Book. As a result of this error, the proper point of commencement of search for survivors was not used, and the error was not discovered until subsequent replotting by the Commanding Officer, showing the correct position. . . ."

Once convinced of the error, Phillips rounded up several of his more senior officers—including Firth and Brown—and shared the bad news. No one else was to know just yet. No one but the radio operator, who was ordered to send the new coordinates as often as the spitting transmitter and puny auxiliary generator would allow.

Meanwhile, Phillips prodded his crew to work even harder to get the port motor launch into the water. He ordered that the pieces of wood that had been ripped from deck structures be roped together for makeshift rafts, and directed his sailors to patch up the leaking whaleboats and stock them with food, water, and fuel for the motors that were still working.

In addition, he ordered his navigator to promptly plot the course for the nearest point of land on the coast of Australia. If the ship sank beneath them—as it was showing more and more indications of doing—their best hope for survival would be to try to float a fleet of overloaded, leaking boats and strung-together wood scraps through rough seas at least five hundred miles to the southwest. There were islands closer by a few hundred miles, but without a way to navigate or accurately steer, they could easily miss them. Australia would be difficult to run past, assuming they could actually get there.

Phillips went back to work, collecting more information and making notes for his incident report.

He had to be wondering by then if he would live to write it.

When night finally fell, the wind quickly turned uncomfortably cool. The men on the deck who had been suffering in the heat now gathered blankets and moved behind any structure to escape the chilly breeze.

The wind also brought cloud cover. That was disappointing to Captain Phillips. He was hoping to get a better fix on their exact position so that the radio could pass it along. However, with no stars, no moon, just an impenetrable canopy overhead, there was no way to do it.

He still had no way of knowing if the radio messages with the corrected coordinates were reaching anyone. The radioman heard no response from the headset, just crashes of harsh, mocking static.

By dusk of their second day adrift, the looks on the faces of his men told the captain just how close they were to giving up. Sun, salt spray, and oil had left them red-faced, their lips and cheeks dry and cracked, and other exposed skin burned by the sun and wind. Their eyes were weak, distant, especially those of the injured.

Phillips could no longer, in good conscience, talk hopefully about imminent rescue as a means to keep spirits up. He knew help was not simply delayed. Because of the position error, salvation had become less and less likely. He and those who knew the truth simply would not talk about it.

Amid the discouragement and misery, though, one positive fact kept the crew's hope alive: their ship was still afloat.

The *Neosho* continued to take on water, and the severe buckling of the deck plates confirmed she was under intense and increasing stress from the sea and her own bulk, forces that could, at some point, break her in half. Yet for the first time since the crew had begun tracking it, their thirty-degree tilt had not increased at all in several hours, at least not enough to notice, despite the snafu while releasing the anchor.

The *Neosho* was still floating, and she seemed determined to continue doing so. Like a battered but empty oil drum, she remained buoyant. The wretched survivors aboard the injured hulk still had a deck beneath their feet, listing, sun drenched, wave swept, oil covered, and miserable as that platform might be.

As long as their ship refused to give up, then at least those men who rode her still had a chance to survive.

That is, if they did not surrender before their vessel did.

CHAPTER TWENTY-ONE
Drifting

By the morning of May 9, Louis Verbrugge had finally given up on any possibility of getting the ship back under power. The captain and just about everyone else aboard the *Neosho* had come to that realization the day of the attack, but the engineer refused to accept that he could not somehow resurrect the boilers from cold death. He had held out hope that he would be able to get them to produce enough reliable power to provide lights and more energy for the radio transmitter, for air-conditioning for the worst injured, and for some semblance of pumping ability to slow the flooding and to deliver refrigeration to preserve food. They were already losing precious provisions to spoilage.

Another of the engineer's goals was to have enough power to lower the port motor launch the considerable distance from where it hung on its davits and down to the water. That appeared to be yet another impossible task.

Verbrugge began figuring alternate ways to make use of that perfectly good boat. With another sunrise and no rescue ship in sight, it was looking more and more as if they would need to be able to use it. The engineer figured it was his job to make it possible.

Captain Phillips was disappointed when first light revealed no ships in the distance. He had remained awake most of the night, making plans for abandoning the *Neosho*. As valiantly as the ship seemed to resist sinking, she could not possibly stay on the surface much longer. Not with the serious damage she had suffered. Phillips was convinced that when she did go down, it would be in a hurry, possibly breaking up all of a sudden, as the *Sims* had done. She would take most of them with her if they had not already scrambled into the few boats and crude rafts they had at their disposal.

Phillips's mood likely darkened farther when a pharmacist's mate reported three more men, all *Neosho* crewmen, had died on the deck during the long night. Another hasty, gloomy burial ceremony was assembled, with long-faced sailors looking on, each likely wondering if it was now the deceased who were the more fortunate ones.

After the bodies had been committed to the sea for eternity, there was a noticeable shift in the emphasis of assigned duties. The men were called upon to prepare to leave the ship, and to make the whaleboats habitable for the many days it would take to reach land. The captain and his officers told the men they were only making contingency plans, in case the oiler did abruptly give up the ghost.

The men were beginning to wonder. Were the ship's officers telling them the full story? Was there some reason now to doubt their imminent rescue other than the fact that it had not yet happened?

As best Phillips could determine, the ship was drifting northwestward at about a knot and a half. They desperately needed to get an accurate position in order to send out their coordinates multiple times before the crew moved to the boats. Even the weak auxiliary transmitter was better than what they would have once they left the *Neosho*. Once in the whaleboats and raft, there would be no radio at all. Thomas Brown was assigned the job of determining their precise location.

Meanwhile, Verbrugge reported to the captain that he believed, with the proper rigging, he could muscle the port launch down the sloping deck and into the sea. He would need to requisition enough healthy men to assist him in such a brute-strength task. Phillips told the engineer to gather all the men he needed and get to it.

Seaman Bill Leu was one of the sailors who joined Verbrugge's party. First they crafted a complicated series of lines and chain hoists. Then, while slipping and sliding precariously on the oily, canted deck, trying all the time to keep from falling overboard, the sweating, straining men began the laborious task of winching the boat down, slowly and carefully, into the sea from the high side of the ship.

The sailors toiled all day to lower the boat down the port side. Once near the water, they had to be especially careful to keep the waves from throwing the vessel against the hull and damaging it, or filling it with water and sinking it. Finally, the boat was at a point where they felt they could tie it up, just out of reach of the sea. Exhausted and with nightfall coming quickly, they secured the launch as best they could. They would complete the operation the next day.

Meanwhile, Phillips had not given up on cutting loose the

anchor, trying to remove its weight and allow the ship to lift a bit more above the waves. Men scrounged around below and brought up some hacksaws. They went to work, sawing away at the thick metal chain until their hands bled. When the pain was too much, when the sun's heat made a man too dizzy to carry on, another sailor stepped in and commenced to grind away at the same spot in the same big link. When a blade became too dull to make any progress, it was tossed to the deck and they watched as it slid down into the sea. Then they went back to work with a replacement blade.

It was a maddeningly slow process. They could hardly see any progress at all.

Then, suddenly, the link was weakened to the point that it snapped open with a loud *ching*! The men jumped clear as the chain rattled through, clanking noisily against the hull. The stubborn anchor finally fell clear, plunging to the bottom of the sea.

Though Phillips commended both dog-tired work parties for their great accomplishments, he did not mention that the inclinometer showed only a degree or so of improvement in the list of their sloping deck once the anchor had been deep-sixed. Or that having use of the additional boat would have minimal effect on their likelihood of making it to Australia. Even small victories helped morale immensely.

At just after 1000 hours on their second full morning adrift, Lieutenant Brown reported their position to be latitude 15 degrees, 35 minutes south, longitude 156 degrees, 55 minutes east. Phillips's estimate of their drift had been right on the money. Since the attack, they had wandered almost a full degree of latitude to the north and more than a degree of latitude to the west. That was almost seventy miles from where they started. Factor in the error of about sixty-four miles for the wrong position originally reported and that meant that what remained of the *Neosho* and her crew were a long way from where any search might be going on.

Unless, of course, someone was actually hearing their weak radio signals. They could only pray that was the case. Regardless, the transmissions now contained their newly determined position.

At 1300 hours, Brown took another sighting. He reported they were drifting a bit faster now, but at a knot or two, it would take many days to hit New Guinea or the Cape York Peninsula of Australia. Even if the *Neosho* remained buoyant enough to float, even if she was not sent to the bottom by a sudden storm, they would have run out of medicine, food, and water long before then, and many more of the wounded would die.

Captain Phillips continued to consult with his officers, to speak with the pharmacist's mates about the condition of the injured. As the day wore on, with no sign of aircraft in the skies or ships on the horizon, they leaned more toward making final preparations to take to the whaleboats the next day and risk heading southwest, toward the Australian coast. They could make better speed. It was a long shot at best, but it still looked like the only chance they had to save the crew.

Only one boat now had a working motor. The others' engines had simply given up. Men went to work rigging masts and sails on all three. The patch on the lone whaleboat from the *Sims* was in bad shape, so they used more pieces of life vests and gobs of tar to try to strengthen it. More provisions were brought over to the boats from the ship, even though every nook was full already.

With precious little room, space would be at a premium when all remaining 120 or so men moved to the boats and rafts. All the vessels and the makeshift rafts would be tied together, while the whaleboat with the working engine, plus the newly available motor launch, would tow the ragged little flotilla. The crude sails would be used to assist.

When the sun fell on May 9, Lieutenant Brown took yet another navigational fix, this time using the stars. They had continued to drift at about the same rate, but had turned more to the southwest. Was the stubborn hulk going to start migrating in a big circle now? They were at the mercy of the currents.

Winds had also picked up late in the day and the seas were once again growing rough. Distant thunderheads put on a frightening fireworks show well into the evening, but no rain fell on the ship. Everyone kept an eye on the starboard side, watching how the waves broke over the deck until it was too dark to see. Then they could only hope and pray that some unseen rogue wave would not swamp them in the dark of night, sending the wreck to the bottom before they could scurry off her.

Facing another precarious, grueling night on the deck, the mood of the men had tumbled. Phillips urged his officers to try to instill hope among the crew, a feat that was becoming more and more difficult, even for Brown and Verbrugge, the most chipper among them. The officers felt their own outlooks dimming.

Some men now openly scoffed when their officers promised, halfheartedly, that their savior ship was just over the horizon, awaiting first light so that it could whisk them off the *Neosho* and take them all home.

All night, the ship heaved and pitched, making it difficult for even the most exhausted among them to find sleep. Sea spray and oil continually bathed them, spoiling the last of their clean clothes, blankets, and mattresses.

During that wretched night, two more men died. One was the gravely wounded Noel Craven, Jack Rolston's high school buddy from back in Missouri.

All the while, the Southern Cross constellation impassively looked down on the men from amid all the other brilliant, winking stars. Its familiar shape formed a mocking crucifix in the black, moonless sky.

It was midafternoon for the men who were on their second full day adrift in the four tied-together life rafts. The relentless sun continued to bake the sixty-eight survivors as they lay still, too exhausted to move.

Carley life rafts were first developed in Australia way back near the turn of the century, and still remained the choice of most merchant and military ships around the world. They consisted of an oval-shaped copper frame covered with cork and then canvas, painted with waterproof paint. The floor was made of wood grating, which offered good footing but little comfort or a dry place to rest. The rafts were light enough to be easily thrown over the side of a ship and were virtually unsinkable, even if damaged by gunfire. Fire was another matter, though, as the men on the *Neosho* had seen firsthand. They made good kindling. When the suicide plane hurled onto the deck, blazes quickly devoured half the ship's available rafts.

In the awful heat of the afternoon, someone lying near Jackie Rolston leaned over the edge of their raft, dipped up a double handful of seawater, and slurped it down. He loudly smacked his parched lips, grinning broadly.

"No! Don't do that!" William Smith shouted, startling half-asleep men in all four of the rafts. "That salt water will kill you. Don't you know that?"

"So will thirst," the man replied, and dipped up another double handful and gulped it down. "I know that, for damn sure. Besides, it ain't so bad and it is wet."

Several men grabbed the sailor's arms, trying to keep him from drinking any more seawater.

"Hang on, man. Help is on the way," they told him.

"We'll see a plane or ship any minute now."

"That stuff will make you go crazy."

The sailor just smacked his lips again and grinned, his eyes glassy and red-rimmed, dead skin hanging from his mouth.

Several of his raft mates glanced from his dazed face to the vast stretch of water that surrounded them as far as they could see in every direction. Some men tried to swallow, but their mouths were too dry. Their throats burned even worse than before. Others intently watched the man who drank the seawater, looking for any signs of distress.

The sailor did not go crazy. There were no convulsions.

Another man finally reached over, wet his own hand in the Coral Sea, and licked the salty drops of warm water from his fingers.

Aboard the destroyer *Henley*, both Commander Austin and Commander Smith were frustrated. Since leaving Nouméa, they had been steaming at top speed during the day, continuing to run a back-and-forth course to confuse any enemy aircraft or submarine they might encounter. At night, they had to cut speed to about fifteen knots to avoid running into anything floating in the sea that did not show up on the radar.

Both men wanted to get as quickly as they could to the position where the *Neosho* and the *Sims* had reportedly come under attack. Then they would look for oil slicks and debris, and assess where any survivors could have drifted. Nothing gave them reason to believe that the tanker might still be afloat. Not after the *Monaghan* crew found nothing at all in their aborted search the previous day.

They made decent time during the day of May 9, even as the crew aboard the *Neosho* was wrestling with the port motor launch and sawing through the anchor chain. Then, at about midnight that night, the destroyer got exasperatingly detoured.

They received distressing word that they were on a course that would take them directly into the area where an enemy aircraft carrier had been reported. Whether the spotting was accurate or not, Austin had no option. He did not want to attract the attention of a carrier, its aircraft, or its escort vessels. A mere destroyer would have little chance in that kind of showdown.

Austin told Smith to order a course that would take the *Henley* away from the enemy flattop—a move that would point them in the opposite direction from where they expected to locate the oiler or her lifeboats and rafts filled with survivors.

Though it was crucial that they learn what had happened to the replenishment vessel, the escort, and their more than five hundred men, there was no choice about this maddening diversion. The tin can ran in the wrong direction for several hours until the commanders were sure they had bypassed any possible encounter with the supposed enemy carrier.

Then they turned back to once again steam toward the hole in the ocean where all those men might be depending so desperately on the *Henley*. After all, she was just about their only hope to survive the hell they had likely been living for the past three days.

CHAPTER TWENTY-TWO
First Hope

Captain Phillips was determined to keep occupied every able-bodied man still aboard his sinking ship, no matter how tired or disheartened that crew member may have become. There was plenty to do: finishing the task of helping Louis Verbrugge get the motor launch in the water without swamping it; removing the now-useless motors on the two whaleboats to get rid of deadweight; cleaning up the decks where men had defecated, vomited, and bled during the night; provisioning the boats; manufacturing makeshift rafts to replace the life rafts that had burned up or gone overboard during the attack. Phillips was aware, too, that these chores were more than mere make-work. They were important tasks, ones that might help save their lives.

They served another valuable purpose as well. They helped to keep his men's minds off what was becoming more and more a hopeless situation.

Their list to starboard had not changed much during the night, but that was small comfort. When the sun rose at dawn on May 10, everyone could tell that the *Neosho* was riding even lower in the water. Their valiant ship had not yet given up, and she had already amazed them all with her endurance. Regardless, she simply would not be able to float much longer. The sea was certain to claim her soon.

The captain conducted the now-familiar burial ceremony early that morning for the latest two men who had died during the night. There was no thought of dispensing with the ritual, of simply jettisoning the bodies like the ship's trash.

Someone pointed out that it was Sunday. Few had noticed. The first attack had been on the morning of Thursday, May 7. That made this the fourth day that they had been adrift.

They had no chaplain onboard. There would be no services that day. Men took the opportunity to pray as they could and if they so desired. Someone commented that God must have forgotten them by now. Others shushed the man, but only halfheartedly.

The tropical trade winds and current still determined their course. Those arbitrary forces seemed to be pushing them almost due west on this day, even farther from the position where they had been ambushed by the Japanese.

Verbrugge, with the help of Bill Leu and the same group of tired but willing sailors from the day before, finally succeeded in lowering the port launch into the water. They brought her around to the starboard side and began loading provisions for the impending cruise.

Captain Phillips hardly bothered scanning the horizon anymore, looking hopefully for smoke from a ship's stack or for Allied aircraft. After four days they had not seen a single

Captain John Spinning Phillips, commanding officer of the USS Neosho.

Neosho crew member Fireman Third Class William Leu, whose later accounts of the attack on his ship and their destroyer escort, USS Sims, along with the four days adrift on the sinking oiler, contributed greatly to the telling of this story.

The USS Neosho (AO-23) just after commissioning, August 1939.

Pearl Harbor's Battleship Row early in the Japanese attack of December 7, 1941. The *Neosho* is at far right, still moored and off-loading volatile fuel.

The view down Battleship Row during the attack. At left, listing to port, is the USS *California* (BB-44). At right, the *Neosho* backs away from the mooring after chopping lines.

With the *California* in the foreground, the *Neosho* gets under way on a run across the harbor to reduce danger of fuel explosion at Ford Island.

The *Neosho* alongside and refueling the aircraft carrier USS *Yorktown* (CV-5) on May 1, 1942, a week before the Battle of the Coral Sea.

The *Neosho*'s crew battles heavy seas while refueling the *Yorktown* just a few days before the oiler was mistaken for a carrier and attacked by the Japanese.

The destroyer USS *Sims* (DD-409), the *Neosho*'s escort during the Battle of the Coral Sea.

The *Yorktown* steams in the foreground with the *Neosho* just beyond and the *Sims* in the far distance.

In this photo taken from a Japanese dive-bomber, the *Neosho* is on fire following the attack on the morning of May 7, 1942.

Another photo from a Japanese attack aircraft of the *Neosho* ablaze and heavily damaged but still under power.

Chief Watertender Oscar Peterson, who received the Medal of Honor posthumously for his brave actions during the attack on the *Neosho*.

Four survivors of the *Neosho* are rescued after nine days adrift on a raft with no food, water, or shelter. This copy of the photo was obtained from survivor Jack Rolston, who had written on the image to indicate himself.

airplane, friendly or enemy. Had they drifted out of the main areas where each fleet searched for assets of the other? It was certainly possible that those ships and planes were, or already had been, involved in a life-or-death battle up north.

There was the chance, too, that rescuers had looked hard in the wrong place. Then, with no signs of survivors, they decided that nobody had lived through the sinking of the two ships. The search might have been abandoned, the ship or ships sent on to more pressing business.

Still, why had some of the land-based aircraft not happened upon them by now? Even accidentally? The PBYs out of the Allied base at Nouméa? Or even a plane flying a scout mission from one of the Australian airfields?

Reports in Japanese war archives indicate that IJN aircraft did, indeed, spot the drifting *Neosho* on May 10. Yet senior officers decided it was not worth the ordnance or effort to finish her off. She would be allowed to sink on her own. No record exists that anyone on the oiler ever saw the enemy aircraft.

Was it possible that the men struggling to stay alive on the deck of the *Neosho* and the survivors out there somewhere in the rafts were the only human beings left in that entire quadrant of the Coral Sea?

Several of the more seriously wounded men on the group of rafts died during their second night drifting. It was so dark that nobody could tell until the sun came up. With no medicine, painkillers, or even a sip of cool water to wet their dry, split lips, there was nothing their fellow sailors could do for them. A few more of the injured slipped into death before the sun even had time to climb halfway up the morning sky.

Jackie Rolston, with the help of Ken Bright, Grove Hough, and a couple of other men, managed to pull their deceased shipmates over to the edge of the raft. Someone said a few biblical words from memory, and the sailors grunted and strained until they could slide the bodies over into the sea.

Someone made a bad joke, something about how they should not be throwing perfectly good meat overboard. Nobody laughed.

With nothing weighing the bodies down, the lifeless shipmates continued to drift alongside the rafts most of the day, as if reluctant to leave the company of their friends. For a while, the floating corpses were a mocking reminder to the living that they would soon end up the same way.

Small fish began to nibble and nudge at the bodies, a macabre feeding that eventually attracted bigger fish. They tugged at the lifeless human flesh with enough force to make it appear as if the corpses were moving on their own, jerking, gesturing, struggling. Then the fish finally carried the remains of the dead shipmates out of sight.

One raft lost some of its buoyancy and took on water when sizable waves broke across the sides. Men used their shoes to bail briskly. Under the direction of Seaman William Smith—who had proceeded to take charge when no one else seemed willing or able to—they moved some of the men from that sinking raft over to another that was already seriously overcrowded, but was at least entirely above water.

As of about midday on Sunday they had been in the rafts seventy-two hours with no water, food, or shelter. Every man was badly sunburned, parched, and weak. Most of their strength as well as their will had long since been sapped. It took every man, working together, to jettison the bodies of the dead men over the side, in order to balance the men who had come over from the foundering raft.

Out of desperation, quite a few men had begun to drink seawater, some more, some less, despite the admonitions of the others. Several were now painfully sick, writhing about, suffering seizures and screaming craziness. Surrounded by sea, there was nothing to echo back their cries. The noise of their hollow shrieks died out instantly, erased by the vast emptiness around them.

One of the most severely stricken sailors finally fell quiet and died. His kidneys, poisoned by salt water, refused to function. He was quickly shoved over the side so that another suffering man could lie down in his spot.

All the while, the rafts full of haggard men continued to drift beneath a searing sun, little more than flotsam on an empty, uncaring sea.

After the scare from the reported Japanese aircraft carrier, Commander Austin dared to put the *Henley* back on course at a speed of twenty knots, even though they were still surrounded by inky darkness. Lookouts strained harder, searching for obstacles that might pop up in their path. When the sun came up, Austin pushed the destroyer's speed even higher. They had lost a good six hours trying to dodge that ghostly flattop. Now they needed to make up time and distance if they were to locate and rescue any survivors of the *Sims* and the *Neosho*.

There was another worry. Intelligence confirmed that the MO Carrier Striking Force—now with only the *Zuikaku* as its main component—had refueled at Rabaul and returned to the area where the main battle had been fought two days before.

The remaining forty-five operational aircraft off the carrier's decks would be ranging out, looking for what was left of the American fleet, intent on finishing the job they had begun. They would be only too happy to take down an Allied destroyer should they discover the *Henley*. By herself, in such an encounter, the warship would have no more chance of survival than her sister destroyer, the *Sims*, had.

As with most of the key players in the *Neosho* story, the men on the *Henley* were quite familiar with the oiler. Since she was based at Nouméa, the destroyer had not been fueled by the *Neosho* as regularly as the members of Task Force 17, yet the *Henley* had also been at Pearl Harbor on the morning of December 7, when she created her own bit of accidental history.

Early that morning, before the attack, the *Henley*'s acting captain, Lieutenant F. E. Fleck—both the commanding officer and executive officer were ashore at the time—had given the order to sound quarters for muster, a call for all hands to assemble on deck. In this case, it was so those who wished to could go ashore for church services. A relatively new, untrained sailor mistakenly sounded General Quarters instead, sending all crew members to their battle stations.

That careless mistake proved to be a lucky one. With men already at their battle stations when the Kates and Vals roared out of the morning sky, the *Henley* became the first destroyer to fire an antiaircraft barrage in World War II. Later, the destroyer was in the middle of the harbor, guns blazing, dropping depth charges on what was believed to be a mini-submarine, when the *Neosho* made her dash through hellfire to reach the relative safety of Merry Point.

Now the crew of the *Henley*, including Austin and Smith, had to wonder if they would ever see the *Neosho* again. All they had to do was check the date and hour to realize that, if the oiler had sunk, any possible survivors were certainly running out of time. Any sailors swimming in the water were certainly dead by now. Men on life rafts or in whaleboats would be on the ragged edge of survival, even if they had managed to carry over some rations. If the *Neosho* had gone down the previous Thursday, anyone who lived through the sinking would be in bad shape by now.

At midday on May 10, the *Henley* was still 150 miles away from the doomed ship's last known position. Yet those coordinates were in doubt after the *Monaghan* had found no trace of the ships. Even if any survivors were still on rafts nearby, the destroyer could not reach the vicinity until at least the next morning.

Neither veteran officer was optimistic. Still, both of them were determined to try.

"1230: Single aircraft sighted, approaching from about 240 degrees."

Just after midday on Sunday, a member of one of the *Neosho*'s work parties paused, stood up to stretch his aching back, and wiped his face with the filthy sleeve of his oil-soaked shirt. He cocked his head sideways.

"Any of you hear that?"

"What? My stomach . . . ?"

"No. Listen."

A faint, distant buzzing could be heard from the southwest. Could it be?

A sailor with binoculars spun in that direction and scanned the sky.

"Airplane! Good God! Airplane!"

From the bridge, Captain Phillips heard the uproar and wheeled around to see for himself. Sure enough, it was an aircraft.

Ours or theirs? he wondered, then decided it did not matter. They had to make certain the plane's crew saw them, just in case they were friendly.

Some sailors on deck were not so sure. "We look up," Seaman Bill Leu recalled, "and here's an [airplane] and the rear gunner has his machine gun [pointed at us] and he's laughing. Jeez, it scared the hell out of us until we found out it was an Australian."

"Signalman, get the light working! Identify us."

The signalman quickly attached auxiliary power to the signal light and, in less than half a minute, began flashing away in the direction of the rapidly approaching aircraft.

Two engines. It had two engines.

"Send up the distress flag!" Phillips ordered. The international distress signal.

Now he could tell that the plane was a Lockheed Hudson. That made it almost certainly Australian. And thank God the newcomer was now blinking his own light, returning their signal.

"He wants to know if we are in distress," the signalman translated.

"Tell him we sure as hell are!"

The sailor blinked away, relaying his captain's pointed reply. The airplane flew on over the oiler, still a couple of thousand feet high. Then, just before disappearing into a thick cloud bank, he turned in a broad circle, flew back toward them, and made another pass directly overhead. He did not acknowledge their distress signal or position report, and was still a bit higher than Phillips would have liked.

The plane kept going, back in the direction from which it had come. In less than a minute, he was out of sight. No matter how hard they listened, the men on the *Neosho*'s sloping deck could no longer hear the hopeful buzzing of the Hudson's twin engines.

PART SIX
SURVIVAL

There, then, he sat, holding up that imbecile candle in the heart of that almighty forlornness. There, then, he sat, the sign and symbol of a man without faith, hopelessly holding up hope in the midst of despair.

—Herman Melville, *Moby-Dick*

CHAPTER TWENTY-THREE
Dashed Hopes

For the first time in four days, smiles lit up the faces of the men stranded aboard the sinking tanker. Finally there was reason for hope.

The Aussie plane had seen them. That much they knew for certain. They had exchanged light signals. Though the aircraft had not acknowledged their predicament, the plane's crew had to know the vessel foundering in the water below was in trouble. No ship in good condition would be so severely listing, trailing oil, and drifting in the Coral Sea—enemy waters—with no escort.

Now, as soon as it was prudent, the plane's crew would hopefully report the American ship's presence back to their base. If things worked the way they were supposed to, the Australians would send the message to General MacArthur's headquarters. South West Pacific HQ would then relay the message to Pearl Harbor. Pearl Harbor would forward the information to Task Force 17—if such a thing still existed by this time—as well as to the American and Australian land bases in the area. All those entities might assume it was the *Neosho* that the Aussies had seen wallowing around out there.

Then, finally, help would be on the way. Hopefully, that help was already nearby, already looking for them, and could arrive quickly. Then, if they had not found the more than one hundred men in the life rafts, they could continue looking for them, too. The rafts had likely drifted farther than the considerable bulk of the *Neosho*. Still, those poor souls could not be that far away.

Yet there was no assurance that protocol would be carried out as it should. Many potential snags could hinder how the Hudson's report might be interpreted and passed along.

First, MacArthur had been named supreme commander of Allied Forces in the southwest Pacific only three weeks before the Coral Sea showdown. He was still building his command, an odd mixture of officers who had escaped with the general and his family from Bataan in the Philippines two months before, along with some handpicked members of the Australian military. Rumblings of distrust had already been heard— the flamboyant general had taken over a role many felt should have gone to an Australian, not the formerly retired American who had been chased out of the Philippines in the dark of night.

Secondly, MacArthur's headquarters had first been established in Melbourne. Yet at the time of the *Neosho*'s sinking, his command was in the process of being transferred almost a thousand miles north to Brisbane. The general felt the southern coast of the continent was too far removed from his area of operation.

Also, the Battle of the Coral Sea had actually occurred in

the portion of the Pacific near the demarcation line between MacArthur's command and that of Admiral Chester Nimitz, who oversaw his area from back in Pearl Harbor. There was still some confusion over what action belonged in whose area.

The situation was rife with possibilities for miscommunication. Phillips and his officers were likely aware of that. There is no indication, though, that anyone speculated out loud about it happening. No one seemed to doubt that the news of their finally being spotted would result in anything other than a quick rescue.

The men were smiling again. Even if Phillips harbored any concerns, he would not have voiced them. Instead, he thought of a way to build on the welcome jubilation the appearance of the aircraft had set off.

He ordered men to go below and bring to the deck several hot plates, coffeepots, and bags of coffee. He instructed Louis Verbrugge to rig precious auxiliary power so the hot plates could be plugged in and to go ahead and fire up the auxiliary generator with no worries.

For the first time since breakfast on the morning of May 7, every man had fresh, hot coffee to drink. As much of it as they wanted.

The sighting of the airplane and the caffeine from the fresh coffee worked wonders for morale. There was even the occasional sound of laughter among the men. They still worked hard, but despite the heat and humidity, the constant roll of the hulk, the slippery, canted deck, and the moans of the injured men, they had found renewed energy.

Captain Phillips's notes and eventual incident report, though, suggest that the seasoned commander well knew they were not rescued just yet. Help might still have to come from five hundred miles away or more, and the condition of their ship continued to worsen by the minute. The possibility still existed that the *Neosho* would break up and sink before anyone could get there.

They still had some freshwater in the storage tanks, but a sudden shift in the infrastructure could break a weld or seam and allow oil or seawater to contaminate it. They would continue to make sure the containers of water on the deck were kept filled, just in case, and that each boat had a good supply, even if it required men to continue taking risky trips below to get it.

The increased buckling and deformity of the deck plates continued to serve as a frightening indicator of just how seriously their vessel was damaged. The distortion had grown noticeably worse by the afternoon of May 10, especially behind the bridge, toward the stern, where the most damaging of the bombs had exploded. It would not have surprised Phillips or any of his senior officers if the stern section simply broke away. If that happened, they would possibly sink in minutes.

The inclinometer seemed to offer something else positive. The list of the ship had subsided substantially, enough that even men who were working on the deck had noticed it, and happily so. Verbrugge, Phillips, and others suspected that bit of good news hid a far more ominous development.

An inspection team was dispatched below before dark to check on flooding levels in the various compartments. Their report was sobering and confirmed their worst fears. The captain made certain the news was not shared with the rest of the crew.

Sure enough, water had come up dramatically since the last look, especially in the engine room and the fire room. The lean of the deck was diminishing only because they were settling in the water. The sea was now rushing into the ship faster, sinking them more quickly. Who knew how much longer this gallant girl could tread water?

Out of earshot of any of the men, Phillips held a quick meeting with his officers.

"We have to be ready to take to the boats in a hurry," he told them. "Make preparations for that. It will help us anyway if we have a rescue vessel and have to get everyone off then." He turned to his engineer. "With less of a list, we may be able to reach the starboard whaleboat now. We'll need it if we can get it. See if it's damaged or what our chances might be to get it launched and provisioned so we can make use of it."

"Will do."

Next he made eye contact with Lieutenant Commander Brown.

"Tom, you made any progress on plotting us a course?" He had asked the navigator to find the most direct route to land.

"I have, Captain. I have a bearing for Willis Island. I'll keep adjusting it, depending on our drift in the meantime. If we miss Willis somehow, we'll be headed for Cairns Harbor if we are lucky. Or at least somewhere on the Australian coast, and we'll pray we hit land somewhere where there's water and an apple orchard and lots of girls in bathing suits."

"How far is that, Tom?" someone asked.

"Two hundred sixty miles to Willis," Brown answered.

The officers studied the deck for a long moment. A few of them likely knew that Willis Island was only about a quarter mile long, less than twenty acres in area, thirty feet in elevation at its highest point, and damned easy to drift right on past without their even seeing it. If they missed the island, it would be another 280 miles to Cairns.

No one knew what kind of speed they would be able to make, mostly under sail power, boats packed with more than a hundred men, towing a crude raft or two. It would have to be a journey of a week or more. Could they live in open boats that long? Would their limited provisions hold out? Or would a storm capsize them and end the journey before they had the opportunity to find out?

The odds were heavily stacked against them.

"Okay, let's get to work," Phillips finally told them. "Make sure we have navigation gear in each of the boats in case we get separated by a storm or the current. We have the lists of who goes in which boat, and that'll assure we have somebody who can use a sextant in each one. Weapons, handguns, and rifles should now be placed in the boats as well, just as we have discussed. And make sure that we divide up the worst of the wounded so the others can help care for them." The captain paused for a moment. "Any questions?"

"Are the men going to be all right with abandoning the ship if it's still afloat?" someone asked.

Phillips certainly knew what the officer was thinking. Having the men working on the details of any option other than the sudden appearance of a rescue ship would be demoralizing for them all. Still, they had to be prepared for whatever might happen. With darkness falling, more than five hours had passed since the Aussie Hudson had buzzed the ship, flashed its signal light, and then flown away, out of sight. The officers had overheard their men happily speculating that help would certainly appear on the horizon within an hour or two, taking wagers on direction of arrival, time, and type of ship, and even talking about what they would do on liberty once they were back on solid ground.

Yet now those same men were facing another brutal night

on the pitching decks of their dying ship. Now their officers were coming back to them, asking them to continue to slave away in this miserable environment, still making preparations to abandon the ship and then try to sail over five hundred miles across rough seas in those little launches with two working motors among them.

It had likely occurred to Phillips and the others that, unless the ship was obviously sinking in a hurry, many of the men would never willingly crawl into those smaller boats. They knew what their chances would be out on the vast sea. Since the elation of being sighted by the Aussies, some men might well ignore orders to abandon ship, deciding instead to risk riding it out on the hulk. At some point, the captain and his officers might have to decide how much detail of the ship's condition they were willing to share with the enlisted men. Decide how far they would go to make sure their commands to move over to the boats were obeyed.

Since the initial rush of men over the side during the attack, all of those who were left had served valiantly, had done all that was asked of them and more. Would they be willing to follow that final order to get off the *Neosho*?

At the same time, Phillips had to also wonder if his officers would do the same. Could he count on each of them?

They could well learn the answer to those tough questions the following afternoon. That was now the captain's target for abandoning ship.

But for now, Phillips and the *Neosho* officers had a more immediate problem of diminished confidence. Both the exhilaration of seeing the aircraft and the welcome kick from the coffee had worn off as the broiling sun dipped low and no ship appeared. Cold reality was once again claiming the spirits of the crew.

"Just keep doing what you can to keep their frame of mind positive," Phillips ordered. "If the ship stays afloat tonight, we'll be off her decks tomorrow, one way or the other. Either way, we're going to need the men who are able to be ready to work even harder than they have so far. We need their strong backs and their undivided attention. Tomorrow, we either get rescued or we take to the whaleboats and strike out for Australia."

Phillips did not have to take a vote to see which outcome his officers preferred.

Sundown no longer brought much relief for those wretched survivors trapped in the knotted-together rafts. Their burned skin still crawled, as if someone were rubbing salt into their blistered flesh. With the darkness came a chill wind, and their shivering only made the pain worse. Their empty stomachs growled and ached. It was hard to open dry mouths and cracked, bleeding lips to try to breathe in damp air. Humidity was the closest thing to a drink any of them had enjoyed since jumping into the sea.

It had rained on them almost every day for the two weeks after they arrived in the Coral Sea. Yet not even a sprinkle had fallen since Thursday, and now it was Sunday.

The badly leaking raft, devoid of passengers, had nearly filled with water, threatening to drag down the other rafts lashed to it. It was now little more than an albatross around their necks. The lines had swollen and the knots were difficult to untie with shaking fingers that had lost most of their strength and dexterity. No one had a knife to hack or saw the ropes. Men took turns pulling at the tangled loops until the sunken raft was finally, blessedly untied and allowed to drift away. But the ghostly thing seemed reluctant to sink. Instead, deflated, it floated along beside them, like the bodies of the men who had died and been cast away.

More and more men. By dusk on the tenth, better than twenty had died. That was almost a third of them.

Some had been wounded, burned badly, and they slipped deeper and deeper into unconsciousness until they stopped begging for relief, then simply ceased breathing. Others, in thirsty desperation, gulped handfuls of ocean water. With their bodies already terribly dehydrated, it did not take long for them to start having violent seizures, thrashing about, dry-heaving, talking out of their heads, losing control of what little they had in their bowels.

Their screams and howling were awful to listen to, other-worldly. Then it would be just a little time before they went blessedly quiet, limp. They were dead, their bodies too desic-cated to sustain life.

Jackie Rolston, Ken Bright, and Grove Hough kept to themselves as much as they could manage in such close quar-ters. They tried to keep each other's dispositions positive, but the three friends had long since run out of stories from back home, out of songs they could remember, out of girls' names from school, or the scores of last year's basketball triumphs.

The three friends tried to convince themselves that help was still possible, that they would eventually be spotted from the air. Odds were that they would accidentally wander into the path of a passing ship and get themselves fished out of the sea. There would be water, tea, coffee, soup, and biscuits on that ship, even salve for their scorched skin.

They tried to lie as still as they could, barely breathing, not using any more energy than absolutely necessary to suck in and blow out the salty air. Their only exertion was to help push lifeless bodies over the side when someone on their raft died. Then they took turns using one of the few paddles to shove the dead men farther away so that they would no longer have to see their open, staring eyes. The hope was that a body would float out of sight, hidden by the waves, before the damned fish began pounding away at the poor man's blistered flesh.

The three friends made a pact that when they were rescued off the raft—not "if," "when"—one of the first things they would do when they had shore leave was go see Noel Craven's folks. Maybe they could make the family feel better, telling how he had died bravely doing his duty, fighting the Japs, and how he had—as far as they knew—gone quickly, without suffering.

If, amazingly, the *Neosho* had survived the attack, they had surely buried Noel at sea and with a proper ceremony, with taps and a rifle salute. Not with just a shove into the water and a nudge with a boat paddle like the sorry send-off to eternity the poor boys on these rafts were getting.

But more likely, "Fat Girl" had gone down that first night. Everyone on the rafts agreed on that point. They had seen the drubbing she was taking. The captain had ordered them to abandon the ship. No vessel could have survived. That meant Noel's body had still been consigned to the sea, just not in a formal, traditional way.

It also meant that, despite their misery, their pain, and those who were dying slow, horrible deaths all around them, the men who had made it to the rafts were still the more fortunate ones. At least they still had a chance to be rescued, even if help was already three days tardy. Had a chance, unlike those poor sailors who likely had been caught up in the whirlpool when the *Neosho* went down.

By the time it had grown too dark on that Sabbath night

for any man even to make out the faces of his raft mates, Jackie was growing more and more concerned about Grove Hough. His friend had begun babbling, imagining he was back home, playing ball. He had started thrashing about and spouting gibberish. Jackie had not seen him drink seawater, but Grove was in a bad way.

Then, unexpectedly, Grove would pop back to some semblance of lucidity for a while. He was his old self again. The cooler night air seemed to help. Then their friend fell into a fitful sleep. Jackie and Ken did not bother him.

No need to. They had no water to give him. No yeast roll or slice of ham or fresh, plump orange, all the things they had talked about looking forward to when salvation finally came. They were now fresh out of words of encouragement, too.

They had used up most of their hope as well. By now, hope was as precious and just as hard to find as a swig of ice-cold water.

Still they tried to tell themselves that the next day would be a new day. First light might bring a relentless sun but it could finally bring help, too.

Such redemption was becoming more and more difficult to visualize. It was getting harder and harder to remember how cool water felt when it touched a man's chapped lips, how it swished around the tongue when he took a mouthful, how it went down his gullet, blissfully soothing a parched throat on the way.

It was becoming almost impossible now to remember how it felt to have once held hope.

Jesus, please. Water. Just a passing rain shower. Anything to give them hope.

Just a few drops of cool, wet, lifesaving hope.

CHAPTER TWENTY-FOUR
Ours or Theirs?

The sea was relatively calm for their last night on the sinking tanker, as if the deep sensed victory and was ready to claim the prize. The soft rocking of the ship was almost comforting. The cool trade winds were actually soothing. Near daylight, word came that no one had died in the darkness during the night. No bodies would be cast adrift in these waters before the crew of the oiler finally left the ship and their fallen comrades behind.

Even so, the last night on the *Neosho* was in some ways their worst yet. The captain and officers had spread the word the evening before that they would leave her this day, regardless. It was a miracle their ship had remained afloat this long. Some sailors had figured they were relatively safe as long as they stayed aboard something as big and buoyant as the tanker. The unknown, the hardships and their likelihood of survival on the boats, was hell to contemplate throughout the long night. Few slept.

In the darkness, some sailors talked among themselves, wondering if they might simply ignore the captain's orders to abandon the ship. They were reluctant to leave the hulk as long as she was still on the surface. Hell, she might last another three or four days with all that air down below in the storage tanks, offsetting the inflow of seawater.

Disobeying an officer's orders was not something a sailor did easily or naturally, especially the Old Man's direct commands. But a few men decided to simply refuse to leave, to stay on the *Neosho*. They would have a greater chance at being found, even if they risked eventually facing some kind of military justice. At any rate, the odds were better than trying to do the backstroke all the way to Australia.

That resolve weakened with the first rays of sun on the morning of May 11, their fourth day at the mercy of the trade winds and currents. Dawn revealed just how much more their ship had settled in the water. As sunlight winked through the wave tops, every man could see their tanker was done for. Soon the crew would crowd into the few boats they had and try to make it to some faraway piece of land. Even the lowest-ranking enlisted man understood what their chances were once they enacted that plan. There would be no going back to what was left of the ship. That ragtag fleet of three whale-boats, the motor launch, and a home-crafted raft or two would be much harder to spot from some passing PBY or ship than would the *Neosho*, even if she now had the sea lapping at her railings, port and starboard alike.

Commander Leonard B. Austin continually scanned the horizon, tirelessly looking in all directions for any sign of the missing destroyer and tanker. Just as had been the case for the last two days, there was nothing to see but open sea and puffy clouds building in the distance as the sun began to heat the water below.

At 0630, USS *Henley*'s navigator confirmed they were finally at the last known position anyone had heard reported by the *Neosho*. Though the sea was relatively calm, they saw no oil slick, no floating debris, and no bodies. No sign a massive ship had been bombed and sunk anywhere near this spot.

Now Austin and Commander Smith, the destroyer's skipper, began a series of calculated turns, heading generally in a predetermined direction. They were trying to cover as much territory as they could before night once again caught up with them. They were basing their assumptions on observations of sea state, direction of the currents, and the trade winds, the only clues to which direction and how quickly a sinking tanker or its life rafts might drift away from them.

May 11 would be a crucial day. If they found no trace of the two vessels, they would have to consider whether or not it was worth the risk to keep the lone warship out there in plain sight any longer. Everyone was aware she was a sitting duck on a relatively calm pond with little cover provided by the weather. The PBY aircraft, of course, would be making their regular patrols through the area. If the *Henley* gave up, the flying boats would still keep an eye out for the missing tanker, but that would be about it. There would be no more formal search by a surface ship.

At some point—and a point that would soon arrive—they would have to declare that both ships had sunk with all hands lost. If there were survivors in life rafts or motor launches, they would be at the mercy of the sea and sun.

"Come to course two-nine-zero," Smith ordered, changing

their base course yet again, just as he had been doing all morning. The bow of the ship nudged twenty degrees closer to due west.

All the while, every man they could spare was on deck, in the rigging, on the bridge, looking for any clue they could see that would give them a reason to continue the hunt.

Earlier in the day, the *Henley* had received a cryptic message that had made its way from MacArthur's HQ in Australia all the way through a maze of commands and radio operators to Pearl Harbor, then to Task Force 17, to Nouméa, and finally back to the Coral Sea. The previous day, an Australian Hudson had seen a lone unidentified vessel in roughly the same area where the *Henley* was now operating. The ship the Australians spotted was afloat but appeared to be without power. She could have been experiencing problems, but the Hudson had been marginal on fuel and the aircrew could not stay around long enough to communicate with the vessel. The pilot suggested that word be sent to the Americans. They might want to have someone investigate the status of the unidentified ship.

The coordinates the Hudson had reported put that unknown ship not far at all from where the *Henley* was now located. Finally, Austin's men had some new information to factor into their calculations, a direction in which to hone their search.

Then, at 0930, a young, sharp-eyed sailor let out a whoop. Something different was in the water, dead ahead.

There was no mistaking it. They were passing an oil slick—a big one, the type that could have been left by a replenishment vessel, her storage tanks damaged by enemy bombs.

Latitude 16 degrees 07 minutes south, longitude 156 degrees 15 minutes east.

There was no way to determine how recently the slick had

been left. No way to tie it directly to the *Neosho* or the *Sims*. No way to even know if this might actually be all that was left of the two vessels and their half-a-thousand crew members.

Commander Austin had a gut feeling, though. The report from the Aussie Hudson backed up his intuition.

They were close. Tantalizingly close.

He scanned the skies. If only they had some eyes up there. High in the sky. Eyes that could see much farther than he could from down here, so near sea level.

Faces were grim during John Phillips's midmorning officers' meeting. All final preparations for leaving the *Neosho* were to be completed by 1200 hours. A final sweep of the ship was to be conducted, making certain all classified documents had been destroyed. Officers were to be in their assigned boats by 1400, ready to take on the wounded first. Once they had been made as comfortable as possible, the rest of the crew were to move into the boats to which they had been slotted and begin carrying out their designated duties.

No personal effects or property were to be brought onto the boats. There would be no room. If a sailor had a photo of a girlfriend or wife that fit into a pocket, fine. But nothing else.

For once, the sea was cooperating. The swells were not bad at all. They should be able to tie the boats up and get men into them without as much risk as there might have been during the previous three days, when the waves were far more treacherous. Everyone kept an eye on the sky, though. Ever since the day of the attack, they had been blessed with relatively calm weather. A storm this afternoon could cause problems, especially if it blew up at the wrong time.

Phillips checked the ship's clock as the meeting broke up: 1130. How many times had he looked at that clock's face?

Soon it would be gone, along with the rest of the ship he had so proudly commanded since the previous August, before this damn war had even started. The ship he led had done her job well. She had miraculously dodged the enemy at Pearl Harbor, and had valiantly tried to do the same thing in the middle of the Coral Sea. Yet she continued to persevere, to stay afloat, to keep her crew alive as long as she could.

John Phillips was not the sentimental type, but he would later admit a bit of sadness at the prospect of never seeing his ship again. He likely felt a wave of sorrow when he imagined leaving the *Neosho*, looking back at what little of her remained above the surface of the sea as they sailed away.

As Bill Leu had said almost a year before, she was a big ship, a good ship.

Phillips was making what he probably assumed would be his last notes while on board and serving as captain of the *Neosho* when he heard an excited shout from someone on the other side of the bridge.

"Say again!" he called out.

"Aircraft, sir! About ninety degrees!"

All the men within earshot instinctively whirled around, shielding their eyes from the sun. Sure enough, there was a speck on the horizon, in relief against a towering white cloud.

An airplane, clearly coming in their direction, growing larger by the second.

Ours or theirs? Ours, and they would certainly be saved. Theirs, and it could mean an explosive and fiery end to their harrowing drift.

Leonard Austin could hardly believe his luck. Just as he was wishing—maybe even praying—for an aircraft to come along and help, a plane appeared. Only an hour after discovering the oil slick, a Catalina swooped in, dipping its wings as a greeting. The pilot waved enthusiastically as he flew less than a hundred feet above the *Henley*'s bridge.

With a few quick words on the radio, the destroyer reported the oil patch and its coordinates. They also passed along the news about the Hudson's reported sighting of the distressed ship the previous day, including its position at the time. Then they relayed their hunch that if the *Neosho* still existed, her hulk would most likely be drifting west-northwest from their current position.

The plane's crew confirmed receipt of the helpful information. For the first time in four days, they had firm data, not incorrect positions. The PBY would use the *Henley* as a base point and begin searching immediately.

The plan was for the plane to search as long as it had enough fuel—about midafternoon—before heading back to Nouméa. Meanwhile, they would cover as much open sea as they could manage.

Of the various types of aircraft that could have answered Austin's prayer for eyes in the sky, the PBY Catalina was absolutely the best for the job at hand.

Dubbed "flying boats" because of their ability to land on water as long as it was not too rough, the aircraft had exceptional range, which had already made them invaluable in the Pacific. They were slow but quite effective, especially for patrolling, looking for any enemy assets. They were especially skilled at spotting submarines and picking up downed fliers in the sea. Their wings were mounted well above the fuselage, and the engines sat near the main body of the plane, out of the way of the crew as they scanned the sea below. With large blister windows on each side at the plane's waist, they were well suited for searches and antisubmarine warfare. Catalina crew members had quickly taken to affectionately calling their odd-looking craft "Dumbo," after the hero of the Walt Disney animated movie that had been released in October 1941.

Austin, Smith, and the rest of the men aboard the *Henley* could only hope that the second part of their prayer would be answered: that "Dumbo" would spot the *Neosho* before running low on fuel. With luck, the ship's location would be close enough and the discovery soon enough that the destroyer could do something about it.

It was a PBY! Cheers rang out up and down the length of the *Neosho*.

A Catalina. An American plane. Not a Japanese divebomber.

The sailors made a hurried attempt to get the signal light powered up and to flash some semblance of identification code at the airplane. After four days and with the codebooks destroyed, there was no way for the *Neosho* to know what the response should be, but it did not matter. By the time they had the light ready to go, the PBY had approached, circled twice, dipped its wing several times, and then flown away.

In minutes, he was gone, out of sight.

The weary men on the ship cheered, laughed, slapped each other on their backs, in spite of a sense of déjà vu. The Hudson the previous day had obviously seen them and departed as well. So far, there had been no reason to believe the Aussies had sent help their way.

This was different. It was an American plane. The pilot, too, had clearly seen them, waggling his wings to make sure they knew it, before he flew off into the distance.

Help would come for sure. After four days of hell, they were about to be rescued.

On the bridge, Captain Phillips wrestled with a crucial decision. Though he was elated that another plane had found them, and confident that word of their situation was probably already being radioed back to someone who could do something about it, there remained many uncertainties.

Where was that potential help? How long would it take for their saviors to arrive? Could the crew be rescued before the *Neosho* sank?

Now that their ordeal was seemingly so near finished, would help come in time? Or would they still need to take to the whaleboats as they had planned, before their gallant ship— the one that so far had refused to die—finally gave up with a gurgle and a groan and plunged to the bottom?

PART SEVEN
WIT'S END

They that go down to the sea in ships, that do business in great waters; These see the works of the Lord, and his wonders in the deep.

For he commandeth, and raiseth the stormy wind, which lifteth up the waves thereof.

They mount up to the heaven. They go down again to the depths. Their soul is melted because of trouble. They reel to and fro, and stagger like a drunken man, and are at their wit's end.

Then they cry unto the Lord in their trouble, and he bringeth them out of their distresses. He maketh the storm a calm, so that the waves thereof are still.

Then are they glad because they be quiet; so he bringeth them unto their desired haven.

—Psalms 107:23–30, King James Version

CHAPTER TWENTY-FIVE
EMERG VICTOR

"Ship! Ninety degrees!"

The men on the *Neosho* had been waiting four long, dreary, nerve-racking days to hear those shouted words.

It had been little more than an hour since the PBY had buzzed them, and no one really expected to see help for many more hours. Some knew it could be days yet. Even now, with a ship sighted, some still feared the worst. The vessel steaming their way from where the sea met the sky might be a Japanese cruiser or destroyer, come to see what manner of wreck was floating out in "their" territory.

Yet when it finally drew closer, the silhouette was unmistakable—a U.S. destroyer. A trail of smoke rose from her single stack, confirming she was steaming at top speed to rescue them.

As she chugged even closer, men with binoculars could tell

it was the *Henley*, a ship some of them had already known from Pearl Harbor.

Captain Phillips checked his ship's clock one more time: 1323. He duly noted it.

It was a mere thirty-seven minutes before the time at which they had planned to start putting men in the boats, evacuating the ship. If another hour had passed beyond that self-imposed deadline, the *Henley* would have found the *Neosho* to be nothing more than a ghost ship. Would their rescuers have quickly found their little armada of whaleboats, or would they have drifted too far by then?

"Signalman!" the captain shouted. "Make your light ready."

But the man was already at his station.

"Ready, sir!"

The destroyer was close enough now. Phillips wanted to be sure her skipper knew what she had found and what her condition was.

The signalman began to flash:

HAVE YOU ANY INSTRUCTIONS FOR ME X SHIP IS A TOTAL LOSS X SETTLING GRADU- ALLY X WHAT ARE YOUR ORDERS

• • •

Commander Austin had grown more and more nervous, even as they awaited word from the search plane. The sky was bright, almost clear, and visibility was unusually good for this latitude. Austin knew the smoke from his stack could be seen from a long distance away. Enemy scout planes were certainly in the area, scouring the ocean for the *Yorktown* and the rest of Task Force 17. Lurking beneath the sea were I-boats, Japanese submarines that could be lining the destroyer up in their scopes right then—and the Americans would not know it until it was too late.

Regardless, when the PBY returned to the *Henley* not long after zooming out of sight, she brought good news. The *Neosho* was a mere fifty miles away at that very moment, survivors dotting the deck of the hulk.

Austin asked Smith to order flank speed and not to fool with any sort of erratic deflecting course. He had no way to know what shape the tanker might be in, or the condition of the men who had survived an attack brutal enough to cripple the ship and sink her escort. The *Neosho*'s survivors had spent four days adrift. Some were surely hurt.

The *Neosho* was riding so low in the water that she was difficult to spot at first. But then her stack appeared, the deck below it, and the bridge deck. Her distinctive profile made it easy to identify as an oiler.

"I think she's glad to see us," Commander Smith offered as he watched the ship grow larger in his binoculars. The tanker's light flashed furiously, as if her crew were afraid the destroyer heading her way might still miss them and steam right on past. The flickers confirmed her identity and related that she was sinking. The destroyer's signalman relayed the message to the captain, including Phillips's last words, the request for orders.

"Tell him no orders," Austin snapped. He wanted to quickly get to work, bringing over the survivors. He absolutely did not want to spend any more time than required out here in the open, on a clear day, bobbing stationary next to a dead-in-the-water skeleton. An enemy submarine or torpedo bomber, if either should happen along, could make quick work of both of them.

In minutes, they had already crossed the stern of the tanker. Men on the deck of the destroyer were soon sending lines over to the *Neosho*, preparing to quickly heave to. Bedraggled sailors lined the railing of the drifting ship in an orderly manner, queuing up to begin moving to the few boats available to shuttle them over to the destroyer. Their captain had been organizing and practicing just such an operation for the past two days.

"If that's all of them . . . ," Austin started. He paused. Five hundred men had been aboard the two ships, but he could see not many more than a hundred coming over now. ". . . it shouldn't take us long."

Meanwhile, as if to confirm Austin's observation, Phillips's signalman flashed away, giving details of the number of survivors, how many were wounded, and more.

"Signalman, interrupt him. Tell him to expedite the transfer of the survivors. We need to make short work of this. He'll have time to write that up on the trip to Australia. Hoist the 'emergency' flag!"

As men on both ships worked to pack men from the *Neosho* into one whaleboat after another, lookouts continued to keep glasses on the sky, scanning for planes, while others watched the wave tops, looking for a periscope. Men manned the guns and depth-charge mounts on the destroyer, ready to try to defend themselves.

The PBY pilot, confident he had directed the rescue ship to its objective, was now some distance away. He did not want to attract any undue attention to that spot in the sea. Instead, his crew remained as long as they could, watching for enemy ships or submarines in the area so that they could give the *Henley* the heads-up.

So far, they had seen nothing.

• • •

Back on the *Neosho*, Captain Phillips fully understood Austin's urgency. He had no doubt about the division commander's intent when the EMERG VICTOR flag was hoisted. It was a not-so-gentle prod. The flag meant not only that a ship was in trouble and an emergency had been declared; it also meant, "Get crackin'!"

Nobody was more anxious than Phillips to get his men safely off the oiler and aboard the destroyer. He urged his officers to expedite the operation, just as they had planned to do if the ship had shown signs she was rapidly sinking.

The men took little coaxing. The *Neosho*'s crew made quick work of ushering sailors into the boats and across the short distance to the *Henley*. The previous day's preparation for abandoning the ship paid off. The first boat full of survivors left the *Neosho* at about 1345. At 1415, John Phillips stepped into the last one, leaving his command behind.

After each whaleboat was emptied of its final load of passengers, it was scuttled. They had some trouble sinking the last boat. The damn thing just would not go down, no matter the number of holes they punched in its bottom. Smith finally told them to forget it, to just set the boat adrift. There was no time to tarry.

Later, in his incident report, the ever-fastidious Captain Phillips would explain in detail why the boats and even the provisions and weapons stored in them were ultimately scuttled or lost. They had unwittingly become a potent symbol of their survival. The preparations had kept them too busy to spend time contemplating their fate. Now it was difficult for the *Neosho*'s demanding skipper to simply dispatch the boats and all they stood for into the maw of the sea.

After handshakes and sincere expressions of thanks,

Phillips and Austin moved to a private spot for a quick discussion. Phillips gave a rundown of all the tanker's structural issues, including the latest reports of flooding in the engine room, fire room, and pump rooms. The ship could not be saved, of that he was sure. Even though they needed to move on, they should first attempt to scuttle the vessel.

Phillips knew that neither Leonard Austin nor the United States Navy would have any interest in salvaging the ship, considering her condition, where she was located, and just how dangerous such an effort would be. They had drifted within range of shore-based enemy aircraft, Japanese submarines were known to be operating in the area, and an enemy carrier—the one that had delayed the *Henley*'s appearance on the scene—had been reported to be not that far away. The two seasoned skippers briefly discussed trying to bring over what undamaged equipment they could easily remove from the *Neosho*. That idea was mutually and hastily quashed.

The only logical choice—to prevent the enemy from happening upon the ship and removing sensitive equipment, or to avoid the tanker's possibly becoming a navigation hazard if she continued to float—was for the *Henley* to do what she was designed to do: sink a ship with her torpedoes and guns. Phillips formally asked the captain of the *Henley* to "expedite sinking." It turned out not to be an easy request to fulfill.

At about 1428, the *Henley* first launched a torpedo at the hulk from point-blank range. Those on deck could clearly hear the loud metallic clang when the fish struck nose-first the hull of the ship, right at the waterline.

It did not explode. The torpedo was a dud.

The Navy had experienced no small amount of frustration so far in the war with the reliability of both its Mark 14 torpedoes, used by submarines, and the Mark 15 torpedoes fired by surface ships. The failure rate, estimated to be north of 50 percent, was especially disconcerting to submariners since the trail of foam the impotent torpedoes left in their wake pointed right back at the boat that had launched it. The undamaged enemy ship knew exactly where to start dropping depth charges. Malfunctioning torpedoes were no small source of frustration for surface warships, either, when half their weapons turned out to be duds.

Another torpedo was sent off from the *Henley*'s launch tubes a few minutes later. This one ran true as well, and when it struck the *Neosho* amidships, it exploded with a thundering *waarrrumph*! Seawater and deck plates shot high into the air.

Phillips, Austin, and Smith waited. The tanker still showed no signs of sinking.

"Use the five-inch guns," Austin suggested.

The *Henley* carried four of the big guns on her deck, and the crews opened fire. By actual count, they expended 146 rounds over the next twenty minutes or so before the stubborn tanker finally went down by the stern at 1522, May 11, 1942. It took almost an hour after the first dud torpedo had been launched to finish the tanker.

Bill Leu remembers his shipmates standing along the deck rail of the rescue destroyer, sadly watching the *Neosho* take her second merciless pounding in four days. Some sailors wept openly, without embarrassment, grieving for their lost shipmates as well as their resilient ship.

True to her nature, the *Neosho* obstinately refused to die until the very end.

Exact numbers would vary slightly in the innumerable reports that would follow. The best estimate is that 123 men were hastily carried over from the *Neosho* to the *Henley* that afternoon, including 104 crewmen from the tanker, 14 sailors—including Robert Dicken and Vito Vessia—who survived the sinking of the *Sims*, and 5 more—among them Ed Flaherty—who had come aboard as passengers from the *Yorktown* and the *Portland* on the night of May 6.

Six men from the *Neosho* and one from the *Sims* had died of their wounds while awaiting rescue. They were buried at sea along with others killed in action during the May 7 attack.

Of the 293 men aboard the *Neosho* at the beginning of the first enemy attack on the morning of May 7—including the 5 passengers—only 109 were rescued by the *Henley* on May 11.

As the *Henley* moved away from the debris, bubbles and oil marking the spot where the tenacious tanker had so recently been floating, the rescued men had another reason to soberly reflect. As they all gathered together on the deck of the destroyer and looked at each other's faces, a harsh fact likely hit them for the first time.

They had survived. Barring an enemy plane or submarine, they would make it to safety, and would likely have some leave back home before a new duty assignment. They would be able to visit with family and friends, eat home cooking, and tell tales of what they had gone through out there.

But so many faces were missing. Faces of buddies, shipmates.

The men had been so busy, preparing to abandon ship, or working to keep her afloat, or caring for the wounded that they had had little time left to think about how many of their brothers on the *Neosho* had been lost back on May 7. They likely did not know the exact number.

Their captain did. He had the count right there in his notes. It was a matter of simple subtraction: 158 good men.

Some were dead in unreachable parts of the ship, finally buried at sea with help from the *Henley*'s shells. Some had gone overboard—many in panic—when they thought the order had been given to abandon ship. Others decided for themselves, orders or not, that their best chance for survival was to dive into the flaming sea.

In addition, sailors off the *Sims* were still out there, drifting on a raft.

Lieutenant Bradford, Ensign Hargis, and others who had pulled many of the *Neosho* sailors from the oil-covered water believed at least half had been deposited on or swum to the seven life rafts. Some had been badly burned—from bombs, the suicide bomber crash, or when they dived into the blazing oil on the sea's surface. Their chances of surviving long on the rafts were slim.

The men in the whaleboats had, of course, seen others floating, drowned or dead from their wounds. They were still technically missing, but they would never be rescued or their fate never be designated as anything other than "missing in action, assumed killed in action."

The crew of the *Henley* confirmed that they had seen no rafts during all their zigzag searching, nor had they heard of the recovery by any other vessels of any men on rafts. If eighty or ninety or a hundred men were still out there, they would be dangerously close to death by now. They had been meandering for four days without water, food, medicine, or shelter.

Despite the critical condition of several of the men rescued by the *Henley*, and no matter Commander Austin's desire to leave the area and head toward Brisbane as soon as they could, everyone knew they had to at least make an attempt to find those men who might still be alive on rafts.

Austin ordered a winding, zigzag course that would follow in reverse the same path the *Neosho* had drifted since May 7, as verified by Tom Brown's frequently entered determinations of their positions.

Meanwhile, the men who had been brought over from the oiler tried not to think about the fate of their missing shipmates. For the first time since May 7, though, the surviving officers and crew members from the *Neosho* and the *Sims* actually had time to think about other things.

They could now contemplate the fact that they had somehow survived this awful affair even as their friends remained immersed in the horror of it all, drifting aimlessly along out there in their own special, unimaginable hell.

CHAPTER TWENTY-SIX
Praise and Dereliction

The sea obstinately refused to yield any clues for the searchers. One hundred fifty-four enlisted men and four officers had leaped into the burning sea around the *Neosho* on May 7. Many had ended up on the life rafts, but so far, there was no sign of any of them—nor of survivors from the *Sims*—as the USS *Henley* methodically crisscrossed the area. Austin employed established procedures for searching for men in the water, maximizing the area they covered in minimal time, but no traces were found. Not an empty life belt. Not a raft. Not a body. More than half the men of the *Neosho* had seemingly been swallowed up by Jonah's whale. The murky sea jealously held its secrets.

All the while, the destroyer's crew kept searching, with one eye on the sea and the other on the sky. The fact that there had been no trace so far of an enemy presence meant only that it would likely be less time before there was.

The *Henley*'s medical officer and the pharmacist's mates

from both ships worked over the severely wounded. On May 13, while the exasperating search droned on, two of the sickest men died. One was a sailor off the *Sims*. The other was Chief Watertender Oscar Peterson, the brave sailor who was severely burned as he crawled his way to a series of steam valves and miraculously managed to close them, saving countless lives. Both men were buried at sea, and finally a bugled version of taps and a rifle salute could honor the dead.

Meanwhile, another drama was playing out aboard USS *Henley*, mostly in the cabin to which John Spinning Phillips had been assigned. As the *Neosho* skipper later wrote, he had decided not to reprimand several of his officers as long as he and any of his crew remained in jeopardy. He felt he had good reason to admonish them, but there would be opportunity for that later.

Phillips was convinced that the decision to put off their admonishment had been the proper one. Even those he was certain had performed the most poorly while under attack had ultimately proved to be of great help during their four-day ordeal while adrift. Still, as captain of the ship, Phillips wanted to determine why discipline had broken down under his command, why certain officers had failed, why over half his crew had abandoned ship without a specific order to do so—and why most of those men in the latter group might yet pay for that action with their lives.

Phillips began to prepare his full incident report even as the search for castaways continued, wanting to have it well under way before they arrived in Australia and his superiors began asking pointed questions. First, he made certain to specifically commend and praise in his report several crew members whose actions had been especially noteworthy.

About Francis Firth, his executive officer, Phillips wrote,

"He was [a] heroic example of unselfishness, insisting upon treatment of all other injured personnel first. Despite his burned condition, he continued to offer his services in the trying days subsequent to May 7, 1942. His conduct was considered extraordinarily courageous and outstanding."

Lieutenant Commander Thomas Brown, the gunnery officer, kept his crews firing at their attackers as wave after wave of enemy airplanes dived on them before he became acting XO when Firth was injured. He, too, was irreplaceable during the horrible days before their rescue. "[Brown] was invaluable in making suggestions for the improvement of conditions on board, and in the final preparations for abandoning ship," the captain wrote.

Also specifically commended were Machinist's Mate Harold Bratt, who used good judgment by trying to keep his men in the fire room while the compartment above was filled with lethal steam, and Machinist's Mate Wayne Simmons, who stayed at a critical feed pump throttle when most men would have run for their lives.

In addition, Pharmacist's Mates Robert W. Hoag and William J. Ward were mentioned, as was Oscar Peterson, the chief watertender. Phillips did not yet know of the heroic efforts in the water of another Pharmacist's Mate Robert Tucker.

In all, about three dozen crew members were specifically recommended for commendation and, in some cases, promotion. That list ranged in rank and seniority from a mess attendant to the ship's executive officer.

As the vexing search continued for his missing crewmen—men who might have been saved shortly after the attack had rescuers not been looking in the wrong area, based on incorrect coordinates—Phillips called for his navigator, Navy Reserve Lieutenant Henry Bradford, to come to his cabin.

The incorrect plotting was the least of Bradford's sins, as the captain saw them. The calculations should have been checked several times, Phillips told Bradford. But the captain was truly angered at Bradford for leaving the bridge during the attack without orders. While Bradford was supposed to be acting as officer of the deck, he instead dived overboard, despite knowing no order to abandon ship had been issued. What's more, Bradford had done little to help the other men in the water once he had climbed into and taken command of one of two available whaleboats, Phillips claimed. Later, before his report was submitted, Phillips had the opportunity to read through Bradford's written comments on all the events for which he had been chastised. The captain would eventually apologize for his comments about what Bradford did once he was in the water. He had actually performed admirably there in view of the circumstances, Phillips decided. But the captain added, "[I] in no way condoned Lieutenant Bradford's dereliction of duty as outlined . . ."

Two other Navy Reserve officers, Lieutenant Bill Driscoll and Ensign Robert Hargis, were reprimanded, first verbally while still aboard the *Henley* and then in writing in the captain's final report.

Driscoll, serving as the communications officer, was not diligent enough in making sure that contact reports and correct positions were continually being sent out during the attack. "He did not display the qualities of a leader, and did not inspire courage or confidence in those who came in contact with him," Phillips pointedly wrote for the record.

Hargis, as the assistant gunnery officer, stood accused of leaving his assigned position overseeing his gun crews, then not staying at his assigned station on life raft number four during the height of the bombing. Instead, he attempted to lower the whaleboat. He had, according to reports, made no effort to try to keep panicked sailors from throwing life rafts over the side and jumping in after them.

In his verbal reprimand of Hargis, the captain also accused him of disobeying a direct order to tow the life rafts back to the ship. Phillips would later back off on the last charge. The sea had simply been too rough at the time, there were reports of sharks, and oil on the surface of the water around the tanker was still burning vigorously. Many men might have drowned or been seriously injured or burned if he had tried to bring them in as originally instructed.

Eventually, the three chastised officers would seek a formal investigation in an attempt to remove the captain's comments from their records and allow them to tell their side of the story. All three had come to active duty from the Navy Reserve. Many reservists had been called to action when the war broke out, leading to clashes between them and experienced naval line officers. Some doubts about competence, experience, and training were justified. Most were not. The reality was that the Navy needed all the help they could get to fight the Japanese. Those men who had trained and remained ready for call-up contributed mightily, especially in the war's early days.

The three officers maintained—as did some of the enlisted men who were never asked to speak on the record—that they had clearly heard a command to abandon ship and were merely following orders. Not "Prepare to abandon ship." "Abandon ship." That was the primary reason why the reserve officers wanted a complete investigation into those few hours of chaos on the tanker. They felt they had obeyed the captain's orders to get off a doomed vessel, just as their men had. It was not to be, though.

Phillips and his superiors ultimately decided that pressing the point against these three men would not bring back anyone killed in action on either ship. A court-martial would not refloat the *Neosho* or the *Sims*. Their captain noted in his report that "all [three officers] conducted themselves in a creditable manner in the face of the enemy at Pearl Harbor on December 7, 1941, and . . . were subjected to a terrific and continuous attack by dive-bombers, with concurrent shock and numbing of faculties." The entire matter of dereliction of duty and disobeying direct orders was eventually dropped.

Almost three days after locating the *Neosho* and rescuing her remaining crew, and after spending every hour of those three days searching for other survivors from the two ships, Commander Austin ultimately directed the *Henley* to break off the hunt and proceed at top speed to Brisbane.

Austin was not completely giving up. He knew that another destroyer, a sister to the *Henley* and a member of Austin's division, USS *Helm* (DD-388), had already left Nouméa and was steaming toward the spot where any survivors might still be found.

There were good reasons for changing horses. Paramount was that several survivors needed more medical attention than could be provided aboard the destroyer. Also, Commander Austin had other pressing business to attend to.

Soon he and his destroyers would join seventy other warships in the invasion force that would put 16,000 Marines ashore at a little island named Guadalcanal, along with some other nearby hot spots. Planning for that operation was well under way in mid-May of 1942.

The *Henley* still searched for signs of the missing men even as they made for Australia. They stopped and examined an oil drum that had been rigged as a raft, but nobody was on it. Captain Phillips did not believe it was anything that came off his ship, anyway.

Then, not long after they had turned toward land and night had fallen, a sailor on deck was certain he heard someone shouting, calling plaintively from some distance out in the water.

Smith circled back to the area. With the ship stopped, they listened intently, peering into the night, burning more lights than was prudent. They tried desperately to determine if it really had been someone hailing them from a raft.

One sailor suggested sheepishly that the sound the man heard was not a human cry at all. They had been working on an auxiliary water pump, which had screeched and groaned. That was almost certainly what the man had heard.

The *Henley*'s crew doused the lights, pointed the destroyer's bow back to the west, and steamed on for Brisbane.

In the wake of any incident resulting in such heavy loss of vessels and men, a great deal of effort is always made by the Navy to determine precisely what happened. In the case of the *Neosho*, the primary source for this detail was, of course, Captain Phillips and his surviving officers.

The Navy would have no such testimony when it came to USS *Sims*. Only the enlisted men who made it into the leaking whaleboat and onto the hulk of the oiler would be able to tell their stories. Once the *Sims* survivors arrived in Australia, the seriously injured, including John Verton, were taken away to a hospital. Their accounts would have to wait.

Vito Vessia and Robert Dicken were debriefed immediately.

"They interviewed us in singles," Vessia later related. "It appeared that none of them were pleased at the lack of reasoning as to why none of the ship's officers survived."

Vessia began his testimony by describing his captain's odd behavior after the near miss at 0900 the morning of May 7, which some reported threw Hyman to the deck and caused a head injury. It was Vessia's opinion, and that of other members of the deck crew of the destroyer, that the captain should have ordered them to abandon ship much sooner. Had he done so, in Vessia's view, many more lives could have been saved. They were also convinced that the captain was not following the evasive course that was always used when they were operating in enemy waters, possibly due to that bump on the head.

The seaman noted that his interviewers did not seem to want to hear too many of his thoughts or explanations. That was especially true after he mentioned the course in which they were steaming at the time of the subsequent attacks.

On the other hand, Robert Dicken's account would eventually become the official incident report of the action that day. As we have seen, it varies somewhat from the observations of John Verton and Vito Vessia.

"I have questioned *Sims* survivors for more data but no further information [is] available," Dicken wrote in the last line of his report, which listed the "Subject" as "Personal observations of SIMS #409 disaster."

An interesting bullet point was included when the report on the loss of the *Sims* from the headquarters of Admiral Nimitz was sent to the secretary of the Navy in July 1942: "Apparently only four dive-bombers attacked the *Sims*, yet three of them made hits. This percentage of hits on a high speed maneuvering ship, especially on a destroyer, is extraordinary and has few if any parallels in this war."

The report went on to speculate that the remarkable success of the Japanese pilots might have been due to their "pressing the attack home to a very low altitude without regard for their own safety."

Or could it have been, as Vessia and others vigorously maintained for the rest of their days, that the *Sims* had not actually been taking evasive measures at the time?

Certainly, details and observations made during such an occurrence can be different when coming from various viewpoints. It should be noted as well that the men spent the four days following the few minutes of intense action under extreme conditions, uncertain if they would survive. One should not be surprised or critical when versions of stories are not identical.

John Verton, his digestive system nearly ripped from his body by an explosion as his ship went down while he treaded water nearby, spent the next month after his rescue recovering in a hospital in Australia. No representative from the U.S. Navy ever spoke with him about the incident, nor did anyone ever officially seek his testimony about what happened on the morning of May 7, 1942. Had they done so, his account would have been identical to those of Vessia and the others.

It would not be until the middle of June before Verton's family received word that he had survived the sinking of his ship and was still recovering from his injuries.

Anytime he told the tale of his ordeal and amazing survival, Verton would always give credit to his friend, Vito Vessia, who, while manning the tiller of a leaky little whaleboat, saved his shipmate's life.

CHAPTER TWENTY-SEVEN
The "Hundred Hour Rule"

As was the *Neosho,* the *Monaghan,* the *Henley* and the *Sims,* the destroyer USS *Helm* was at Pearl Harbor when the Japanese attacked. And like the other destroyers, her crew eventually found themselves involved in the fate of the oiler.

On December 7, the *Helm,* under the command of Lieutenant Commander C. E. "Blackie" Carroll, had just pulled into West Loch Channel to perform a rather mundane chore—getting the iron ship's acquired magnetic signature degaussed by the de-perming buoys there. They used high-amperage electric current pulsing through copper wire to degauss, or erase, the ship's magnetism so that compasses and other sensitive gear would work properly, and so that the ship would not attract magnetic mines so easily. That task put the destroyer over a mile from Battleship Row that morning and likely saved the ship from the fate of several of her sister tin cans. The *Helm* had two of her whaleboats, filled with crew members, in the water when men on the destroyer's deck spotted the first enemy airplane zooming down in a shallow dive over Ford Island.

With her guns blazing, the *Helm* took off, leaving the two boatloads of men behind at West Loch. In case of an attack, her designated position was the entrance to the harbor. As she hurried that way, her guns provided covering fire to protect the battleships, the obvious primary targets of the sneak attack. After passing the gate vessel at the harbor mouth, crewmen spotted the conning tower of a small two-man submarine just outside the main ship channel. Carroll ordered the gunnery crew to open fire on this new target, chasing it off a ledge and into deep water.

The submarine got snagged there. One Japanese crewman drowned, while the other escaped the submersible vessel and made it to the beach, where he became the first prisoner of war of the United States in World War II.

There was another interesting note to the *Helm*'s action at Pearl Harbor. Early that morning, assuming it would be another routine day, "Blackie" Carroll brought with him to work his thirteen-year-old son, Chester Todd Carroll. The boy had no idea he would be an eyewitness to history that day. Nor did his father.

When the dive-bombers appeared so unexpectedly, there was no way to get the boy ashore. Only later, after the storm had calmed, could Carroll evacuate his son from the warship—via boatswain's chair—and send him home to his mother. Carroll and his boy were the only known father/son shipmates present during the Pearl Harbor attack. Young Chet later served in the Navy during the Korean War.

On May 13, 1942, as he took his ship out of Nouméa in New Caledonia, Blackie Carroll was just as determined as his division commander, Leonard Austin, had been to get to his latest task of racing to the search area and locating any survivors of the *Neosho* and the *Sims*. He also was just as aware as his boss that this was dangerous territory. Any hunt had to be a mix of speed and caution.

The *Helm* had just completed another eerily similar rescue mission only a week before. On May 5, two Japanese torpedoes from the submarine I-21 struck a Liberty ship (a merchant vessel operating with the Navy), the SS *John Adams*, off New Caledonia. She was carrying two thousand tons of gasoline from Nouméa to Australia, and the resulting explosions and fire were horrendous. Five Navy gunners aboard died. Incredibly, the remainder of the crew, forty-five men, escaped the fiery vessel. *Helm* picked up thirteen of them from their life rafts on the morning of May 9. All the remaining survivors were rescued by other ships. The *John Adams* was the first Liberty ship lost during the war.

Carroll and the crew of the *Helm* could only hope this search turned out as well.

"This vessel departed Noumea at 1922 GCT, 13 May, 1942 and proceeded towards the designated search area at speed of advance 13.5 knots," Carroll later wrote in his action report. "Search was commenced at 1950 GCT, 15 May, 1942, speed 20 knots, zigzagging; speed of advance 19 knots."

Soon this latest search vessel was deeply involved in its own monotonous hunt, with absolutely nothing to show for its risk and trouble. With no way to know if the rafts had drifted in the same direction and speed as the half-sunken oiler, Carroll had to assume they had, and began searching there, ranging out in the general direction of where the wind and current might have pushed them.

After a full day, the *Helm* and her crew had found nothing. They knew that anyone on those Carley rafts would be in serious condition by now if they were still miraculously holding on to life.

Rescuers looking for survivors at sea observed the informal "hundred hour rule." Anyone without drinkable water for a hundred hours—just over four days—would have little chance of surviving, even in a moderate climate. Hopefully, the survivors had drifted through rain showers, captured enough water to sustain them, found seaweed to eat, or managed to catch fish or turtles. That was the only way others similarly adrift for longer periods than that had managed to make it.

Even so, the Coral Sea certainly did not have a moderate climate. Out here, in this heat and humidity, with the sun's rays so direct and unrelenting this close to the equator, it would be amazing if anyone was still alive. Those aboard the *Helm* probably dreaded what they might find if they ever did locate one of the rafts.

Then, on the second day of their search, they did just that.

"At 0325 GCT, 16 May, sighted the broken half of a Carley life raft, floating a few feet below the surface."

It was astonishing that anyone even spotted the raft, considering it was below the water and was almost the same color. They slowed, took a look, and then hooked the wrecked raft and tugged it closer. They found no body, no indication that it had ever been occupied.

There was also no way to tell if it had come from the *Neosho* or the *Sims*. Still, it was a first positive sign. Maybe the others were nearby. Maybe they were still afloat. Maybe they held some living sailors. Maybe this was not the only one still floating after all the others had sunk.

Carroll made a note of their find and they promptly resumed the search with renewed vigor.

• • •

Jack Rolston had lost all sense of time. He had no idea how long it had been since they obeyed orders to abandon ship before the *Neosho* followed their escort to the bottom. How long it had been since they had lashed several rafts together and taken a count. How many hours had gone by since the first man had died. How long it had been since the last one had passed away.

There had been sixty-eight men on the group of rafts that had been lashed together. That did not count the men on other rafts who had opted to not tie up with Rolston, Hough, Bright, Smith, and the rest of the "68." Now, however long ago that had been, the number had dwindled to just four. Four men left of the sixty-eight.

There had been talk early on, while they still had some strength and numbers, about using their paddles and trying to navigate toward the southeast, toward New Caledonia and Nouméa. Yet with no navigational gear, they would have to rely on the sun to set a course, and could easily drift right past the islands and into the South Pacific. Someone else argued that they should try to paddle to Australia, to the west, where they would be more likely to hit land.

But another man pointed out that the Australian coast was better than five hundred miles over rough waves and through enemy waters. It would be impossible to try to go anywhere else but where the seas wanted to take them. The better plan would be to rest, conserve their energy, and wait for rescue in the area where somebody would certainly be searching for them.

So they had done nothing but drift. They allowed the currents and trade winds to carry them wherever they so desired.

On the second day, rumors spread that some men had

managed to snatch canteens of water before they dived off the ship. A few more had grabbed waterproof knapsacks of food. When confronted, though, the guilty men admitted they had already drunk what they had, that they had already eaten the food in the dark of night, when no one could see them.

It was all gone. Every drop. Every crumb.

Anger flared among the group that the men had not shared the precious water, had not allowed them to ration it and make it go farther. But no one had the strength or will to fight about it.

Besides, rescuers would be there before they died of thirst. How long did that take? Men told tales of survivors living for weeks on rafts. Did they have water onboard? Did it rain? However they did it, that was proof that it was possible, something to keep them hoping.

Four or five days were about it, someone else offered. That quieted the discussion for a bit. Even so, it was only the first day. Or was it the second? Help would come before they died of thirst. Before four or five days had passed.

Then, in desperation, the first man drank seawater. When he did not immediately start frothing at the mouth, several more slaked their thirst with the briny mix.

The sky remained clear. Where were the tropical showers they had come to expect in this part of the world? The sun's rays were terrible, piercing their skin like hot needles.

Twice they saw aircraft in the sky above them. They waved, but without flares to fire, smoke to release, or flags to wave, the aircraft were too high, too far away, to make out the rafts in an expansive sea so far below them.

When the one raft began to sink and they brought those men over, they tried to pull it out of the water and use it for a shade for the more seriously wounded among them. Somehow it got away from them and drifted away, most of it underwater. No one had the muscle power anymore to paddle out to the damned thing, to bring it back and pull it up out of the sea. It was just too heavy, filled with seawater.

Men became frenzied, hallucinating, laughing crazily, vomiting, and swooning, their eyes rolling back in their heads as they writhed in violent seizures. They were the ones who drank ocean water. Some suddenly stood and jumped into the sea, trying to catch imagined grouper or flounder, or to swim out to meet a loved one who called and beckoned to them from the heat haze.

They soon drowned, of course. Nobody could reach them. Nobody had the strength to swim out and try to wrestle back a delirious man.

Then others, the wounded first and finally the ones who had been in relatively good shape when they were pulled into the raft, began to die. Some went peacefully, quietly fading away. Others died horribly, kicking, screaming, begging for life.

Too emaciated to continue to live, Grove Hough quietly took his last breath, lying between Rolston and Ken Bright. The two men were too dehydrated to conjure up any tears. They summoned enough of their precious strength to pull Grove over the lip of the raft and slide him gently into the sea. Using what mental faculties they could muster, they recited a verse or two from the Bible as their friend slowly drifted away, already attracting the attention of hungry sea life.

Rolston wanted to cry. He had become hardened to watching men die around him, but this one was different. Grove was his friend. Jackie lay back in what was now becoming a roomy raft and closed his eyes, imagining soda pop, beer, and ice water. He figured Ken was doing the same. His lone remaining friend was just as tired and withered as he was, lacking the strength to grieve.

Only four were left. Rolston, Bright, William Smith, and Seaman Second Class Thaddeus Tunnel.

In the relative cool of the evening, they decided to release the other rafts. They were filling with water and could drag them down. They hung on to only one, somehow managing to pull it over their heads to give them some shelter from the ruthless sun.

Weakly, they discussed what they would do when they sighted a ship or plane. None of them was certain he could invoke enough energy even to stand, much less jump and wave to attract attention. They knew it would be difficult for anyone to see the raft by itself, that it would dramatically help their chances if someone could just stand up.

"Maybe I can get to my feet," Smith finally offered. "I could use the paddle like a crutch. You fellows can help balance me. Then they'll see us. We'll be okay."

So that was the plan. Now all they needed was for a ship to appear, and to be close enough that the four skeletons on the raft could see it. Close enough also so that the men on the ship could discern out there in the vastness of the sea one ragged, propped-up scarecrow, waving weakly at them before he collapsed back to the slatted floor of his wretched little raft. See them before they passed right on by and continued the search somewhere else.

"At 0357 GCT, 16 May, sighted an empty NEOSHO whaleboat. This boat, which was full of water, had been rigged for sailing. The boat was sunk by ramming. At 0740 GCT discontinued search for the day due to darkness."

It was only about a half hour after spotting the half-sunken Carley raft when someone saw the drifting boat. Blackie Carroll assumed this was one of the motorized whaleboats that had been used to move men off the *Neosho* and over to the *Henley* five days before. That meant they were in the vicinity of where the oiler's crew had been rescued and the big ship had been blasted with shells until she finally sank.

But that also put the *Helm* in roughly the same area where her sister destroyer had already searched at length for men on rafts. Now, what made anyone think they would have any more luck than Austin, Smith, and the *Henley* had?

No matter. It would be twelve hours before they would have enough light to resume the search. They would give it one more day, even though the fear was growing that no one could have survived out here this long, or that the rafts had sunk and would never be found. After another day, the USS *Helm* had other business to attend to elsewhere.

Carroll ordered his crew to ram the half-sunken whaleboat and send it to the bottom, leaving, so far as they knew, no further trace of USS *Sims* or USS *Neosho*.

CHAPTER TWENTY-EIGHT
The Scarecrow on the Surface of the Sea

Sometime during the night, the raft that had so far kept them from drowning began taking on water. There was little worry that it might sink, as these rafts were very buoyant, but in their gaunt condition, the four men soon gave in to violent shivers, which robbed them of any strength they had left. They knew they had to somehow get out of the water and dried off.

Rolston and Smith, with what modicum of energy they had left, managed to work the second raft—the one they had used for shade for the last day or so—beneath all four of them, on top of the leaking raft. They struggled to drag Bright and Tunnel out of the water and onto the second raft. They could finally dry out their clothing and hopefully stop trembling for a while, yet now they would be at the mercy of the harsh sun once it came up in the morning.

Maybe, when it got hot, they could crawl back between the rafts without slipping into the sea and drowning. Maybe it would finally be a cloudy, rainy day, and bucketfuls of fresh, potable water would fall from the sky.

Maybe that rescue ship they had been waiting for would dramatically appear on the horizon and they could prop up Smith with the paddle and signal for help.

"At 2000 GCT, 16 May, resumed search."*

As had the *Monaghan* and the *Henley*, the crew of the *Helm* knew they would soon have to break off the search. This day, they decided, would be their last, whether they found survivors or not.

Lieutenant Commander Blackie Carroll did not give up easily. He had served in the U.S. Army in World War I, and then entered the U.S. Naval Academy in Annapolis, graduating as an ensign in the Navy in 1924. He then served on a gunboat on the Yangtze River in China and aboard a captured Spanish-American War cruiser, all before coming to destroyers in 1936. The *Helm* was his first command.

He had refused to allow his ship to be bottled up in West Loch or even in Pearl Harbor when the enemy attacked on December 7. Fighting the entire way across the harbor, the *Helm* became the first ship to exit into the Pacific during the mayhem of that awful morning.

Still, his orders this day in May, more than five months later, were clear. His intuition and experience backed them up, even if his heart and soul did not. There was little chance they would find any American sailors out here, and a considerable chance the Japanese would find the destroyer, all alone and without likelihood of help showing up. If that was a single

---

* Note that Carroll and Helm used Greenwich Coordinated Time in making notes and compiling the eventual incident report. The designation "2000" would have been about sunrise on May 16 in the Coral Sea.

plane or even a small contingent, the *Helm* had a decent chance of evading their bombs and torpedoes and fighting them off. If it was a bigger group, the rescuer might be in need of rescue.

Almost two hours passed after it became light enough to resume the search. Then the quiet was shattered when a man on deck spotted something out there among the whitecaps.

"At 2145 GCT sighted a life raft with men on it. This raft was sighted by the rangefinder operator during a sweep of the horizon with the director."

Afterward everyone would agree—if William Smith had not been standing, using the boat paddle as a crutch, propped up like a scarecrow, partially supported by Jack Rolston lying beneath him, the rangefinder operator on the *Helm* would likely have never seen them and their pitiful, stacked-up rafts.

It still took the destroyer a few minutes to reach them, lower a boat, and row out to where the sad-looking men waited patiently. None of them was able to climb into the whaleboat; all had to be carried over.

"At 2210 lowered a boat, towed the raft alongside, and took aboard the . . . men," Carroll later wrote. "These men were all in critical condition due to exposure, and were placed in the care of the Medical Officer."

Only two of the haggard survivors were lucid enough to talk, and only after they had guzzled down some water. Smith and Rolston were then able to answer the obvious questions.

Yes, they were survivors off the *Neosho*, the last of a group of sixty-eight men who had tied a group of rafts together and floated since May 7. Carroll wanted to know if there might be other rafts out there close, also filled with men similarly at death's door. The two survivors were not sure. There had been another raft or two from the *Neosho*, they knew, and rumors of one from the *Sims* that had a few men on it. But they had not seen anyone else since the first night. No other rafts.

Locating these four men and hearing from them that there had been other rafts were enough to keep Carroll and his destroyer looking. They continued the organized search to the west of the oiler's last known position, assuming any other rafts would have floated roughly the same distance and in the same direction as this one had.

They found nothing.

Ken Bright died that night. He was buried at sea the next morning. Jackie, still fighting for his own life, did not even have a chance to tell him good-bye. All three of his Missouri friends were now gone, committed to a watery grave.

Two hours after Bright passed away, Lieutenant Commander Carroll ended the search and immediately set a course for Brisbane. The other three men needed more medical attention than he could offer on his ship, and he knew his luck in avoiding the Japanese could be running thin.

As they steamed for Australia, Carroll learned more about the ordeal these three men had undergone. He was especially impressed with the actions of Seaman Smith, and included a mention in his otherwise succinct action report:

"SMITH, W.A., Sea. 2c, deserves special mention and great credit for his courage and spirit at the time of the rescue. The men on the raft sighted the ship before they themselves were sighted. Although greatly weakened by exposure, being even too weak to wave anything, SMITH got himself to a standing position in order that the raft might be more readily sighted, and remained thus, propped up with an oar, until taken off. It was his standing figure which first caught the attention of the man searching through the rangefinder. It is the opinion of the Commanding Officer, based on necessarily brief observation of, and conversation with, the survivors, that SMITH assumed the leadership of the group and by his courage and will to live materially contributed to the survival of the other men."

Thaddeus Tunnel would soon pass away in a hospital in Brisbane. Jack Rolston and William Smith both lived, eventually heading home for leave and then on to other duty in the Navy.

At this point in the war, the tracking of men killed or missing in action and the notification of next of kin were spotty. Sometimes this was for security reasons. Other times it was simply the system catching up with a rapidly changing and nearly overwhelming military bureaucracy. Sometimes families received bad news quickly. Other times, men had died or been declared missing for weeks or months before notification was given.

Jack Rolston's case was typical. Though he was in a hospital in Brisbane, slowly recovering from the nine-day nightmare, his family still had no idea of his whereabouts or condition, or even that anything had happened to his ship.

Their last letter from him had come on April 3, five days after his eighteenth birthday, a couple of weeks before the *Neosho* joined Task Force 17, and four days short of a month before the day the ship was attacked. The envelope, as usual, bore no mark that might indicate from where it had been mailed. In the letter, Jackie wrote about how good the food was on his ship and included a photo to prove that the Navy was fattening him up. It showed a young, smiling sailor proudly wearing his dress white uniform.

Rolston's father and bedridden mother next heard word of their son in a terse telegram dated June 13, 1942, almost a month after their boy had been pulled from the raft in the Coral Sea. It came from Rear Admiral Randall Jacobs, chief of the Bureau of Naval Personnel.

"The navy department deeply regrets to inform you that your Son Jackson Rolston Jr seaman second class USN is missing following action in the performance of his duty and in the service of his country. The department appreciates your great anxiety and will furnish you further information promptly when received."

One can only imagine the agony this news caused his parents. Jack was an only child. His mother was often very ill and spent most of her time in bed. Now all they knew was that their teenage son was missing out there in the midst of a brutal war. They also likely knew such a pronouncement usually meant he was dead but his body had not yet been located. If he was lost at sea, that was almost certainly the case.

Though they checked newspapers and listened to radio broadcasts, they discovered no clues about where he might have been when he was lost. Simply too much action was reported in too many exotically named places from the Coral Sea to Midway. There was also no mention of the ship he was on, USS *Neosho*.

Then, a few days after the telegram came, news stories began to appear in papers around the country about the *Neosho* and her loss in the Coral Sea. An Associated Press dispatch that ran in the Kansas City papers on June 15 told of the attack on the tanker and USS *Sims*, noting that the destroyer was sunk immediately and the *Neosho* continued to stay afloat due to her large fuel storage tanks—long enough for her crew members to be rescued, the reporter added.

The story's lead, though, was about how the enemy had not been able to sink the ship, even with three devastating attacks. The headlines read: "NEOSHO Sunk by US Warship," "Sailors Report Japs Could Not Down the American Tanker," and "Warship's 'Mercy Shot' Finishes the War-Torn Supply Craft."

Survivors of both ships were taken to Brisbane, the article reported, and reached the port the very day the story was filed, June 15. (We know that was not the case. The bulk of them had actually reached Australia a month before.) The article did add a note that one local boy had been killed in the attack: Noel Craven, the seventeen-year-old son of Mr. and Mrs. Leroy Craven of East Eighth Street in Smithville, "the first navy volunteer here after Pearl Harbor."

The Rolstons were now aware that Jackie's ship had been sunk in a vicious attack by the enemy, that one of his friends had died, and that their boy was, as far as they knew, still missing. Their only hope came from the fact that their son was not listed in the local versions of the news stories as being a casualty.

Ten days after the telegram and a week after the discouraging newspaper account, they checked the mailbox to find another letter, the envelope addressed in a familiar hand. Again, the outside bore no indication of its mailing location or even the date it was sent. It could easily have been mailed before their boy became "missing following action."

The letter, though, brought glorious news.

Jackie told them he had survived the sinking, that he was in a hospital, and that he was doing okay, recovering from what he described as back injuries. That was it. No mention of witnessing his friend's death on the ship, of watching helplessly as two other friends slipped away, or of the desperate days on a drifting raft. There was not even a hint of where the hospital in which he was recuperating was located.

But what he told them was plenty enough for his parents—Jackie was alive. The letter was dated June 17, 1942.

How the local paper heard about the Rolstons' great news is unknown, but a few days later a large photo was featured of a smiling Jackie in his uniform from before his ordeal, and a short story about the happy parents, including their elation at the receipt of the letter from their son. The headline read, "Tears of Sorrow Now Turn to Tears of Joy."

War stories with happy endings were hard to come by. The newspaper played it to the hilt.

At about the same time Rolston's parents received the missing-in-action telegram, another message was delivered to Mrs. Flossie Hough in nearby Rich Hill, Missouri. It was the same report: the Navy regretted to inform her that her son, Grover Hough, was missing in action, but they promised to send her any updates when available. There would be only one more update, though, and it would come months later, well after she knew Grove's fate. The death of her boy was confirmed.

On July 24, a full month after receiving the wonderful letter from Jackie, the Rolstons received a second telegram from Rear Admiral Jacobs. As with the telegram to Flossie Hough, this one also shared news that a family already knew. It was welcomed gloriously anyway, and especially for its detail. For the first time they knew how to contact their boy.

"The Navy department is pleased to inform you that your son Jackson Rolston Jr seaman second class USN previously reported as missing is now known to be a survivor. Following the sinking of the USS Neosho he was rescued and transferred to the Naval hospital Pearl Harbor Hawaii. You may write to him in care of that hospital via the Post Master San Francisco.

The Navy Department regrets the anxiety caused you by the previous message and shares with you the joy you must feel upon hearing of your Sons [sic] good fortune."

Over the next weeks, the happy parents exchanged several letters with Jack. Then he told them he would be released from the hospital soon and would have some leave time, enough to come home for a few days. Jackie would be headed to Missouri by train and later gave them the day and time he would most likely arrive at the Kansas City terminal.

The family—Mr. and Mrs. Rolston, along with both sets of grandparents—arrived at the station early, several hours before Jackie was supposed to come home, just in case the train was running ahead of schedule. Jack Sr. lifted his ill wife from their car and carried her in his arms into the terminal. There they staked out a comfortable spot from which they could see the tracks, waiting to catch the first glimpse of Jackie when he stepped off the train. They anxiously watched the list of arrivals and departures, checking for delays as times were updated.

His train came in right on schedule, but their son was not aboard.

More trains from the West Coast pulled in throughout the rest of the day and into the early evening, yet there was still no sign of Jackie.

Mrs. Rolston grew more tired as the day wore on. So did Jackie's grandparents, who had kept watch with them all day long. Jack Sr. finally sent them home to wait. He again lifted up his frail wife and carried her back to their car.

The fretful father waited and waited, maintaining a continuous vigil, sleeping on a bench in the terminal, but making sure he was awake anytime an eastbound train rolled in.

Then, on Saturday night, after more than fifty hours, Jack Rolston Sr. looked up to see a slender, pale young sailor walking his way across the terminal. It was Jackie.

After hugs and handshakes, the boy apologized profusely. He simply had no idea his dad would be waiting there for him all that time. He had taken a last-minute detour to visit some shipmates who had also survived the sinking and were on leave down in San Diego. He actually ended up hitchhiking most of the way to Missouri.

One newspaper article of young Rolston's return was headlined, "Jackie Rolston, Once Lost at Sea, Returns Home," and gave a brief but highly inaccurate account of what had happened out there in the Coral Sea. Like other stories, it claimed that Rolston had been on the raft for fourteen days before being rescued. It also maintained that there were five hundred men on the tanker and that four hundred had been rescued. That may have been a factual error by the reporter, but it was more than likely a number provided by the Navy in an attempt not to give the enemy the true human loss in the attack.

Jackie Rolston did not—and legally could not—correct the errors. Instead, he pointedly refused to talk about any of what had taken place. He happily spent time with his family before he was to report back for duty in San Francisco in less than a week.

As the local newspaper reported, "The parents . . . took him yesterday noon to the home of his grandparents, Mr. and Mrs. Frank Price, in Platte County, for a family reunion and fried chicken." The paper noted that Jackie visited the parents of his friend, Noel Craven, just as he, Ken Bright, and Grove Hough had vowed to do while still back on the raft.

He also called on the mother of Grove Hough, and did

something the Navy had not yet done to that point. He confirmed for her that her son was not missing, but had died on the raft.

"Although the Navy department still reports Hough as 'missing in action,'" a local newspaper article reported, "Ralston [*sic*] confirmed that he helped bury Hough at sea."

From all outward appearances, Jackie Rolston's ordeal was now over.

That, of course, was not the case. The man's torment would not end until the day he died.

Many years after his ordeal, Rolston gave a short interview to an oral historian but otherwise spoke little about what happened back then, not even to his family. In 2003, the nephew of Seaman Bill Leu, Del Leu, was doing research for a tribute to his uncle on a Web site. He contacted Rolston for information on his service aboard the *Neosho* and his experiences on the raft. The old sailor seemed eager to help and even forwarded documents, newspaper clippings, and articles. He invited Leu to call him anytime if he wanted to learn more.

A month or two later, the younger Leu again contacted Rolston with some follow-up questions. Jack Rolston's attitude was completely different by this time.

He told Leu that his original inquiry had reopened some old wounds he thought had long since healed. Ever since he had brought out the clippings and documents and sent copies of them to Leu, he had been continually reliving the horror of the days on the raft. The dreadfulness of watching his friends slip away and die before him—over sixty years before—had all come flooding back.

He requested that Leu not call him again. The palpable sadness in Jack Rolston's voice was obvious to Leu, even over the long-distance telephone connection.

"Of course, I felt absolutely terrible about this," Leu said later. "I learned how scars from an incident like this might never heal, even decades later."

He promised Rolston he would not contact him again and wished him all the best.

Leu not only kept his promise but he also removed all mention of Rolston and the rafts from the Web site. He did not want anyone else to see the information, somehow get in touch with the old sailor, and rekindle an experience the man had obviously been trying to put out of his mind for a long, long time.

In 2012, Del Leu learned that Jack Rolston had passed away a couple of years prior.

"I debated whether or not to post his story and that of the 'raft of 68,'" Leu said. "But then I remembered a specific part of Jack's letter to me in 2003."

At the time, Rolston had written that he was sending Leu the copies of the documents and the few remembrances for a reason. He wanted others to know about those men on the raft, what they had gone through, the sacrifice they had made. He simply did not want them to be forgotten.

"After thinking about that, I decided to put the information back on the Web page as a tribute to Jack and to . . . the men who perished on that raft," Leu writes on his Web site. "He was the last of the sixty-eight men, a sad and little-known story that has been lost to the waves of time."

EPILOGUE
Beyond the Bow

Bill Leu's relationship with a fat girl named *Neosho* was not yet over. After his convalescence in Australia, the Navy sent him back to the United States for fifteen days of shore leave, plus five days' traveling time, far more than he needed to journey home to Skykomish and back to San Diego.

Even considering the solemn circumstances, Leu experienced a wonderful homecoming. Friends and family clamored for details of his shipwreck adventure. He could not tell them much—the Navy forbade sailors to give out information that might somehow find its way to the enemy. But the real reason he did not talk more was because he had caught a bad case of laryngitis when he came ashore in California.

The local newspaper ran a story about Leu's homecoming under the headline, "Skykomish Boy to Be Honored at Dance." The story briefly alluded to the adventures "the former Sky Hi basketball star" had seen, which "included plenty of action and experience."

"Bill and the tanker he was on escaped under fire from Pearl Harbor December 7, but was not so fortunate in the Coral Sea battle," the story reported. "He lost his ship and was five days at sea before being picked up and taken to Australia."

The dance in his honor was held at the Masonic Hall on a Saturday night, with an admission charge of fifty cents. "Proceeds of the dance will be put in a fund and used to put an [sic] entertainment for the boys that come home from action. And also to swell their pocketbooks before they leave."

When his furlough ended, Leu reported back to the naval station in San Diego and picked up his papers for his next duty assignment, which he had heard was to be new construction on a brand-new oiler. He almost fell over when he saw the name of the ship to which he was to be assigned: USS *Neosho*.

This ship was designated AO-48 and had started life as the USS *Catawba*, a *Kennebec*-class tanker, built originally for and operated by the company that would someday become Mobil Oil. She was launched two days before Christmas and sixteen days after Pearl Harbor in December 1941. When the Navy acquired the vessel in July 1942, they renamed her in honor of her lost sister tanker.

Bill Leu was soon back on the "black gang," plying familiar waters up and down the West Coast, to Hawaii and beyond, replenishing the fleet. Except for a turn serving under a "crazy, mad engineering officer" and coming down with appendicitis while on liberty in Hollywood, Leu had nothing like the traumatic experiences he suffered on his first ship. Even the bad appendix episode had a silver lining, resulting in better duty for him, and at one point the Navy even tried to convince him to become an officer.

He was serving on a ship in the Marshall Islands when the Japanese surrendered. After the war, Leu returned to Skykomish and eventually put what he learned in the engine rooms of Navy ships to good use. He went to work for the Great Northern Railroad as a train engineer.

He remained active in the group of former *Neosho* sailors and attended many crew reunions around the country as well as commemorations in Hawaii, proudly wearing his "Pearl Harbor Survivor" baseball cap. Still, even without the complication of laryngitis, Leu was like many other veterans. He did not speak much with his family about his experiences in World War II, and especially about those grueling days on the torrid deck of his sinking ship.

At least he did not speak much until his nephew Del came along and started asking questions. Thankfully, he took the opportunity to tell us—from an enlisted man's point of view—what it was like to endure a sneak attack that started a war. Then he described how it felt to have a ship withstand a massive assault, to almost capsize beneath him, and then to miraculously remain afloat somehow until help came along and rescued him.

Finally he told us how it was to climb right back up onto the horse that threw him—a horse with the same name—and keep her under power as she took him once more to war.

Bill Leu passed away in 2003.

Harry Ogg, who was raising the ship's flag on *Neosho* when the first Japanese aircraft flew overhead at Pearl Harbor, left the tanker before the Battle of the Coral Sea. He was crossing the country, heading for a new construction in New York City, when he heard word about the loss of his former ship.

Ogg was later sent to serve aboard a minesweeper, the USS *Hazard* (AM-240), and eventually was back in the South Pacific. His ship saw duty in several hot spots, but perhaps the most satisfying was to sweep for mines off the shores of Korea and Japan to make the way safe for the occupation forces that came in after the signing of the peace treaty. The *Hazard* today is a museum vessel, moored in the Missouri River at Omaha, Nebraska.

Ogg left the Navy in the summer of 1946 after six years of service. He later served as president of the Corpus Christi chapter of the Pearl Harbor Survivors Association. At one point, he was embroiled in a controversy surrounding the filming of the 2001 movie *Pearl Harbor*, starring Ben Affleck, Kate Beckinsale, and Josh Hartnett. The producers announced they were going to use the USS *Lexington* (CV-16) as a "stand-in" for a Japanese carrier in the movie. Note that this was the immediate successor to the *Lexington* that had been lost in the Coral Sea. CV-16 was named after her sister ship while she was still under construction during World War II as soon as word came that CV-2 was lost. She became a museum ship sitting in Corpus Christi Bay in the early 1990s.

"I think it's a disservice to the many men who lost their lives at Pearl Harbor, Coral Sea, and other battles," Ogg told a reporter for the *Honolulu Star-Bulletin*, who noted that Ogg was stationed on the oiler *Neosho* on December 7, 1941. "You can't have a Japanese war flag flying on a U.S. warship."

Ogg lost his battle with the moviemakers. The ship was used as intended, but not without much protest by him and his group.

He eventually retired from a career at the Reynolds Aluminum Company facility in Corpus Christi. In June 2014, the City Council of Corpus Christi assembled at the nursing facility where Ogg lives to present him with a certificate of appreciation, recognizing him as one of the few remaining survivors of the Pearl Harbor attack. They also voted to declare June 26, 2014, as "Harry Ogg Day" in the city.

"I served my country and I'm glad I did," he later told an interviewer. "I'm proud that I did."

As noted, Chief Watertender Oscar Vernon Peterson died from his injuries six days after the attack on the *Neosho*. He was aboard the *Henley*, en route to Australia, and was buried at sea a hundred miles off the coast. For his heroism, Peterson was posthumously awarded the Medal of Honor.

The citation read in part, "For extraordinary courage and conspicuous heroism above and beyond the call of duty while in charge of a repair party during an attack on the U.S.S. *Neosho* by enemy Japanese aerial forces on 7 May 1942. Lacking assistance because of injuries to the other members of his repair party and severely wounded himself, Peterson, with no concern for his own life, closed the bulkhead stop valves and in so doing received additional burns, which resulted in his death. His spirit of self-sacrifice and loyalty, characteristic of a fine seaman, was in keeping with the highest traditions of the U.S. Naval Service. He gallantly gave his life in the service of his country."

In 1943, the destroyer USS *Peterson* (DE-152) was named for him in his honor.

Peterson had been a kid when he joined the Navy in 1920 and spent the rest of his life at sea. Even so, he and his wife, Lola, had two sons. Like other players in this saga, Peterson was a snipe, a blue-collar sailor, one of the men who did the dirty work to keep his ship under steam and moving. He was the type who simply did his duty, sometimes against what appeared to be overwhelming odds.

Even after dying a hero, Oscar Peterson's mighty contributions and posthumous recognition seemed to have been mostly overlooked.

For reasons unknown, his family did not receive his Medal of Honor in a formal presentation ceremony as was typical at the time. Instead, the medal and accompanying certificate simply showed up in the mail, addressed to his widow. Customarily, at the time of the ceremony, a marker was usually placed in a local cemetery or public place in the recipient's hometown to commemorate his or her bravery. There was no such marker for Oscar Peterson.

That oversight was eventually remedied, but only partly, and not until much later. In 2010, sixty-eight years after his heroic actions, a special observance was held in Richfield, Idaho, where his family had relocated after Peterson's death. By then, both his widow and one of his sons had passed away. A large crowd of more than 850 family members, veterans, dignitaries, and military representatives gathered for the event at the local Church of Jesus Christ of Latter-Day Saints chapel.

Rear Admiral James A. Symonds, commander of Naval Region Northwest, presented Fred Peterson, Oscar's surviving son, with a forty-eight-star American flag and a Medal of Honor as he sat in the front row of the church. A marker, a U.S. flag, and a Medal of Honor flag—all to be cared for by the local Veterans of Foreign Wars group—were placed at a local cemetery.

"The thing that got me, I'd put everything back past it," Fred Peterson told a reporter covering the ceremony. "Then it all came back up again. It kind of hurts, kind of like opening up a wound again. I guess I should be big enough to accept it."

Fred Peterson's wife added, "He was the only one burying his father today."

"The aftermath to Lola must have been devastating," Admiral Symonds told the crowd, referring to Peterson's widow. Then, in a tribute to all those who waited for their men to come home before learning they would not be doing so, the admiral added, "I believe she would have benefited greatly by a presentation with more ceremony, with more importance, than receiving her husband's medal in the mail. The same can be said for her efforts to get a grave marker that befits a Medal of Honor recipient. It certainly took far too long to make it happen. She sacrificed much for her country, in a different way, but in no less a terrible way than her husband."

Peterson's heroism might still have been mostly buried with him at sea had it not been for a board member of the Idaho Military Historical Society. Gayle Alvarez discovered the oversight that had occurred seven decades earlier, and petitioned the Department of Veterans Affairs for some kind of formal recognition of Oscar Peterson's sacrifice.

Her efforts led to the long-delayed ceremony and the placement of the permanent marker. Finally, it was assured that the Navy chief's amazing bravery would no longer be passed over and ultimately forgotten.

Owing in part to the recommendation in the action report submitted by John Phillips, Lieutenant Commander Francis Firth was awarded the Silver Star for his actions aboard the *Neosho*. The citation read, in part: "For gallantry . . . while serving as Executive Officer on board the Oiler U.S.S. NEO-SHO (AO-23), during an attack on that vessel by enemy aerial forces during the Battle of the Coral Sea on 7 May 1942. Although knocked down and rendered unconscious when a Japanese plane made a suicide dive into the NEOSHO, Lieutenant Commander Firth, upon regaining consciousness, made his first and only consideration the safety of personnel in his vicinity. In spite of severe burns about his face, hands and arms, he continued his unselfish devotion to duty during the tense days following the attack."

Firth recovered from his injuries and went on to become the captain of USS *Napa* (APA-157), an attack transport ship that saw action during the invasion of Iwo Jima. He eventually retired from the Navy as a rear admiral.

Francis Firth died in May 1985.

There were more Silver Stars and other medals of valor awarded to the crew of the *Neosho*.

One went to Harold Bratt, the sailor who fought to keep the men in his compartment from certain death if they panicked and tried to climb out through the steam-filled boiler room above them. His Silver Star citation said, "When a bomb exploded in the fire room, tearing open the main and auxiliary steam line, boiler casings and boiler tubes, Motor Machinist's Mate First Class Bratt, who was on duty in the compartment just below, quickly made a correct assumption of existing conditions. By his leadership, quick thinking and action under most difficult circumstances, he was able to save the lives of two men under his charge."

Another Silver Star was awarded to Wayne Simmons, the machinist's mate who remained at the feed pump throttle throughout the Japanese attack on the oiler. Simmons had a girlfriend, Bernice Lybbert, waiting for him back home in Utah. A terrible week or so passed between her hearing of the loss of the *Neosho* and receiving word from Simmons that he was okay. When he finally left Australia and got his leave during the summer of 1942, Harold sent word to Bernice for her to meet him in Las Vegas. He wanted to take care of something before he went back out there where the war was raging.

Wayne and Bernice were married in a civil ceremony before Bratt returned to sea duty, and Bernice went back to Utah to resume her job as a schoolteacher. She later moved to San Diego, became a "Rosie the Riveter" in an industrial plant, and waited for the rare and quick occasions when she could visit with her new husband when his ship brought him to the mainland.

Simmons served on other ships and in some of the Pacific's hottest spots but was never again injured. He was discharged from the Navy in 1946. The first thing on the agenda was something he and his wife believed was another bit of unfinished business. He and Bernice were determined to have another wedding ceremony, this time in the Mormon temple in Salt Lake City, to validate the earlier civil union in Las Vegas.

One of their five children joined the Navy and served a tour of duty in Vietnam.

Engineering Officer Lieutenant Louis Verbrugge's Silver Star citation related that, "Despite difficult conditions aboard his ship because of severe aerial attacks by the Japanese, and with the ship in imminent danger of capsizing, [he] remained in the engineering spaces until assured it was impossible to restore power."

Verbrugge had been as aware as anyone that the oiler could have flipped over at any time. Still, he had not hesitated. His job was to try to get them under power again if that was humanly possible.

Thomas Brown, the gunnery officer who remained at his position when it must have seemed that the world was ending right there on the decks of the *Neosho*, and who acted as XO when Francis Firth was injured, was awarded the Navy Cross. The citation reads, "The President of the United States of America takes pleasure in presenting the Navy Cross to Lieutenant Commander Thomas Markham Brown, United States Navy, for extraordinary heroism and distinguished service in the line of his profession as Gunnery Officer aboard the Fleet Oiler U.S.S. NEOSHO (AO-23), when that ship was attacked by Japanese aircraft in the Coral Sea on 7 May 1942, and as acting Executive Officer during the trying days when she was in a sinking condition. His conspicuous courage and resourcefulness during the engagement was directly responsible for the destruction of three enemy planes and the damaging of at least four others. In the days subsequent to the attack, when preparations were being made to abandon ship, he assumed and performed the duties of Executive Officer in a thorough and efficient manner."

Brown later had the opportunity to command his own ship when he placed the destroyer tender USS *Everglades* (AD-24) into commission in May 1951. Before retiring from the Navy, he eventually achieved the rank of rear admiral.

He died in July 1970 and is buried in Arlington National Cemetery.

As previously mentioned, Pharmacist's Mate Third Class Henry Tucker was posthumously awarded the Navy Cross. He was the sailor who swam from raft to raft in heavy seas, treating the men with the worst of the burns, and who was never heard from again.

Tucker is still classified by the Navy as "missing in action, presumed killed in action."

The swashbuckling pilot Stanley "Swede" Vejtasa's heroic work continued beyond his amazing action at the Battle of the Coral Sea. He would eventually receive three Navy Crosses for valor and skill in carrier battles. Vejtasa was the only pilot to be so honored in both dive-bombing and in air-to-air combat, making him one of the true aces of the Pacific war.

The Montana native had joined the Navy Reserve in 1937 and was commissioned an ensign in 1939. Before he retired, he served not only during World War II but also the Korean War and the Cold War. In Korea, he was the air officer on the carrier USS *Essex* (CV-9). In November 1962, Vejtasa became captain of the USS *Constellation* (CVA-64)—the only ship in U.S. naval history to be authorized to display her designation numbers in red, white, and blue—bringing him full circle, commanding a vessel similar to the ones off which he had once flown. Similar in purpose, perhaps, but certainly much larger and more sophisticated.

In 1965, Vejtasa became commander of Naval Air Station Miramar near San Diego, home of some of the Navy's most famous flying squadrons. There, he continued to find seat time in the latest aircraft, including the F-4 jet, again a craft that might be similar in purpose but radically different from the Douglas SBD-3 Dauntless planes he flew off *Yorktown* twenty years earlier.

"Swede" Vejtasa retired from the Navy in 1970. He passed away in January 2013 at the age of ninety-eight. According to his wishes, his ashes were scattered at sea.

• • •

The three men who brought their destroyers into harm's way to look for the *Neosho* and the *Sims* and any possible survivors eventually went on to distinguished service for the rest of the war and beyond. So did their ships.

Lieutenant Commander William Burford, the captain of USS *Monaghan*, had already received the Navy Cross for his leadership in sinking that Japanese mini-submarine in Pearl Harbor in the midst of the December 7 attack. After unsuccessfully looking for the *Sims* and the *Neosho* survivors, he took the *Monaghan* to the Battle of Midway as part of Task Force 16. There Burford and his crew once again had a run-in with an enemy submarine that had mortally wounded an already impaired *Yorktown*. This time, although the destroyer's depth charges apparently did some damage, the I-boat escaped.

Later in the war, Burford was promoted to the rank of captain and awarded the Legion of Merit for his work as the western Pacific representative of commander-destroyers during three months in 1945. According to the citation, "His initiative, perseverance, and outstanding ability made possible the rapid repair of battle-damaged destroyers when they were urgently needed for the final blows against the enemy. Despite frequent Japanese air attacks, he successfully carried this staggering task to completion, thereby greatly contributing to the crushing defeat of the foe."

Burford passed away in October 1968 near Seattle, Washington.

Burford's former command, USS *Monaghan*, eventually met a most unusual and tragic end, not from enemy fire but at the hand of Mother Nature. In December 1944, the destroyer was taking part in the liberation of the Philippines. Her primary role was to provide escort for the fleet's oilers. Bad weather interrupted the refueling of the destroyer. Most of the ship's ballast water had already been pumped out to allow for taking on the fuel. That left the *Monaghan* top-heavy.

With little warning, bad weather turned into Typhoon Cobra. Waves and wind were so powerful that the ship actually flipped over onto her starboard side and immediately sank. Only thirteen men got off and eventually found themselves in a life raft on roiling seas. Over the next three days, men jumped into the sea or were pitched off the constantly capsizing raft. A couple more drank seawater and went insane. Still others, injured in the ship's sinking, died. Planes flew overhead, but a tiny raft in heavy seas was almost impossible to spot.

They were finally seen by an aircraft and rescued by the USS *Brown* (DD-546), a sister destroyer. Two hundred fifty-seven men who had been aboard the warship were declared missing in action and never seen again. Two other U.S. Navy ships were lost in that terrible storm.

Only six men off the *Monaghan* survived the three-day ordeal on the raft.

As previously noted, soon after leading the search for the *Neosho* survivors, Commander Leonard B. Austin took the ships of Destroyer Division 7 based in Nouméa, New Caledonia—including the *Henley*—and participated in the invasion at Guadalcanal. He was awarded the Legion of Merit for that action as well as for later duty as commander of Destroyer Division 22. His citation mentioned that "(Austin) saw action in the first landings on Guadalcanal as part of Task Force SIXTY-TWO, undergoing several heavy air attacks, directing the bombardment of enemy shore positions and taking an active part in rescue operations following the Battle of Savo Island."

He also made flag rank before retiring from the Navy. He

passed away in August 1973 and is buried in Arlington National Cemetery near Washington, D.C.

USS *Henley* remained mostly in the waters of the South Pacific until, after skillfully dodging two enemy torpedoes fired from a submarine, she was taken down by a third fish while operating off New Guinea on October 3, 1943. By then she was skippered by Commander Carlton Adams, but still carried some of the crew members who had helped in the rescue of *Neosho* survivors.

The *Henley*'s crew, too, quickly took to life rafts as their ship sank, but only for a short period of time. They used flashlights to signal, and several other destroyers rescued them early the next day. One officer and fourteen men were reported missing in action. Two hundred twenty-five were saved, including Commander Adams, even though he had been wounded.

After his tenacious search for any survivors of the *Neosho* and the *Sims* in the Coral Sea—and the disappointing discovery of only four men on the raft—Commander Chester "Blackie" Carroll took USS *Helm* to her next job. After depositing the rescued men in Brisbane, Carroll and his crew took up patrol duty up and down the Australian coast as part of British Task Force 44. After that, they saw action at Savo Island and Guadalcanal as part of the first offensive amphibious assault in the Pacific.

When he was relieved as commander of the *Helm*, Carroll went to new construction, taking the destroyer USS *Abbott* (DD-629) through sea trials and to the Caribbean, looking for German U-boats. He later commanded Destroyer Squadron 96, Task Unit 94.3.9 in the Bonin Islands, and Destroyer Squadron 6. He was later a military adviser to the government of Taiwan during the tense early 1950s.

After achieving the rank of rear admiral, Carroll retired from the Navy in 1954 with thirty years of service. He received both the Silver Star and the Bronze Star for his actions in World War II.

Carroll passed away at the age of eighty-seven in June 1987. He was buried at the Fort Rosecrans National Cemetery at Point Loma, California, near San Diego.

USS *Helm* went on to see more action in such hot spots as Iwo Jima and Okinawa. During the Iwo Jima campaign in February 1945, she was yet again called upon for rescue duty. The escort carrier USS *Bismarck Sea* (CVE-95) came under a brutal attack in which the Japanese used their latest desperate tactic, kamikaze planes. Of her crew of 925, a total of 318 were lost. Over the next twelve hours, the *Helm* and other ships managed to pluck more than 605 men from the oily water, despite darkness, heavy seas, and continued attacks by the enemy.

The destroyer would later be dispatched to search for survivors of the tragic sinking of the heavy cruiser USS *Indianapolis* (CA-35) in the Philippine Sea in July 1945. About 900 men went into the shark-infested ocean when the ship sank. They were there for four days with no life rafts, food or water. Only 316 were still alive when they were ultimately rescued.

After being decommissioned in June 1946, the *Helm* was used as one of the "target ships" during atomic tests at Bikini Atoll in the Pacific. The destroyer was the recipient of eleven battle stars for duty during the war, from Pearl Harbor to the Coral Sea to Okinawa. She was eventually sold for scrap in October 1947.

Her rescue of the four survivors on *Neosho's* "68 man raft," if even mentioned at all, is merely a single line in most published histories of the ship.

• • •

Most of the men went unrecognized for what happened in the Coral Sea. For them, their survival would have to be reward enough. They simply shipped back home, took a few days' shore leave, and then reported back to new duty. There was still a war raging.

Most of the men kept quiet about their experiences for the rest of their lives. A few of them talked much later, mostly to oral history collectors or to reporters looking for Veterans Day copy or human-interest stories.

Some stayed in touch with the families of shipmates who did not make it. Some relatives reported that those shipmates' families became as close as blood kin.

Others pointedly avoided such powerful reminders.

Some shared odd details with relatives. One sailor maintained for the rest of his life that whenever he was in a swimming pool for a while, he began to smell oil and had to climb out. He had spent time in the sea, surrounded by burning oil.

One surviving crewman refused ever to eat canned pears again. It seems that when work parties went below on the stricken *Neosho*—often having to dive into water in a flooded compartment to find and bring up food—they retrieved far more canned pears than anything else.

When one of the survivors arrived home for leave, he pointedly told his family they had better ask any questions they had about his experiences right then and there. He vowed to never talk about it again.

Relatives confirmed that he never did.

As for those who never returned, and who are still listed as missing, there have been rumors over the years—none of which have been validated—of survivors not only of the *Neosho* but of other vessels lost at sea who ended up on rafts or boats and eventually washed up onshore, primarily in Australia. Some of those men, stories claim, were still alive. Some died shortly afterward but others were eventually nursed back to health.

Some claim that other men somehow made it to remote islands, got ashore, and lived a Robinson Crusoe existence until they finally died or were rescued.

One wife of a missing *Neosho* sailor told family members that she once received a letter from a woman in Australia claiming her husband and another man had been rescued from a raft that washed up nearby. She was supposedly taking care of them. Other family members recalled hearing the same or a similar story, but the wife has long since passed away. No such letter was ever found. No husband ever showed up, and the man remains "missing in action, presumed killed in action."

None of these supposed survivors ever returned home. The rumors were likely nothing more than hopeful thinking.

History would not treat kindly two of the other participants in the story of USS *Neosho* and USS *Sims*.

Rear Admiral Frank Jack Fletcher, the commander of Task Force 17 at the Battle of the Coral Sea, has long been saddled with the reputation for being timid and indecisive. One indication that is often cited was his almost fanatical insistence on ensuring a constant fuel supply for his fleet. There were charges of nepotism as well, since he had served under his uncle, Admiral Frank Friday Fletcher, during World War I.

Whether that reputation was deserved or not, Admiral Fletcher himself may have contributed to that perception. His papers were lost in combat and he declined to work with naval archivists to restore them from existing documentation. Additionally, he refused to be interviewed by Rear Admiral

Samuel Eliot Morison, who wrote *The History of United States Naval Operations in World War II*, which many consider to be the definitive work on the subject.

Some historians now say such harsh judgment of Fletcher came too soon after the war ended, and without enough overview or understanding of the situation that Fletcher faced at the time.

The fact was, when the Japanese attacked Pearl Harbor, the Medal of Honor recipient, along with his longtime Navy contemporaries, were facing challenges no one could have anticipated. As previously noted, Fletcher was not an aviator, yet he was in command of Pacific Fleet aircraft carriers at a time when such warfare was relatively new. Many now say he relied on more experienced aviation officers to advise him until he learned the ropes, literally learning by doing.

Fletcher also found himself in the midst of a raging storm from the first day of the war, with little opportunity to do more than react. He spent at sea all but 50 days of the initial 290 days of the Pacific war, and all of that was in or near waters controlled by the Japanese. Most consider that time to be a period during which the Imperial Japanese Navy was at its strongest, too.

Still, despite those raps against him, Frank Fletcher led his ships to victories at Midway and the Eastern Solomon Islands (though some still say he was too cautious there or the victory would have been more clear-cut), and a virtual victory in the first-ever battle of its type in the Coral Sea. Those, of course, were the first three carrier battles in history. There were no textbooks on the subject to study beforehand.

At that time, Fletcher, his staff, and his counterparts on the Japanese side were developing tactics through on-the-job experience.

At the time of the Battle of the Coral Sea, Frank Jack Fletcher was already fifty-seven years old. He graduated from the U.S. Naval Academy in 1906 and had commanded his first ship in 1909. He earned his Medal of Honor in the Mexican Revolutionary War way back in 1914. He brought another era's experience to a war in which an entirely new kind of combat was being employed. Considering his eventual record, and with the benefit of more investigation, it is likely that history will be more kind to him going forward.

After the bombings of Hiroshima and Nagasaki and the signing of the peace treaty with Japan, Fletcher took charge of Hokkaido, the northernmost Japanese Home Island, overseeing the Allied occupation there.

Before his retirement from the Navy as a full admiral in 1947, Fletcher served as chairman of the General Board of the U.S. Navy, a sort of general staff overseeing the administration of the service branch.

He died in 1973 at the age of eighty-seven and is buried in Arlington National Cemetery. The destroyer USS *Fletcher* (DD-992) is named in his honor.

On the Japanese side, the one individual who played not only one of the more significant roles in the Battle of the Coral Sea but certainly one of the biggest in the fate of the *Neosho* and the *Sims* was Rear Admiral Chuichi Hara—"King Kong"—commander of the IJN's 5th Carrier Division.

Many in the higher reaches of the Japanese military took issue with how the fiery commander approached, conducted, and ended the battle. Especially vexing to them was the time wasted trying to deliver aircraft off the carrier decks to Rabaul as well as his hurried run back to Rabaul for refueling after the action on May 8. Critics felt he should have instead aggressively pursued what was left of the Allied fleet as they retreated.

And, of course, there was Hara's decision to send most of the airplanes he had available to attack what turned out to be a destroyer and a tanker, not one of the big Allied aircraft carriers. And to okay pursuing the assault on those two targets even when it was clear those ships were not what they were so frantically seeking.

After the Battle of the Coral Sea, Hara would again face Admiral Frank Jack Fletcher and the American fleet in the Eastern Solomons. That would be declared another defeat for Hara's fleet.

In 1944, Hara was abruptly reassigned to command the Japanese base on the isolated island of Truk, little more than a speck in the Pacific Ocean. At one time, the island had been a major operational base for the Imperial Japanese Navy. That had changed by the middle of 1944. The enemy had already removed many of their bigger warships from the island before a major Allied attack in February 1944, dubbed Operation Hailstone, virtually ended the tactical importance of the remote atoll.

By the time Hara assumed command, and though the base was officially designated as the "4th Fleet," there were no warships at all assigned to the base. Because the island was so remote and of such little value, the Allies simply ignored it except for harassing air strikes when planes happened to be in the area. Hara had effectively been sent away to a backwater assignment, a garrison whose 130,000 troops and civilian workers faced near starvation much of the time. He remained there until the end of the war.

Hara later described his duty on Truk in blunt terms.

"The seasons do not change. I try to look like a proud vice admiral, but it is hard with a potato hook in my hands. It rains every day, the flowers bloom every day, the enemy bombs us every day, so why remember?"

When the Japanese surrendered the base to the Allies, the ceremony, with Hara in his best dress whites, took place aboard USS *Portland*. There is a tie to the *Neosho* there, of course, since the *Portland* was one of the ships from which passengers had ridden the boatswain's chair over to the *Neosho* on May 6, 1942.

After the war ended and Truk was formally surrendered, Hara was immediately arrested. He was charged by the Allies with committing war crimes. Those included allowing the execution of U.S. airmen who had been captured during an attack on the Truk base, something that actually occurred before he ever took command of the base. Regardless, he was convicted and sentenced to six years at a prison in Tokyo.

When the Allies released Hara from prison, the man who had been such a key cog in the sneak attack on Pearl Harbor, and who churned the waters of the Coral Sea frantically looking for Fletcher and the Allied fleet, spent the rest of his life lobbying for pensions and other relief for the Japanese men and their families who had been imprisoned for war crimes.

After the war, Hara would quite famously say of the Pearl Harbor preemptive strike he helped launch, "[It] did not fit any thinking that I knew to be right." He believed that "we won a great tactical victory at Pearl Harbor and thereby lost the war."

Hara lived a long life. He was seventy-four when he died in February 1964.

It would take a while, but John Spinning Phillips would one day get to indulge his love for the game of golf.

After his rescue and arrival in Australia, Phillips continued to hone his incident report, including backing off a bit on the harshness with which he had initially judged some of the Navy Reserve officers under his command. Most of the men he recommended for formal recognition or promotion of rank would eventually be so rewarded.

It was not uncommon for captains to make specific recommendations in their incident reports to fix things that had not gone right or to recommend better ways of handling similar situations in the future. John Phillips seized the opportunity to do just that with his report.

Little else could have been done to try to survive such a concentrated attack by scores of enemy dive-bombers. Yet Phillips added some very specific actions he felt were important to help avoid an incident such as the one that had befallen his ship and crew. From the nature of his comments and the wording of his proposals, we can surmise that the veteran captain was especially bothered by the loss of the men on the life rafts.

He suggested, "That all life rafts be painted yellow, and provided with a tarpaulin which can be quickly slipped off; tarpaulin to be painted the color of the surrounding structure. The *Neosho* life rafts were painted grey and were extremely difficult for the men in the water, and personnel on board ship, or for searching ships or aircraft, to locate in the water.

"That all life rafts be provided with a telescopic stick, similar to a fishing rod, of sufficient strength to permit a flag to be bent on the top, to assist men in the water, and searching boats, ships and aircraft, to locate the raft.

"That all ship's boats be fitted for sail, and that a mast, spars, canvas and running tackle be provided in the boat."

From his final recommendation, it was also clear something else was bothering Captain Phillips: the confusion and chaos surrounding his order to prepare to abandon ship.

He wrote, "That the words 'ABANDON SHIP' be deleted from all preliminary orders given: that the preliminary order be 'FALL IN AT (or MAN) BOAT AND RAFT STATIONS,' and that the words 'ABANDON SHIP' be used only when it is desired to accomplish just that, namely, for all personnel to leave the ship."

Based in part on the *Neosho* incident and her captain's recommendation, the Navy did eventually modify its procedure. Now, when there is any chance that it will be necessary to abandon a vessel, and if there is adequate time, the order is for the crew to muster at assigned positions near lifeboats and rafts. Then they are to await the clear order—the words "Abandon ship!"—to launch the rafts or boats and get off the doomed vessel.

Perhaps the most telling indication of how deeply the tragedy of the two vessels affected the captain would not come until he was back in Pearl Harbor, ready for his next assignment.

Phillips, the veteran ship captain, the experienced commander, a man whose skills his Navy and country so desperately needed, was immediately offered another command.

He declined to accept it.

Some former crew members speculated that losing all those men, particularly the ones who died so slowly and horribly on the drifting rafts, left him with no desire to take a ship to sea again, and especially not to war.

In a December 1975 article in the *Washington Star* about his death, Phillips is quoted as having said, "We figured we were so far behind the battle area that nothing could possibly happen to us. We were protected by one destroyer and were just cruising along, waiting to refuel the ships in the battle.

"But all of a sudden, we were discovered by Japanese planes," he continued. "That was it. In a few hours the destroyer was sunk with the loss of almost 300 men. My ship was not sunk but it was a derelict. My losses were almost as great as the destroyer's."

Though he was pressed to helm a ship once again, Phillips held firm and never returned to sea. He spent the remainder of the war in the Intelligence Division of the Navy. He returned to his academic service after the war, teaching college-level courses. He eventually retired from that post and the Navy in 1947 with the rank of rear admiral.

In addition to the Navy Cross that he was awarded for the action at Pearl Harbor, Phillips later received the Silver Star for the leadership he displayed in the ordeal in the Coral Sea. The citation noted that he "insured the welfare and safety of the wounded and supervised abandoning operations. His coolness, courage and inspiring leadership throughout this battle reflect the highest credit upon Rear Admiral Phillips and the United States Naval Service."

With the war and the Navy behind him, Phillips settled with his wife, Nancy, in Arlington, Virginia, and later moved to Fort Lauderdale, Florida. He turned to golf.

Phillips, a man who had spent most of thirty years at sea or teaching and supporting men and women who would go there, quickly had his hands in dirt and grass. He adapted to retirement by actively helping oversee the greens at the Army Navy Country Club in Arlington, on the same ground once occupied by the Civil War–era Fort Richardson. He was later an honorary member of the Golf Course Superintendents of

America, was elected president of the D.C. Golf Association, and was the northern Virginia representative of the Virginia Golf Association.

Phillips died in December 1975 and was buried at Arlington National Cemetery, only a short distance from the golf course he loved so much.

AUTHOR'S NOTE

First and foremost, I am a storyteller. Anytime I contemplate writing a work of historical nonfiction, I first look for a captivating narrative with complex characters that will fascinate, entertain, and be of interest to readers. I am not necessarily attempting to write a book that will appeal only to historians, history buffs, or scholars, though I do want those groups to appreciate and learn from my work and any new information I may uncover.

My goal, however, is for my books to be entertaining and accessible to a broad range of potential readers, including those who want a good story populated by everyday people placed into extraordinary situations and doing remarkable things. My focus is the human side of history.

This is why something else I do in my books often earns me criticism from those who would prefer a more scholarly approach. I put words in the mouths and thoughts in the heads of the people who may or may not have spoken those precise words or held those exact thoughts. Few of them are still with us to confirm what was said or how, and even so, those words and thoughts took place over seven decades ago.

I base those quotes and unspoken thoughts on a great deal of research. I am as sure as I can be that they are as accurate as I can make them and reflect the personality of the individual to whom I attribute them. Otherwise, I convey the information in another way or simply do not use it.

I strive for accuracy. Be aware, though, that official incident reports are often full of errors—unintended or not—or based on one man's observations, which may sometimes come with an agenda or be colored by self-interest. Oral histories, valuable as they are, are filled with mistakes, guesses, scuttlebutt, and even self-glorification. Journalistic accounts are subject to errors, too, as well as deliberate military misinformation or censorship at the time.

As always, I very much appreciate the sharp eyes and spot-on suggestions of my sometimes coauthor Commander George Wallace (Ret.), who kindly read a draft of the manuscript, helping to keep me on point and accurate with many details of the narrative. The skipper always assures that I maintain a level bubble.

When I consider a topic for historical nonfiction, my first step is to establish that the subject has not already been adequately and accurately covered. I have taken a pass on several captivating stories simply because I felt they had been well told already. When my literary agent, Jim Donovan, mentioned the *Neosho* incident to me, my first chore was to find other books or articles that had already dealt with this compelling story.

Any author hopes for adequate research material to be

able to write a book, but also looks for aspects of the story that have not yet been satisfactorily related. I found no books at all that specifically tell in detail the tragic but inspiring story of USS *Neosho* and USS *Sims*. Certainly, there has been no book like the one I wanted to write, relating the complete human story of the crew members of the two "decoy" ships.

Three works on the battle served as my primary background source material. They are *The Coral Sea 1942: The First Carrier Battle* by Mark Stille; *The Battle of the Coral Sea: Combat Narratives,* compiled by the Publication Section of the Combat Intelligence Branch, Office of Naval Intelligence; and Edwin P. Hoyt's *Blue Skies and Blood: The Battle of the Coral Sea.* Commander Stille's maps, timelines, and exhaustive lists of assets employed on both sides of the battle were enormously helpful.

Important in getting various viewpoints of the attack on the two ships was an article by Dan Verton, that appeared in *Naval History Magazine*. His father was one of the survivors of the *Sims* and was interviewed for the article, along with one of the other survivors of the destroyer's sinking.

Other primary source material included the actual combat narratives from the Office of Naval Intelligence as collected in the 1943 investigation of the events, the official post-incident reports by various participants, and an informal war diary kept by *Neosho* captain John Phillips and made part of his incident report. Also of value were the full reports of Lieutenant Commander William P. Burford, captain of USS *Monaghan*, the first ship to look for the *Neosho* and the *Sims*; Commander Leonard B. Austin, of Destroyer Division 7, who rode USS *Henley* as she searched for and ultimately located the *Neosho*; and Lieutenant Commander C. E. Carroll, captain of the destroyer USS *Helm*, who rescued the four survivors on the "raft of 68."

The *Nimitz Graybook* was a tremendous aid in understanding and documenting all that was going on at the higher levels of the Navy in the spring of 1942, especially as it affected the Battle of the Coral Sea. This 4,000-page collection consists of volumes of accumulated documents, briefing papers, and other material that show an amazingly complete wartime "diary" of Admiral Chester Nimitz, running from December 7, 1941, through August 31, 1945. The materials, gathered during the war by the CINCPAC staff at Pearl Harbor, are now part of the Papers of Chester W. Nimitz at the Archives Branch of the Naval History and Heritage Command in Washington, DC, and in 2012 were digitized and made available to the public via the Internet as a cooperative effort of the Naval War College and the NHHC.

Vital to the accurate and readable telling of this story were the oral histories and narratives collected from those men who actually experienced it.

One of the most helpful sources was a true labor of love by a relative of one of the *Neosho* survivors. This source provided extensive information on the ship's action at Pearl Harbor, her loss in the Coral Sea, and the eventual rescue of what remained of her crew, much of it as told by *Neosho* crew member Fireman Third Class William A. Leu. Both written transcript and video were kindly provided to the author by Seaman Leu's nephew Del Leu along with permission to use the material any way necessary to tell the story.

Another short oral history as well as documents and other materials collected by Del Leu from Jack Rolston provided firsthand information about his experiences as one of only two survivors from those who were swept away on lashed-together rafts.

Thank goodness Del Leu and others have taken the time and effort to collect and make available to all such valuable reminiscences! By the latest estimates, we are losing five hundred World War II veterans a day. With every warrior we bury—and if we have not made an effort to collect and archive those stories—we are simultaneously interring a lifetime of uncaptured eyewitness history.

With today's on-demand and electronic book self-publishing technology, we now have an unprecedented and remarkable way to capture, archive, and make available the experiences and recollections of those who have lived history. This is not limited to World War II, of course. It includes, for example, those who went through the Great Depression, those who marched in the Civil Rights movement, people who worked to put the first man on the moon, those who created the transistor, and those who worked to usher in the personal computer, the Internet, and more.

There are millions and millions of untold stories out there.

I believe it is crucial that we all help to collect such untold eyewitness history while these people are still alive, and then use modern self-publishing to archive it and make it available to scholars, researchers, authors, and anyone else who wants to read accounts from those who were there, those who experienced history, big and small.

I invite readers to visit a Web site I have created in an attempt to assist in such efforts: www.untoldmillions.net. I call this nonprofit effort the Untold Millions Project.

I am honored to have been able to help tell this remarkable true story of a blue-collar oiler and her devoted escort. Yet as dramatic and inspiring as it is, this was only one of millions of human experiences that are yet untold.

At least now this particular one has been.

Don Keith
Indian Springs Village, Alabama
September 2014

APPENDIX
Survivors and Casualties of
USS *Neosho* and USS *Sims*

These lists of survivors and casualties from USS *Neosho* and USS *Sims* were collected from documents from the Navy Bureau of Personnel, the action and incident reports from the two ships, as well as other sources. Much of the information was compiled by Del Leu for his Web site honoring his uncle, Fireman Third Class Bill Leu, a *Neosho* survivor, as well as contributions from other visitors to his site. Those additions and corrections were all based on official government documents.

Rank and/or grade are unknown for those men where none is listed.

USS *NEOSHO* SURVIVING OFFICERS

NAME	RANK
Henry K. Bradford	Lieutenant/Navigator
Thomas M. Brown	Lieutenant Commander/Gunnery Officer

Charles C. Cook	Lieutenant (j.g.)
William G. Driscoll	Lieutenant (j.g.)/Communications Officer
Francis J. Firth	Lieutenant Commander/Executive Officer
Leonard F. Gearin	Ensign
Robert N. Hargis	Ensign/Assistant Gunnery Officer
Posey N. Howell	Ensign
Estul F. Nessmith	Lieutenant (j.g.)
John S. Phillips	Captain/Captain of Ship
Kenneth S. Terrill	Ensign
Louis Verbrugge	Lieutenant/Engineering Officer

USS *NEOSHO* SURVIVING ENLISTED MEN

NAME	RANK
Sidney Arboneaux	
Harold C. Bagwell	Metalsmith Second Class
Charles Baker	
Wilbert A. Becker	Machinist's Mate Second Class
Herbert L. Bennett	Fireman First Class
Robert T. Boehm	Shipfitter Second Class
Lawrence Boyer	Metalsmith First Class

William D. Boynton	Seaman Second Class
Harold Bratt	Machinist's Mate First Class
Tony Bustos	
Francis E. Chapin	Fireman Third Class
Grover Chessmore	
George E. Cruttenden	Seaman First Class
Harvey L. Dyer	Watertender First Class
Meredith E. Ebbert	Seaman First Class
Frederick W. Fabian	Machinist's Mate First Class
Edward A. Flaherty	Electrician's Mate Third Class
Oswald J. Frenette	
Charles A. Hagewood	Seaman First Class
Jerry Hall	Seaman Second Class
Robert W.Hoag	Chief Pharmacist's Mate
Iris F. Hoffman	Seaman Second Class
Patrick J. Jackson	Boatswain's Mate First Class
William C. King	Construction Electrician's Mate
Uriel H. Leach	Chief Warrant Officer, Machinist
Robert Ledford	Seaman First Class

William A. Leu	Fireman Third Class
Russell Lollar	
John E. Lowe	Storekeeper Third Class
Vernon R. Manners	Boatswain
Nicholas G. Marchese	Ship's Cook Second Class
Lorenza McNair	OC First Class
Arthur R. McPherson	Seaman Second Class
Doug J. Nelson	Signalman Third Class
Elvin G. Newman	Seaman Second Class
James T. Nix	Machinist's Mate First Class
Gilbert M. O'Grady	O-1
Samuel Ogur	Chief Boatswain's Mate
Leopoldo Paloma	Officer's Steward First Class
Thomas J. Parker	Boatswain's Mate
William S. Parker	Chief Radioman
Loren B. Parkhurst	Fireman Third Class
Ralph Patterson	
Albert V. Paulek	Shipfitter Third Class
LeRoy Pearce	

Gilbert Percifield	
Walter J. Perowitz	Chief Machinist's Mate
John J. Peterson	Seaman Second Class
Alex Pupkin	Yeoman First Class
Wallace P. Quillan	Seaman First Class
Junior E. Reigle	
Anthony Rella	
Harold A. Reynolds	Fireman First Class
Jack Rolston	Seaman Second Class
William Romanofsky	Storekeeper Second Class
Cecil Sawyer	
Grant Seward	
Francis J. Shea	Chief Gunner's Mate
Leroy S. Shogren	Apprentice Seaman
Wayne Simmons	Machinist's Mate Second Class
Addison F. Smith	Quartermaster Third Class
William A. Smith	Seaman Second Class
Wilbern L. Stovall	Chief Boatswain's Mate
Lorenzo Tyner	Officer's Cook Second Class
William J. Ward	Pharmacist's Mate First Class

James L. Watchler	Coxwain
James M. Weber	Quartermaster Second Class
Samuel Wells	
Ernest W. Wobrell	Chief Electrician's Mate
John H. Wortham	Mess Attendant Second Class

Note: It is believed 32 more men survived the *Neosho* sinking but those names are not available.

USS *NEOSHO* OFFICERS KILLED OR MISSING IN ACTION

NAME	RANK
Robert T. Allsopp	Lieutenant (j.g.)
John D. Greathouse	Lieutenant (j.g.)
Chan Lyman	Ensign
Oscar J. Peterson	Ensign
Ralph P. Plumb	Ensign

USS *NEOSHO* ENLISTED MEN KILLED OR MISSING IN ACTION

NAME	RANK
Mitchell E. Andrews	Seaman First Class
Beverly Annis	Seaman Second Class

Bruce Annis

Benjamin F. Baggarly | Chief Construction Mechanic

Floyd D. Bailey | Seaman Second Class

Carl F. Baird | Seaman First Class

Frank J. Baker | Seaman Second Class

Frank Balzer | Seaman Second Class

William J. Bannen | Baker First Class

Stuart C. Battenfield | Fireman Third Class

Ernest J. Beech | Seaman Second Class

Louis R. Blackburn | Scaman First Class

Richard M. Blood | Yeoman Third Class

Edward C. Blue | Fireman Third Class

Harry F. Bradshaw | Seaman First Class

Kenneth T. Bright | Seaman Second Class

Leon M. Brooks | Construction Mechanic Second Class

Voris V. Brownfield | Seaman Second Class

Arthur Bunch Jr. | Seaman Second Class

George Bundy | Gunner's Mate Second Class

Dennis D. Burger | Construction Mechanic Third Class

Albert J. Busky | Gunner's Mate Third Class

Thomas H. Cameron	Gunner's Mate Third Class
Louis R. Cardy	Seaman Second Class
Herman E. Carter	Machinist's Mate Second Class
Mark A. Casella	Quartermaster Second Class
Henry T. Chapman	Fireman First Class
Davis M. Charlton	Seaman Second Class
David A. Christian	Fireman Third Class
Richard C. Clark	Seaman Second Class
Willie Coates	
Allie Collette	Seaman Second Class
Leland R. Collier	Electrician's Mate Third Class
Virgil W. Colson	Seaman Second Class
Claud C. Cooper	Gunner's Mate Third Class
Earl I. Couse	Storekeeper Third Class
Ross C. Covina	Seaman Second Class
Pearlin G. Cox	Seaman Second Class
Noel E. Craven	Seaman Second Class
Rex B. Crawley	Radioman Third Class
Lynn J. Creech	Fireman Third Class
Louis B. Crosby	Signalman Second Class

Loren B. Crouch	Storekeeper Second Class
Rex B. Crowley	Radioman Third Class
Russell L. Croxen	Seaman Second Class
Harold V. Cummins	Seaman Second Class
Manuel S. Davilla	Seaman Second Class
August M. D'Hondt	Seaman First Class
Kenneth L. Dowdy	Seaman Second Class
Roland Q. Dudley	Seaman Second Class
Audress C. Dunn	Fireman Second Class
Edmund L. Dunn	Radioman Third Class
James H. Ellis	Fireman Third Class
Fermin Felosofo	OC Second Class
Attilio J. Ferrari	Seaman First Class
Dale F. Flory	Watertender Second Class
William K. Forbes	Radioman Third Class
Howard J. Foster	Fireman Third Class
Robert L. Fredrickson	Storekeeper Third Class
Herman A. Frohnhafer	Seaman Second Class
Delvan C. Gaylord	Electrician's Mate Second Class

Joseph A. Gelinas	Watertender First Class
George W. Goff	Fireman Third Class
Hugh T. Gonia	Seaman First Class
Robert K. Gracey	Fireman First Class
Brevis M. Gregston	Seaman First Class
Dale W. Guthrie	Fireman Third Class
Luis Gutierrez	Seaman Second Class
Julio M. Guzman	Seaman Second Class
William C. Hackworth	Fireman First Class
William Hames	Seaman First Class
Charles A. Hamrick	Seaman Second Class
George L. Hanis	Seaman First Class
James W. Hardwick	Seaman Second Class
Otis A. Hartman	Fireman First Class
Albin M. Haugen	Machinist's Mate First Class
Elliott D. Haynes	Gunner's Mate Second Class
Grover H. Hough	Seaman Second Class
James K. Howard	Seaman Second Class
John C. Hudson	Fireman Third Class
David G. Huntsman	Seaman Second Class

Marchell R. Hurst	Machinist's Mate First Class
Donald E. Hyde	Seaman Second Class
Henry A. Irons	Seaman First Class
Alfred J. Jablonski	Seaman First Class
Ernest C. Johnson	Seaman Second Class
Robert Johnson	Seaman Second Class
Herbert Jones	
Marvin E. Kynerd	Seaman Second Class
Elbert F. Lacy	Signalman First Class
Lewis L. Lane	Fireman Second Class
Llewellyn L. Larson	Seaman First Class
Harold W. Levy	Seaman Second Class
Robert L. Lormis	Seaman Second Class
Clyde B. Lynch	Watertender First Class
Ralph H. Magnuson	Machinist's Mate Second Class
Winston T. Manry	Seaman Second Class
George H. Mansfield	Electrician
Darrel F. Matzdorf	Fireman Third Class
Raymond E. Medow	Seaman Second Class
Earl J. Miller	Fireman Third Class

Thomas R. Miller	Seaman Second Class
Alvia L. Minor	Seaman Second Class
Vimmy M. Mitchell	Steward's Mate Second Class
Anthony M. Mondi	Fireman Second Class
Eugene J. Montanari	Seaman First Class
Christopher Montano	PRT Third Class
Elijah W. Moore	Machinist's Mate First Class
Raymond G. Moreau	Machinist's Mate First Class
Hal A. Nelson	Seaman Second Class
Harrison S. Nobbs	Chief Radioman
Sinforoso Paguirican	Steward's Mate Second Class
Joseph R. Palmer	Shipfitter Third Class
Charles D. Parker	Seaman Second Class
Melvin W. Parmenter	Fireman Second Class
Harry J. Patterson	Electrician's Mate Second Class
Leroy D. Pearce	Seaman Second Class
Oscar V. Peterson	Chief Watertender
Robert L. Peterson	Seaman Second Class
Julian Ponce	Fireman Third Class
Richard M. Prentice	Fireman First Class

Robert H. Pursley	Seaman Second Class
Stanley E. Raimer	Ship's Cook Third Class
James F. Ramos	Seaman Second Class
Floyd T. Resley	Fireman Third Class
William L. Reynolds	Chief Watertender
Emil J. Rogalla	Gunner's Mate First Class
Joseph R. Rogers	Electrician's Mate Second Class
Earnest F. Roland	Fireman Third Class
Gerald W. Routledge	Seaman Second Class
Marshall L. Rowell	Seaman Second Class
Richard H. Rowley	Machinist's Mate First Class
Garvin D. Runyan	Chief Commissary Steward
James E. Saul	Coxswain
Cecil D. Sawyer	Seaman Second Class
Frank A. Scarborough	Seaman Second Class
Eugene H. Self	Yeoman Third Class
Wendell A. Shaw	Boatswain's Mate Second Class
Robert W. Shroyer	Seaman Second Class
Glen W. Smith	
Leonard Q. Smith	Baker Third Class

Samuel H. Soliday	Seaman Second Class
Carl C. Stebbins	Radioman Third Class
Donald A. Stewart	Seaman Second Class
George A. Stewart	Seaman Second Class
Robert E. Stretch	Fireman First Class
Ernest Strouse	Watertender Second Class
Craig L. Strozda	Watertender Second Class
Donald F. Stubblefield	Seaman First Class
Clifford Tatge	Seaman Second Class
John E. Theriac	Fireman Third Class
Leland E. Thompson	
Earl D. Thornton	Steward's Mate Third Class
Leonard A. Thorpe	Fireman Third Class
Philip J. Toner	Seaman Second Class
Victor N. Toney	Seaman First Class
Henry W. Tucker	Pharmacist's Mate Third Class
Thaddeus O. Tunnel	Seaman Second Class
Charles H. Tyler	Storekeeper Third Class
Chester D. Underwood	Machinist's Mate Second Class

John W. Varnum	Ship's Cook Second Class
Jack C. Vogan	Machinist's Mate Second Class
Othello F. Wadley	Steward's Mate Second Class
Prospero E. Walker	Steward's Mate Second Class
Oliver Ward	Warrant Officer
William H. Webb	Gunner's Mate Third Class
Clarence J. Webre	Seaman Second Class
Louis H. Weidner	Signalman Second Class
James B. Wheeler	Seaman Second Class
Robert L. White	Ship's Cook Second Class
Lester L. Williams	Machinist's Mate Second Class
Nelson M. Wilson	Ship's Cook First Class
Edward N. Wolf	Fireman Third Class
George A. Wood	Seaman First Class
Vernon A. Zeddies	Seaman Second Class

USS *SIMS* SURVIVING CREW MEMBERS

NAME	RANK
Vincent F. Canole	Machinist's Mate Second Class
J. Chielewski	Fireman First Class

Robert J. Dicken	Chief Signalman
Silas V. Dugger	Machinist's Mate First Class
George E. Ernst	Fire Controlman Third Class
Arthur C. Gober	Seaman Second Class
Jackie J. Lawes	Seaman Second Class
Edward F. Munch	Machinist's Mate Second Class
Thomas F. Reilly	Watertender First Class
Jones Savage	Fireman Third Class
Marvin W. Scott	Fireman Third Class
Kenneth W. Tevebaugh	Radioman Third Class
John C. Verton	Seaman Second Class
Vito J. Vessia	Fireman Second Class
	Note: No officers survived the sinking of USS *Sims*.

USS *SIMS* CREW MEMBERS KILLED OR MISSING IN ACTION

OFFICERS

NAME	RANK
Robert P. Graham	Ensign
Arthur M. Grindle	Ensign

Wilford M. Hyman	Lieutenant Commander/Captain of Ship
Gustav F. Kerndt	Ensign
James E. McManus	Ensign
Strudwick T. Pennington	Ensign
Melvin E. Radcliffe	Lieutenant/Gunnery Officer
Max Silverstein	Lieutenant
Andrew P. Stewart	Lieutenant/Executive Officer
Lionel J. Tachna	Ensign
Arthur W. Wilkinson	Lieutenant (j.g.)
Clifton F. Wyatt	Ensign

ENLISTED MEN

NAME	RANK
Alfred Adamson	Chief Fire Controlman
Cecil E. Ammons	Apprentice Seaman
Randers H. Andersen	Chief Boatswain's Mate
Robert E. Anderson	Apprentice Seaman
Robert F. Andren	Fireman First Class
James H. Austin	Fireman Third Class
Frank Barnes	Seaman Second Class

Edwin R. Barney	Chief Watertender
Paul R. Barthel	Apprentice Seaman
Donald R. Bean	Fireman First Class
Sylvester C. Bell Jr.	Radioman Third Class
Robert J. Belonga	Seaman Second Class
Joseph S. Bender	Gunner's Mate Third Class
Dennis H. Bennett	Seaman Second Class
Robert L. Bitson	Seaman Second Class
Jerold E. Bonebright	Coxswain
Victor R. Boston	Seaman Second Class
John D. Braiovich	Radioman Second Class
James Brandenberger	Seaman First Class
Frederick R. Brick	Machinist's Mate Second Class
Walter Brodie	Fireman Second Class
Raymond W. Bryant	Seaman Second Class
Albert L. Bugmra	Seaman Second Class
M. Buonassissi	Torpedoman Second Class
Kenneth J. Capistrand	Yeoman Third Class
Thomas K. Carlisle	Seaman Second Class

Dorsey E. Cherry	Pharmacist's Mate Second Class
John K. Christensen	Seaman Second Class
Allen Clark	Chief Yeoman
John F. Clark	Fireman First Class
Joseph D. Clayton	Seaman Second Class
Leo F. Coughlin	Boilermaker Second Class
Donald A. Davis	Torpedoman Second Class
J. Defrance	Machinist's Mate First Class
Hans W. Deguehery	Storekeeper Third Class
Gerald J. Dente	Boatswain's Mate Second Class
Virgil J. Despres	Signalman Third Class
Albert W. Dieckmann	Coxswain
Wilfred J. Dismuke	Seaman Second Class
Clem T. Dixon	Steward's Mate Second Class
Charlie L. Dorrough	Chief Electrician's Mate
Charles F. Doyle	Fireman First Class
Thomas Duckworth	Seaman Second Class
Dorand H. Dumoulin	Storekeeper First Class
Johnny M. Duncan	Seaman Second Class

Roland S. Dunham	Seaman Second Class
Lester W. Duoos	Fireman Third Class
Dupree L. Edwards	Fireman Third Class
James J. Edwards	Torpedoman Third Class
Leonard P. English	Coxswain
Scott W. Erickson	Fireman Second Class
Anthony J. Falzone	Seaman Second Class
Walter J. Faucett	Fireman Second Class
Roger H. Fenske	Seaman First Class
Anthony W. Ferracane	Yeoman Second Class
William F. Fischer	Seaman First Class
James W. Flack	Signalman Second Class
Thurman C. Foskey	Seaman Second Class
Elmer C. Fox	Seaman First Class
Maurice D. Fox	Machinist's Mate Second Class
Harold D. French	Chief Quartermaster
Cecil E. Gardner	Fireman Second Class
Ralph C. Gardner	Seaman Second Class
Russell Gardner	Seaman Second Class
Paul A. Garner	Steward's Mate Third Class

Clayton L. Gibson	Seaman Second Class
Purvis W. Gilmore	Seaman Second Class
Charles W. Gleason	Seaman Second Class
John Goldych	Torpedoman Second Class
Robert Paul Grab	Fireman
Edmund P. Graichen	Chief Machinist's Mate
Martin L. Hansen	Seaman First Class
Leon W. Hartford	Yeoman Second Class
Bernard F. Hebel	Fireman Second Class
Richard O. Heiden	Fireman First Class
James W. Henderson	Seaman Second Class
Willie L. Henderson	Steward's Mate First Class
Lynn Hilton	Apprentice Seaman
Paul G. Hogan	Fireman Second Class
Alvin V. Howard	Seaman Second Class
Frank P. Iessi	Radioman Third Class
John C. Janke	Seaman Second Class
Robert E. Johnson	Fire Controlman Third Class
Clifton C. Jones	Seaman Second Class

Mahlon J. Kelbaugh	Seaman Second Class
Lester Kelly	Machinist's Mate First Class
John R. Kendig	Machinist's Mate First Class
Herbert Kennedy	Seaman Second Class
James J. Kinchsular	Radioman Third Class
Edward W. King	Chief Torpedoman
Eugene J. King	Seaman Second Class
James C. Kosbob	Seaman Second Class
James E. Lamb	Seaman First Class
Edward S. LeBlanc	Fireman First Class
Henry N. Lindberg	Seaman First Class
Alfredo Lorenzana	OC Second Class
Walter Luke	Radioman First Class
Robert T. Lund	Fireman First Class
Francis F. Lynch	Torpedoman Third Class
John T. Martin	Apprentice Seaman
Michael F. Martin	Chief Watertender
Hoyt G. Matthews	Torpedoman Third Class
Roy G. Mattice	Apprentice Seaman
Philip Mattingly	Seaman Second Class

Glenn C. McAlister	Apprentice Seaman
Thomas J. McCarthy	Apprentice Seaman
Frederick McComb	Watertender First Class
James C. McConchie	Chief Commissary Steward
Langford S. McCord	Seaman First Class
Flake V. McCormick	Apprentice Seaman
Louis F. McKay	Apprentice Seaman
Edward E. McKinney	Seaman Second Class
Harrison E. McMillan	Seaman First Class
Joseph S. Meeks	Apprentice Seaman
Virgil D. Meyer	Apprentice Seaman
John J. Miller	Electrician's Mate Third Class
Charles A. Morgan	Radioman Third Class
Ronald B. Morris	Coxswain
Edward C. Morse	Chief Machinist's Mate
Orval J. Myers	Seaman First Class
Paul Nabors	Seaman First Class
Russell E. Neu	Machinist's Mate Second Class

Orville Y. Newton	Seaman First Class
Burton K. Nichols	Seaman Second Class
John W. Norman	Quartermaster Third Class
Wilson W. Odom	Apprentice Seaman
Leo Orzechowski	Gunner's Mate First Class
Rudder B. Padgett	Seaman First Class
George T. Pair	Seaman First Class
E. M. Peleis	Seaman Second Class
Frederick W. Penton	Radioman Third Class
Paul Perryman	Gunner's Mate Second Class
Francis Peterson	Gunner's Mate Second Class
Duane E. Phillips	Seaman Second Class
Edward M. Pieles	Seaman Second Class
Charlie B. Pike	Fireman Third Class
James D. Pike	Seaman First Class
Allen C. Pittman	Fireman Second Class
Cecil C. Pitts	Apprentice Seaman
Burel L. Plant	Fireman Third Class
Manuel F. Polomares	Apprentice Seaman
Johnnie L. Privett	Seaman Second Class

George F. Pruett	Seaman First Class
Clabe W. Putnal	Fireman Third Class
Willis E. Quesenberry	Apprentice Seaman
Maunsel E. Ramsey	Machinist's Mate First Class
Raphael J. Ratti	Fireman First Class
James T. Ray	Ship's Cook First Class
John S. Reistetter	Chief Gunner's Mate
Lawrence H. Renger	Fire Controlman Third Class
Nathan A. Roberts	Fireman First Class
Robert F. Rock	Machinist's Mate First Class
Harold L. Rose	Apprentice Seaman
Harold E. Ross	Fireman Third Class
Harold G. Ruffner	Electrician's Mate Second Class
George P. Ryan	Fire Controlman Second Class
Harding I. Salpeter	Apprentice Seaman
Alfred A. Sanzari	Fireman Third Class
Sidney M. Saunders	Apprentice Seaman
Stanley J. Schumacher	Chief Boatswain's Mate
C. Scott	Carpenter's Mate Second Class

George R. Sellett	Fireman Third Class
Alexander Sentelik	Fire Controlman First Class
Alonzo R. Settlemire	Watertender Second Class
Arthur L. Sheron	Seaman First Class
Arthur S. Shidler	Electrician's Mate First Class
Grady Singletary	Seaman Second Class
Thomas E. Sligh	Seaman Second Class
Glenn N. Smith	Seaman Second Class
Henry C. Smith	Fireman Second Class
Charles E. Smithson	Fireman Third Class
William M. Sneed	Seaman Second Class
David R. Stevenson	Seaman Second Class
Charles R. Street	Fireman First Class
George C. Sutton	Seaman First Class
Walker Tackett	Seaman Second Class
Alvin T. Talbot	Seaman Second Class
James R. Taylor	Seaman Second Class
Curtis Townsend	Seaman Second Class
Joseph G. Troxil	Machinist's Mate Second Class
Thomas L. Turner	Seaman Second Class

William J. Turner	Fireman First Class
Elias Tyrpak	Gunner's Mate First Class
Kenneth F. Valente	Seaman First Class
Daniel K. Vanantherp	Fireman First Class
Eugene J. Vannucci	Fireman Second Class
John Vdouin	Seaman First Class
Robert F. Vinson	Seaman Second Class
Stuart H. Wallace	Seaman Second Class
Vernon C. Watkins	Shipfitter Second Class
Joseph C. Webb	Chief Mechanic's Mate
Garnold R. West	Seaman First Class
Joseph Wheaten	Steward's Mate Second Class
Raymond F. Wickett	Machinist's Mate Second Class
Earl J. Williams	Seaman First Class
Henry I. Williams	Fireman Second Class
Richard S. Williams	Seaman First Class
Mansfield C. Williamson	Steward's Mate Third Class
James Wilson	Seaman First Class
Selmer R. Winnett	Fireman Third Class

Lewis H. Wolger	Ship's Cook Third Class
Louis J. Woll	Ship's Cook Third Class
Pink Worley	Seaman Second Class
John J. Yanek	Gunner's Mate Third Class
William J. Yanny	Watertender First Class
Michael Yanov	Gunner's Mate Third Class
James A. Yates	Electrician's Mate First Class
Orin A. Yates	Electrician's Mate Second Class
Kenneth E. Yerian	Fire Controlman First Class
Oscar Young	Fireman First Class
Robert W. Young	Fireman First Class
Edward V. Zon	Seaman Second Class
John D. Zonik	Seaman Second Class
Otto J. Zoss	Watertender Second Class
Michael S. Zwir	Ship's Cook Second Class

Note: It is believed 12 more men were lost on the *Sims* but those names are not available.

SOURCES

BIBLIOGRAPHY

The Battle of the Coral Sea: Combat Narratives. Washington, DC: Publication Section of the Combat Intelligence Branch, Office of Naval Intelligence, U.S. Navy, 1943.

General Description of USS Sims from the Office of Supervisor of Shipbuilding. Washington, DC: Naval Bureau of Ships.

Hoyt, Edwin P. *Blue Skies and Blood: The Battle of the Coral Sea*. New York, NY: Jove Books, 1984.

Lundstrom, John B. *The First Team: Pacific Air Combat from Pearl Harbor to Midway*. Annapolis, MD: Naval Institute Press, 2005.

———. *Black Shoe Carrier Admiral: Frank Jack Fletcher at Coral Sea, Midway, and Guadalcanal*. Annapolis, MD: Naval Institute Press, 2013.

Rawlings, Charles, and Isabel Leighton. *Fat Girl*. New York, NY: American Brake Shoe Company, 1942.

Stille, Mark. *The Coral Sea 1942: The First Carrier Battle*. Oxford, U.K.: Osprey Publishing, 2009.

Wildenberg, Thomas. *Gray Steel and Black Oil: Fast Tankers and*

Replenishment at Sea in the U.S. Navy, 1912–1992. Annapolis, MD: Naval Institute Press, 1996.

OFFICIAL DOCUMENTS

Action report: Task Force 17.

Action report: USS *Helm.*

Action report: USS *Henley.*

Action report: USS *Lexington* Air Group, Carrier Group Task Group 17.5.

Action report: USS *Lexington.*

Action report: USS *Monaghan.*

Action report: USS *Neosho.*

Action report: USS *Yorktown.*

Action reports: Torpedo Squadron 5, Bombing 5, Fueling Group Task Group 17.6.

Document compendium: *Nimitz Graybook*, gathered by CINCPAC staff, Pearl Harbor, Hawaii, now part of the Papers of Chester W. Nimitz Collection, Archives Branch, Naval History and Heritage Command, Washington, D.C.

Medal citations: Medal of Honor collection, National Archives.

Narrative report: Senior Line Petty Officer Robert Dicken, USS *Sims.*

Numerous post-incident reports, action reports, and other official documentation on the attack at Pearl Harbor.

Post-action report: 25th Japanese Air Flotilla.

Post-incident report: USS *Sims*, staff of Admiral W. L. Ainsworth, Commander Destroyers, Pacific Fleet, and the follow-up report to the Secretary of the Navy from Commander in Chief, U.S. Pacific Fleet, Admiral Chester Nimitz.

Survivors' report: USS *Sims.*

War diary: Captain John Phillips, USS *Neosho.*

ORAL HISTORIES

Seaman Harry Ogg (crew member of USS *Neosho*), collected and archived by the National Museum of the Pacific War Oral History Collection, Fredericksburg, Texas.

Lieutenant (jg) Stanley "Swede" Vejtasa (pilot assigned to Carrier Group Task Group 17.5), collected and archived by the World War II Museum, New Orleans, Louisiana.

Seaman Julius Jay Finnern (crew member of USS *Monaghan*), collected by Eric Koepp, made available on a Web site devoted to the history of the *Monaghan*, www.ussmonaghan.com.

Seaman Newton Brooks (crew member of USS *Helm*), collected and archived by the Veterans History Project of the American Folklife Center, Library of Congress.

Seaman Jack Rolston (crew member of USS *Neosho*), collected by Richard Erickson for the Branson Veterans Task Force.

ARTICLES

Lundstrom, John B. "Frank Jack Fletcher Got a Bum Rap." John B. Lundstrom. Annapolis, MD: *Naval History* magazine, Part One: Summer 1992; Part Two: Fall 1992.

Newspaper story: *Idaho Statesman* (Boise), 2010.

Newspaper story: *Honolulu Star-Bulletin*, 2001.

Newspaper story: *Kansas City Star*, August 1942.

Newspaper story: *Monroe Monitor & Valley News* (WA), 1942.

Newspaper story: *Deseret News* (Salt Lake City, UT), 2010.

Newspaper story: *San Francisco Examiner*, June 1942.

Newspaper story: *Seattle Times*, 1942.

Newspaper story: *Twin Falls (ID) Times-News*, 2010.

Newspaper story: *Washington Star*, December 1975.

Rawlings, Charles, and Isabel Leighton. "Fat Girl." *Saturday Evening Post*, February 6, 1943.

Verton, Dan. "Misfortune at Coral Sea." Annapolis, MD: *Naval History Magazine*, June 2002.

WEB SITES

Congressional Medal of Honor Society: http://www.cmohs.org/

KIII-TV, Corpus Christi, Texas: http://www.kiiitv.com/

Personal Web site of Del Leu, nephew of Seaman William Leu: http://www.delsjourney.com/

Twin Falls, Idaho, *Times-News*: http://magicvalley.com/

INDEX

Index

Index

Index

Index